The Adventure of I

The Adventure of I

A Journey to the Centre of Your Reality

Tania Kotsos

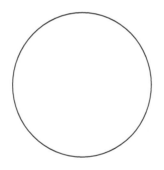

Amarantho House
London, United Kingdom

Dedicated with love to my family and
to William Walker Atkinson

First Edition

First printing, 2013

Paperback Soft Cover Edition - ISBN: 978-0-9576770-0-5
eBook eReader Edition - ISBN: 978-0-9576770-2-9
eBook MOBI Edition - ISBN: 978-0-9576770-1-2

Author's Website:

Mind Your Reality | www.mind-your-reality.com

Cover Illustration: Yaroslav Gerzhedovich

Published by Amarantho House
London, United Kingdom
info@amaranthohouse.com

PREFACE

The Adventure of I is a book that will take you on a journey to the centre of your reality. It has its foundation in the greatest maxim ever passed down to us, which is to 'Know Thyself and thou shall know all the mysteries of the gods and of the Universe'.

The Adventure of I marks the culmination to date of my own knowledge and understanding about the power of the human mind, consciousness, and the mysteries hidden in that vast part of the Universe that is invisible to our physical senses, but that is known to the I that is your Real Self. In the words of Robert Frost, "we all sit in a circle and suppose, while the secret sits in the centre and knows." The secret at the very centre of your being is the I within.

I trust that The Adventure of I will afford you with the breadth and depth of knowledge to transform your life in ways that you may right now deem impossible. My intention in imparting this knowledge was to keep it simple and practical, while also affording you with a deep understanding that facilitates a fundamental shift in your mindset. With this end in mind, I adhered to Albert Einstein's advice that "everything should be made as simple as possible, but not simpler." It has, however, been no easy feat because the simplest story, as the saying goes, is also the hardest to tell.

I encourage you to read this book from cover to cover and not to skip to any one section without having first read what comes before, as it is written in a logical sequential order aimed at maximising your understanding. Bear in mind that any repetition is intended for your advantage because as the saying goes 'repetition is the mother of learning', and for the same reason, to gain the benefits inherent in this knowledge you must apply the exercises in this book persistently.

Finally, in writing this book, I am grateful to my family and friends who have encouraged me. A special thank you goes to my sister, Maria Kotsos, for her tireless editing, and also to Wendy Hart for the final edit. I am also grateful to the reader without whom I would have had little reason to write it, and to the mental giants who, through their writings and teachings, have allowed me to stand on their shoulders so that I too could see reality from a higher vantage point. Above all, I am eternally grateful to the *One Source* of All Power and All Knowledge.

Here's to your adventure.
Tania Kotsos
Athens, Greece

TABLE OF CONTENTS

"Mind is the Master Power that moulds and makes,
And Man is Mind, and evermore he takes,
The Tool of Thought, and shaping what he wills,
Brings forth a thousand joys, a thousand ills.
He thinks in secret, and it comes to pass:
Environment is but his looking-glass."

James Allen, As a Man Thinketh, 1902

PART I
MENTAL SCIENCE

Chapter 1
INTRODUCTION TO THE ADVENTURE OF I

The Adventure of I will take you on a journey of self-discovery. What you will discover is your Real Self that is the I within that holds the key to your directive and creative power as an individual. The I is not outside or separate from you. Rather, it is the Real You as it is that part of you that is eternal, immortal, and unchanging. Inscribed on the Ancient Temple of Apollo in Delphi, Greece, was the maxim 'Know Thyself'. This is the most profound instruction ever passed down to us, and is the foundation upon which The Adventure of I is written. The aim of this book is to empower you with the knowledge of who you really are, and in so doing, to give you the key with which to begin to unlock 'all the mysteries of the gods and of the Universe'.

There exists within you an immeasurable directive power to create the life you desire and become the master of your experience. This power is yours by virtue of your existence as a human being. It is your birthright. You do not have to acquire it or even ask for it. All you need to do is become consciously aware of it and apply it. This power is the power of your mind under the conscious direction of your will, and it is a power more supreme than you have perhaps ever dared to imagine. The intentional and intelligent application of your mind power, under the direction of your will, is the single most important determining factor of the quality of your life. If success were to be defined as the ability to be the master of one's life, then what separates successful from unsuccessful people is how they apply their mind power, under the direction of their will.

However, as is the case with any power, your mind's inherent potential power can be of little or no use to you if you are not aware of it, despite its existence. Think about it this way - before human beings learnt about electricity, they could not harness and apply its power, even though its potential existed all around them, yet today the power of electricity is taken for granted.

Moreover, no one really discovered electricity. Rather, man simply became aware of it and learnt how to apply and use its power for his benefit, but its potential was always there.

What distinguishes human beings from all other creatures is our capacity for self-aware consciousness. In the absence of conscious self-awareness, a human being's physical and mental experiences are directed and determined by the automatic Laws of the Universe, along unconscious lines, as are those of everything else in the Universe. A tree does not have the ability to say consciously 'I will' or 'I will not grow'. Rather, it is the automatic Laws of the Universe that are the cause of its growth. In other words, it grows without any *choice* of its own, and the nature of the tree depends on the nature of its seed, over which the tree again has no conscious direction.

In contrast, human beings have the freedom of choice, which grants us the ability to use our mind's inherent power to think. Through thought, we are able to direct our minds at will, in ways denied to other creatures on Earth. This ability to think, however, comes at a very high price, which is that we subject ourselves to the inherent consequences of our thoughts, both positive and negative. In this way, our greatest advantage is the very thing that, through our ignorance and wrong thinking, is also our greatest disadvantage.

The fact is that all people employ their mind's power to some degree, albeit usually in the way of unconscious or sub-conscious thinking. However, if you do not consciously apply your mind power under the direction of your will, then you have no real advantage over the plant or even mineral kingdoms that are unconsciously subject to the automatic laws of the physical realm. This can be likened to having no advantage over an illiterate man if you are able to read, but never open a book to do so.

Learning to apply the full potential of your mind power is simple but it is not easy. Indeed, it is a lifetime journey and is one of the most challenging objectives you can ever set out to attain. It is for this reason, however, that its rewards are immeasurable and far exceed any effort you may exert in its direction. Having said this, applying the power of your mind becomes considerably easier, and in time effortless, when at the level of self-awareness of the I within. This is because the Real You is at the height of your consciousness and is therefore, that part of you that is most self-aware, and also most powerful in directing your mind. Indeed, when you consciously identify with your Real Self, you can gain direct access to your *full* mental potential as a human being.

In learning to become the master of your life, it stands to reason therefore, that raising your own degree of self-awareness to the I, is the ultimate step towards self-mastery. This is in fact the fundamental difference between The Adventure of I and other books on the subject of mind power. This book is based on what I have called Top-Down-Living, which is to direct your life from higher degrees of self-aware consciousness, which at its height, is your Real Self. This approach is incomparably more powerful than the opposite approach of Bottom-Up-Living, which is an attempt to direct your life at the level of your personality and its sub-conscious programs.

Think about it this way - it is far easier to understand and change the parts of the whole when you can see the whole from above, than trying to figure out the whole, from piecing together the countless parts. This can be compared to completing a puzzle made up of thousands of small pieces. Your chances of completing it, and in the most time-efficient way, increase significantly if you have a complete picture of the puzzle to guide you from the outset.

By applying your mind power at higher degrees of self-awareness, you get to wake up from the unconscious, auto-pilot mode that is behind what appears to be the randomness of your life. Instead, you get to direct your life in ways you never thought possible, to shift out of mere survival mode, and to experience the joy and happiness that is your birthright.

You get to make a new contract with yourself about what is possible for you, by going beyond your self-imposed limitations to the realm of limitless possibilities. You get to direct and create your desires, no matter how far removed your current circumstances may seem from your ideal. Moreover, you find solutions to problems that previously appeared insurmountable, and you experience a love for everything and everyone in the Universe, including yourself, that is beyond anything you may have experienced to date.

Ultimately, by becoming consciously aware of your Real Self, you re-claim the immeasurable power of your mind, under the direction of your will, which enables you to say 'I THINK therefore I AM therefore I WILL', with full authority. In so doing, you become the master of your destiny, which is to actualise the highest potential of a human being that the Greek philosopher Aristotle referred to as attaining «Εντελέχεια» or Entelecheia *(pronounced: endelehia)*.

Entelecheia means 'the attainment of perfection within', or put another way, the actualisation of a thing's full inherent potential. As is the case with any destination, however, to reach Entelecheia you must start at the very beginning of this most wonderful adventure of I that will in time, lead you to the centre of your being's reality where all power resides.

Chapter 2

THE SCALE OF CONSCIOUSNESS

The main premise of this book is that everything in the Universe is energy vibrating at different rates of vibration. This premise of underlying energy, is a common thread found in ancient metaphysical teachings dating back thousands of years, and also underpins today's scientific knowledge of the Universe. The main difference between modern-day science and metaphysical teachings is that the latter assert that this energy is alive with consciousness - that in fact, it *is* consciousness.

However, even this discrepancy is today becoming reconciled as conclusions from the field of Quantum Physics, which is the study of sub-atomic particles, have begun to point to consciousness as a fundamental aspect of the Universe. While this premise of underlying consciousness is developed throughout this book in a sequential manner, this chapter is intended to set the scene so as to facilitate your understanding from the outset.

Metaphysical texts also refer to the consciousness or energy that underlies the Universe as being the Mind of the Universe. Therefore, the words 'consciousness' and 'mind' are used interchangeably to mean the same thing in this book. Having said this, since we are accustomed to thinking of the word 'mind' as belonging only to sentient thinking beings, it is more appropriate to use the word 'consciousness' when referring to those things in the Universe that we are not accustomed to thinking of as having a mind of their own. Nevertheless, the distinguishing quality of consciousness is aliveness, in the sense that all things in the Universe, whether they are things of matter, mind, or spirit, are alive with consciousness.

THE SCALE OF CONSCIOUSNESS

Since everything is consciousness vibrating at different rates, it stands to reason that what distinguishes one thing from another is its rate of vibration, measured in degrees of consciousness. The different degrees or increments of consciousness together make up the Scale of Consciousness of the Universe, and the difference between each degree, is their corresponding frequency or rate of vibration. Put simply, each degree of consciousness on the Scale of Consciousness has a specific corresponding frequency or rate of vibration, be it a rock, a building, a tree, a star, an atom, a single cell, or a thought.

Starting at the bottom of the Scale of Consciousness, lower degrees of consciousness have a lower rate of vibration, and higher degrees of consciousness have a higher rate of vibration. Put simply, the Scale of Consciousness of the manifested Universe is measured in ascending order of frequency or rate of vibration, which is why it is also referred to as the Scale of Vibration. This can be likened to the different musical notes making up a scale in music, ordered by way of ascending frequency of notes, which is the pitch of the note.

Degrees of Positivity
The degrees or increments on the Scale of Consciousness are called degrees of positivity, although not to be confused with the general notion of being positive. Each ascending degree or rate of vibration is more positive than the degrees below it, and less positive than the degrees above it. Another way of saying this is that each degree of consciousness is *positive* to the degrees below it, and *negative* to the degrees above it. This will become clearer later in the book.

It is helpful to imagine the Scale of Consciousness as a vertical scale of 1 to 100 degrees or increments. Higher degrees are found higher up on the scale and are hence more positive, or have a higher positivity, relative to those degrees found lower down. For instance, something with a degree of consciousness at point 45 on the Scale of Consciousness is higher in positivity compared to something at point 30, but lower in positivity compared to something at point 65, such that any degree of positivity is always relative to every other. Put simply, higher positivity is associated with higher rates of vibration and lower positivity, with lower rates of vibration of consciousness.

Having said this, while any one degree of consciousness is above that which is below it, and below that which is above it, it does not mean that it is physically above or below in terms of height and depth. Rather, all degrees of consciousness exist simultaneously, because consciousness is unconstrained by space and time, and hence one degree cannot be said to take place here and another there. Just like two musical notes can be played at once, with the only thing separating them being the pitch or *frequency* of the note, not physical space, thus the different phases of consciousness are a case of degrees of rate of vibration and not physical location.

DISTINGUISHING QUALITIES
There are essentially four distinguishing qualities associated with the varying degrees of consciousness. Specifically, these are density, self-awareness, intelligence, and directive power.

1. Density

The lower the rate of vibration then the denser or more physically solid or tangible the corresponding manifestation of consciousness is. This means that those things with lower rates of vibration are more physical in nature and hence are more accessible to our physical senses, as is the case with matter in the physical world.

In contrast, the higher the rate of vibration, then the more subtle or less dense a thing is. This means that higher rates of vibration are more inaccessible to our physical senses. This explains, for instance, why you can physically see a rock, as it corresponds to a lower rate of vibration and hence a denser degree of consciousness, whereas you cannot physically see a thought, because thoughts correspond to a higher rate of vibration and hence a subtler degree of consciousness.

2. Self-Awareness

The next distinguishing quality of consciousness is self-awareness. All things are alive with consciousness but not all things are aware of their own aliveness. Self-awareness is to be consciously aware of one's own self. Ascending the Scale of Consciousness, higher rates of vibration correspond with higher levels of self-awareness. In contrast, descending the Scale of Consciousness, lower rates of vibration correspond with lower levels of self-awareness, or in other words, greater *unawareness* along unconscious lines.

Put simply, higher degrees of consciousness correspond to higher degrees of self-awareness and lower degrees, to lower degrees of self-awareness. And the more unaware a thing is, the more unconscious it is. For instance, inanimate objects have the lowest rate of vibrations and hence have no self-awareness, whereas human consciousness corresponds to much higher rates of vibration, and so we are self-aware of ourselves as existing.

3. Intelligence

The third distinguishing quality of consciousness is intelligence. Intelligence, in this sense, is not the same as the intellect involved in solving say a complex mathematical problem. The most suitable definition of intelligence, in describing consciousness, is the ability to pay attention consciously. It is only by paying attention to something that you can understand it, know it, and have the power to use, change, or transform it.

All things have potential intelligence by virtue of being alive with consciousness, but not all things can make conscious use of their intelligence. The lesser the ability of a thing to consciously pay attention through its inherent intelligence, then the greater is the unconsciousness of that thing.

Put simply, higher degrees of consciousness correspond to higher degrees of intelligence or ability to pay attention, while lower degrees of consciousness correspond to lower degrees of intelligence, to the point of appearing wholly lacking in intelligence as we know it.

4. Directive Power

The last and most important quality of consciousness is directive power. This is the capacity to use the power of one's will to direct one's thinking. The will of all things is essentially the 'will to live' but not all things have the power to direct their will consciously. In fact, no independent or conscious action can be taken without the will to do so, which means that in the absence of consciously using one's will power, all action to a great extent occurs unconsciously.

Higher degrees of consciousness correspond to higher degrees of conscious use of will power. Moreover, higher degrees of will power are associated with the power to direct change in those things of a lower degree of consciousness. In other words, the higher the degree of consciousness of a thing then the greater its power to willingly direct change in all those things of a lower degree of consciousness relative to its own.

Power in this sense, however, does not suggest force or physical amounts of power. In contrast, it means directive power in the absence of physical force, or in other words, the power to direct change in those things with lesser directive power or lesser positivity. In other words, higher rates of vibration of consciousness are more powerful than lower rates of vibration.

A person's degree of positivity is that person's degree of directive will power to influence those things that are less positive, or negative, in relation to their degree of positivity. So the advice to 'be positive' does not mean to have a happy-go-lucky outlook, or even to think good, positive, and moral thoughts.

Rather, to 'be positive' means to increase your rate of vibration or degree of consciousness by way of self-awareness and the intelligent use of your will power to direct change in all those things in your environment with a lesser degree of self-aware consciousness or positivity relative to your own.

While every degree of consciousness has its corresponding degree of will power, the full potential power of your will belongs to the highest degrees of human consciousness, which is your Real Self. To 'be positive', therefore, really means to aspire to the I within.

The Scale of Consciousness at a Glance

To bring what has been said together, everything in the Universe is energy or consciousness vibrating at different frequencies or rates of vibration, with no physical separation between any two degrees of consciousness because consciousness is unconstrained by space and time. The only distinguishing factor is a thing's corresponding rate of vibration, which is defined by the associated qualities of density, self-awareness, intelligence, and directive power.

Lower degrees of consciousness are physically denser and hence more accessible to our physical senses, whereas higher degrees of consciousness are more subtle and hence more inaccessible to our physical senses. Moreover, the higher the degree of consciousness of a thing, then the more positive it is on the Scale of Consciousness. In turn, higher positivity corresponds to higher levels of self-awareness, ability to pay attention intelligently, and the capacity to use one's will power to mentally direct change in all those things of a lower degree of consciousness relative to one's own.

Looked at another way, the lowest or densest rates of vibration of consciousness in the physical world are found in inanimate objects, which may be alive with consciousness but have no self-awareness or conscious intelligence whatsoever. In contrast, the most powerful human beings, who are able to influence all those things and people in their environment effortlessly, are people of great will power.

However, it is never a case of a physical amount of will power but rather, it is always a matter of *degree of positivity*. Indeed, it is humanity's degree of self-aware consciousness, and hence our capacity to use the power of our will to mentally direct change intelligently, that sets us apart from the animal kingdom. It is also what distinguishes one human being from another. Put simply, while everything is alive with consciousness, not everything lives *consciously*. Anything less than the intelligent and conscious use of the directive power of one's will is synonymous with living largely along *unconscious* lines.

Having set the scene with this introduction to consciousness as the underlying substance of the manifested Universe, we will now look at the anatomy of your own mind or consciousness. This is the first step in the journey that will lead you to the centre of your reality, and to the highest potential of your consciousness as a human being living in the physical world, which is the I within - the Real You.

THE ANATOMY OF THE MIND

Your mind is part of the Scale of Consciousness. There are essentially three levels of consciousness making up your one mind. In order of increasing degrees of consciousness, and hence of increasing degrees of intelligent self-awareness and directive power, the first level of mind is the sub-conscious, the second is the self-conscious, and the third or highest level, is the super-conscious mind that corresponds to the degree of self-awareness of the I within. Having said this, owing to humanity's ignorance, and coupled with our identification with the sensory inputs received from the physical world, the respective functions of these three levels of mind have been ignored and their respective powers have remained scattered and untapped.

Your One Mind

While seeing your mind as having three distinct levels goes a long way towards facilitating your understanding, there is no physical separation. This is because consciousness is not constrained by space and time, and so it is not subject to the division of 'Place A' being separate from 'Place B'. Once again, what distinguishes each level of mind is its respective degree of frequency of consciousness or self-awareness, but each degree blends into the other in such a way as to be inseparable. Put simply, the three levels of your mind are but degrees on the Scale of Consciousness of your *one* mind.

Since your super-conscious mind is the highest on the scale, and hence also the most powerful in directing change, it makes sense that raising your degree of self-awareness to this level grants you access to the full potential of your mind power.

Before you can identify with the super-conscious mind, however, you must first become familiar with the other levels of your mind, starting with your sub-conscious mind.

Chapter 3
LEVEL 1: THE SUB-CONSCIOUS MIND

The first level of your mind is the sub-conscious mind, also known as your subjective mind. You may have read or been told about the limitless power of your sub-conscious mind, and there is great truth in this. But if in ignorance you misuse or fail to intelligently apply its power, it can become the single most destructive influence in your life. Just as is the case with electricity, you may use it constructively to power your home or to power the entire planet, but if misused it can be enormously destructive. For this reason, the importance of learning to use the power of your sub-conscious mind intelligently cannot be over-stated if you are to achieve your goals and create the life you intend for yourself.

BELOW SELF-AWARENESS
The sub-conscious mind is below self-aware consciousness. This is unambiguously implied in the word itself because the preposition 'sub' means below. Therefore, 'sub-conscious' literally means below the awareness of consciousness, which in turn means that the sub-conscious mind is not personally aware of itself being separate from anything else. The lack of self-awareness makes the sub-conscious mind impersonal in nature because there is nothing outside of it to be personal in relation to. Impersonal, in this sense, does not mean without personal beliefs or without personality, but rather it means that the sub-conscious mind does not recognise external relationships of one thing to another as being separate from it in any way.

Moreover, the term 'subjective' means the sub-conscious mind is the *subject*, without any awareness of objects outside of it. In other words, everything is experienced subjectively through its own filters, beliefs, and mental programs. A deeper consideration of the word 'subjective' reveals that it has its origin in the noun 'subject' that means under the control or dominion of another. In turn, the word 'subject' has its origin in the Latin word *subicere*, meaning to place under. It stands to reason therefore that 'sub' in the word 'subjective', tells us that the sub-conscious mind is not only under or below self-aware consciousness, but that it is also subject to it.

Subjective in Nature
The subjective nature of the sub-conscious mind means that it must be directed by a suggestion in order to exert its power in any one direction. Once a suggestion is impressed on the sub-conscious mind,

it is then executed with precision to its final consequences. This can be likened to a seed that, once planted in the soil under the right conditions, will produce a crop in accordance to its nature.

Having said this, what the sub-conscious lacks in self-aware or conscious power, it makes up for many-fold by way of impersonal power. Impersonal power refers to the sub-conscious mind's power to reproduce any message or mental image that is impressed on it, without any *personal* evaluation or judgment of the message or mental image itself. In other words, the sub-conscious sets out to create whatever it is directed to create, which also means it is the creative aspect of your mind. This impersonal creative power is, in theory, limitless but in the absence of self-awareness, this power is limited to and by the messages that are given to the sub-conscious mind. It is humanity's ability to direct and impress images on the sub-conscious mind that sets us apart from the animal and plant kingdoms, but it is also the reason behind the disorderly state of our lives, at both a personal and global level.

Take for example the life of a tree. All growth takes place along unconscious or sub-conscious lines without any independent thought on the part of the tree. In other words, the sub-conscious operations of the tree simply serve to reproduce the nature of the tree that is inherent in the seed. In contrast, human beings impress their own sub-conscious minds through independent thought and so what is produced or created in a person's life, matches the quality of their dominant thoughts, whether positive or negative.

The creative power of the sub-conscious mind to create the life you intend can only be harnessed at a level of self-awareness, the highest degree of which is your Real Self. In order for you to be able to choose and direct your thoughts and emotions consciously, and in a way that serves you, you must rise above their level. Only the I within is above your ever-changing mental contents, as you will learn when we discuss the super-conscious mind.

Deductive Reasoning

The sub-conscious mind is only capable of deductive reasoning. This is a method of reasoning that starts with a general hypothesis, which does not need to be true, but that through observation is confirmed, deduced, and assumed to be true. Deductive reasoning, therefore, is equivalent to an 'if this, then that' function. A simple example of deductive reasoning is: all men are mortal (hypothesis), Socrates is a man (observation), therefore Socrates *is*, or more accurately *must be*, mortal (assumed deduction).

Put another way, assuming hypothesis A to be true, if factor B becomes present, then factor C must follow, but with no concern as to the validity of the initial hypothesis A. This means that any hypothesis impressed on the sub-conscious mind consistently enough is in time adopted and assumed to be valid because the sub-conscious does not rationally evaluate the inputs that are impressed on it, or the consequences inherent in them. As you may well know from your own experience, the problem that arises from deductive reasoning is that you may or may not believe what you are told, but you never doubt what you assume. In other words, what you sub-consciously *assume* to be true is what you *believe* is true, and so your assumed beliefs are rarely, if ever, up for questioning.

Any Suggestion, Any Source

The deductive method of reasoning of the sub-conscious means that any suggestion or message impressed on it often enough, is accepted, reproduced, and carried out with precision to its final consequences. In other words, the sub-conscious mind always produces or creates the outcomes inherent in its assumed hypotheses.

Moreover, the reproduced outcome then serves to confirm the original hypothesis, which in turn, serves to reproduce the same outcome. The more this cyclical confirmation takes place, the more a hypothesis is accepted as being valid and accurate. In other words, matching and re-matching an outcome with its hypothesis makes the hypothesis appear valid, in ignorance of the fact that the outcome itself is inherent in the hypothesis, and not the other way around.

Once again, the impersonal nature of the sub-conscious mind means that it does not personally evaluate or seek to validate the messages and suggestions that are given to it. There is clear evidence of this in the practice of hypnosis where the hypnotised subject is, at a sub-conscious level, under the control of the hypnotist and believes he is whatever the hypnotist says he is, without question.

The Achilles' Heel of the Sub-Conscious Mind

The sub-conscious mind's power to reproduce or create any message impressed on it to its finest detail, without fail, and without any need for critical or conscious reasoning on your part, is the source of its immeasurable, creative power. However, the obvious weakness or Achilles' Heel of the power of the sub-conscious mind is that *any* persistent suggestion, *any* persistent thought, or *any* concentrated mental image is adopted and in time reproduced, irrespective of its nature or its source.

This leaves the sub-conscious wide-open to unexamined, harmful programming. In turn, all the unexamined instructions, messages, and suggestions that are given to the sub-conscious mind make up its countless hypotheses that together reproduce the consequences that are inherent in them. Your sub-conscious mind's hypotheses are your beliefs and the sum of your beliefs make up your belief system, in accordance with which you perceive, create, and experience your life.

The Limitations of the Programs in the System

The potential power of the sub-conscious mind may be limitless but its actual power is limited by and to the programs in its 'system'. In the same way, a computer may be very powerful but its useful power is limited to the programs that have been installed on its hard drive. Likewise, your sub-conscious is capable of actualising any potential possibility, but which possibility is actualised in your life can only ever reflect the messages and mental image inputs that it has been provided or programmed with.

Having said this, the inability to reason or evaluate the inputs that are received, is not an oversight or weakness on the part of your sub-conscious mind's nature, but rather it is central to both its power and its function. This is because the sub-conscious mind is intended to both automatically and impersonally carry out the programs with which it has been programmed, including all your bodily functions, with no need for your conscious input.

Think about it this way - if your sub-conscious mind had to decide or evaluate whether or not your heart should pump blood around your body, or whether to send white blood cells to heal a wound, or whether to walk each time you wanted to walk, then there would be no physical existence as we know it. In other words, the sub-conscious mind is not intended to select or actively partake in choosing its impressions, and this is central to its role and its power.

Moreover, the consciousness that underlies all things and sustains the harmony of the Universe, works along unconscious or sub-conscious lines in accordance with Universal Laws. Therefore, were the sub-conscious mind able to think for itself, then the Laws of Physics would be rendered useless because a ball, for instance, could will itself not to roll down a slope, the sun could will itself not to rise, or a tree could will itself not to grow. Put another way, the order and harmony present throughout the manifested Universe would descend into chaos in the absence of the impersonal operations of the sub-conscious or unconscious mind throughout nature.

THE ROLE OF THE SUB-CONSCIOUS MIND

One of the fundamental roles of the sub-conscious mind throughout nature is to ensure survival in the physical world. This is evidenced in plants that naturally know to seek sunlight, and in animals with their heightened sense of hearing and smell that maximise their chances of survival in the wild. This survival function dates back to our primitive ancestors who faced very real survival challenges on a daily basis, and is essential throughout nature so as to ensure the continuity of all life.

Of course there is no denying that survival is an important aspect of your physical existence. If, for instance, you burn your hand by touching a hot stove, your sub-conscious mind creates a 'pain program' associated with a hot stove, which serves to preserve your existence and keep you safe in the future.

Having said this, even though the direct level of threat to our survival in modern day life has been greatly reduced, the sub-conscious mind when left to its own impersonal devices, still carries out its automatic functions along instinctive lines aimed at survival, because the sub-conscious 'will to live' is shared by all things.

This is all well and good as far as protecting you from physical danger goes, but the problem is, that once imprinted at a sub-conscious level, then your beliefs and mental programs are also instinctively executed with survival in mind.

Moreover, the longer a belief or program has been in place, then the more deeply ingrained it is sub-consciously. This is why so many people struggle to change or even challenge their assumptions and beliefs about life, because doing so is at some level perceived to be a risk to their survival, or in other words, to what they *think they know* to be true about what it takes to survive.

The Sub-Conscious Mind's Automatic Functions

There are three broad groups of sub-conscious automatic functions. The first group includes functions you are born with that are inherent to your physical nature as a human being. The second group includes functions you consciously acquire or adopt through learning, and the third group is your automatic mental programs that are based on those beliefs that you have adopted courtesy of your experiences.

Functions you are born with are largely bodily in nature, such as breathing, digestion, self-healing, waste elimination, the beating of your heart, the continuous pumping of blood around your body, and so on. These functions operate at the very deepest levels of the sub-conscious mind and thankfully there is little you can do to interfere with them directly on a day-to-day basis, although they too are open to direction under the right mental conditions.

Functions you acquire through learning include walking, speaking a language, playing an instrument, driving a car and so on; most of which required conscious input and attention during the learning stage, until such time that they were imprinted on the sub-conscious mind, and so became automatic.

The automation of learned functions at the sub-conscious level is itself intended to enable your self-conscious mind to learn new functions, as well as to allow you to participate in your experience of life consciously, without having to consciously think about walking, speaking, driving, and so on.

Assumed Belief System

It is the third group of sub-conscious functions that has the greatest impact on your life as far as your success and overall happiness are concerned. This third group is your acquired, assumed hypotheses, or in other words, the beliefs that are automatically triggered when certain factors present themselves, and the automatic consequences that follow. To further your understanding, let us now examine how you came to acquire your beliefs, whether consciously or otherwise.

It all comes down to your perception associated with memories, which themselves are stored in the sub-conscious mind. Your sub-conscious mind categorises memories of what happened in your life in a linear fashion. Your perception at the time determines what you *believe* to have happened, which in turn forms the basis of the nature of your memories. Your perception though is nothing more than your personal interpretation of events, which is usually coloured by already existing beliefs that may or may not be valid. In other words, all your experiences are in themselves neutral. It is you that allocates a meaning to them through your *perception*, and your sub-conscious mind then stores your experiences in accordance with your perceptions as specific beliefs or programs to be triggered when similar situations arise.

Once a program is in place sub-consciously, you begin to perceive new experiences through its filters and tend to pass off experiences that contradict the program as being a fluke, too good to be true, or you may not perceive them at all. For instance, if your experience in a past intimate relationship was painful and you inadvertently allowed that experience to affect your beliefs and hence your expectations about relationships, then your future relationships will, unbeknown to you, be run by an underlying 'avoid-pain' program. Moreover, the power of the program is determined by your personal conviction in your belief about what you perceived happened in the past.

The Self-Fulfilling Prophecy of Pleasure or Pain

Remember that the sub-conscious mind does not evaluate or think about its programs but rather, it simply carries them out, along with all the other automatic functions of the body, because that is what it does most efficiently. So even though a new experience may hold the greatest promise, if you are not consciously participating in that experience in the present moment, then the outcome of that experience is likely to be similar to the outcome of its past equivalent experiences, courtesy of your subconscious assumed beliefs.

The result is something of a self-fulfilling prophecy, be it one of pleasure or pain. The irony, of course, is that you are creating the outcome in accordance with your beliefs, and you accept it as being valid because it serves to make you right about what you believed would happen; and in turn reinforces the original belief irrespective of whether the outcome causes you pleasure or pain.

This brings us to the tendency as human beings to need to be right, which comes part and parcel with survival. The need to be right is arguably the single greatest cause of all strife in the world whether on a personal or global level because to make yourself right, you must by definition, make something or someone else wrong, and nobody wants to be wrong. Being right is ranked higher than being happy because survival depends more on being right about what you *think* it takes to survive, than it does on your happiness.

Where Did Your Beliefs Come From?

Since you were not born with your beliefs, the next question to ask yourself is where did they come from or, in other words, how did you learn to perceive your experiences in such a way that specific programs are automatically triggered? Remember that the subjective nature of the sub-conscious mind means that it can and does receive impressions from *any* source, and so it is that you have acquired your beliefs from a huge number of sources. Such sources include your parents or primary caretakers, your childhood environment, culture, religion, schooling, teachers, media, the government, the society in which you live, and so on.

Psychology suggests that most of the beliefs or programs that are running your life today were locked in place by the age of around seven. This is because a child's ability to critically and consciously reason is limited and hence absorbs and accepts new information, or in other words is programmed, with far greater ease than is an adult.

This then suggests that your life is being run in strict accordance with a set of deeply ingrained adopted and assumed beliefs accepted with the discretion of a seven year old child's mind, at best. This then means that if you are not consciously participating in your life in the present moment, then everything you think, everything you say, everything you do, and every perception you have, is simply an 'if this, then that' function of some program being carried out by an automaton whose primary aim is to be right and to survive.

There is no point in assigning blame to anyone, including yourself, for your sub-conscious programs and beliefs, because this would only serve to re-enforce them by handing your directive power over to them. However, it is up to you to take responsibility for your programs and beliefs because, irrespective of whether you consciously chose them or not, they are still yours.

Once again, this is not about blaming yourself in any way but rather, it is about taking conscious control of and responsibility for your life as an intelligent adult, instead of leaving your life in the hands of a seven-year old version of yourself. Taking responsibility grants you the power that allocating blame denies you. Moreover, if you do not take conscious responsibility for the contents of your mind, then you are more than likely going to carry on automatically executing your programs, irrespective of their nature, which really amounts to being the servant and not the master of your mind.

Nevertheless, understanding the subjective nature of the sub-conscious and the tremendous influence that childhood experiences, messages, and beliefs have in creating and locking in place the future programs of the sub-conscious, is reason enough for parents to be very wary of the messages they give to their children. Endeavour as a parent to teach your children well by way of the messages you give them and the example you set.

Re-Programming the Sub-Conscious Mind

Your aim is to be done with those sub-conscious programs that do not support you in taking your life in the direction you intend. Since your sub-conscious mind does not evaluate its inputs and in time accepts any suggestion given to it, then any unwanted sub-conscious program can be overwritten. Re-programming your sub-conscious mind, however, is not easy at the level of your personal self because at this level you are caught up in your physical experience and the automatic script of your sub-conscious mind. Having said this, the good news is there is no need for deep re-programming of your sub-conscious mind when at higher degrees of self-awareness, and none whatsoever if you identify with the I within. You will find that the more you come to know your Real Self and your inherent power, the more those negative or unwanted programs will naturally fall away.

This is the beauty of the Top-Down-Living approach of directing your life compared to the Bottom-Up approach of having to identify a negative program, that you are more than likely unaware of to start with, and then attempt to do away with it. Nevertheless, the first step in this direction is to wake yourself up from auto-pilot mode by becoming consciously aware of that level of your mind that is self-conscious, or in other words self-aware. In so doing, you rise above the level of involuntary reaction to voluntary action.

METAPHORS FOR THE SUB-CONSCIOUS MIND

Here are some metaphors for the sub-conscious mind that will help deepen your understanding. The sub-conscious can be likened to the script of a movie, with the actor acting out the script but without any critical evaluation on his part as to the validity of the script.

The sub-conscious can also be likened to the programmable hard-drive of a computer. Just as is the case with the hard drive of a computer, the sub-conscious mind simply executes the software that is installed on it, irrespective of whether it is a useful program or a destructive virus. Moreover, the hard-drive does not get to choose its own programs.

Finally, the sub-conscious mind can be likened to the soil in which seeds are planted. The crop that is reproduced or created always matches the nature of the seed, but the soil has no choice as to which seeds are planted within it.

The Sub-Conscious Mind in a Nutshell

To bring what has been said together, your sub-conscious is your source of immeasurable creative power to reproduce in your physical reality, with precision, the messages, suggestions, and mental images that are impressed upon it. However, in order for you to harness its subjective power to its full potential, you must become the single, intelligent, and self-aware source of its messages. In other words, you must use your *directive* power of positivity, to direct its *creative* power. The first step in this direction is a step upwards in self-awareness on the Scale of Consciousness, which brings us to the next level of mind that is your self-conscious mind.

Chapter 4

LEVEL 2: THE SELF-CONSCIOUS MIND

Your self-conscious mind is that part of you that is consciously aware of yourself in the physical world as being personally separate from others and as having a distinct personality. It is also referred to as the personal self, as well as the objective mind, because through it, you personally and objectively experience yourself as being separate from all those things outside the physical you, including people and things. Its own point of reference therefore, is the personal self that says 'me', while everyone and everything else is perceived as 'them' and 'outside things' respectively.

Having said this, bear in mind that all levels of mind *above* the sub-conscious are, by definition, *conscious* and *objective*, including the super-conscious mind of the I within. The *self*-conscious mind therefore, is that part of the *conscious* mind operating at the level of the personality, which is the first level of self-aware consciousness.

THE POWER OF ATTENTION

Your self-conscious mind is aware of those things that are within the field of your ordinary consciousness. In turn, your field of ordinary consciousness is captured within the radius of your attention. This means that you are only conscious or *aware* of those things that you give your attention to, whether they are taking place in your outer physical world or in your inner mental world. Put another way, your self-conscious mind consciously experiences and hence is aware of, those physical and mental things which you give your attention to, whether they are outside conditions and things, or inner thoughts and emotions. The greater the field of your conscious attention, then the greater is the field of your conscious awareness. In other words, where attention goes, self-conscious awareness follows.

Your Objective Mind Gives Meaning

It is your objective mind that gives meaning to your experiences and directs your subjective mind with that meaning. This is because your self-conscious mind receives impressions from the outside world in the form of fresh, raw inputs that have no implicit meaning. It then modifies these inputs at lightning speed using emotion, perception, and associated memories to give them meaning. In turn, it sends the adjusted inputs down to your subjective sub-conscious mind, which is akin to directing the sub-conscious to carry out the instructions in the inputs you give to it. The problem is that most people do not consciously evaluate the inputs they receive, and nor do they pay any attention to the meaning that they give them, before the inputs are allowed to pass from their objective self-conscious mind to their subjective sub-conscious mind. In this way, unbeknown to you, you have facilitated the scripting of your sub-conscious programs that are today largely determining the quality of your life.

Inductive Reasoning
Remember that the sub-conscious mind reasons deductively, giving no consideration as to the validity of the starting point, and hence simply carries out the ensuing stages of any message it consistently receives, to its final consequences. In contrast, the distinguishing factor of the objective self-conscious mind is that it is capable of both deductive and inductive reasoning. Inductive reasoning is the opposite of deductive reasoning. It is the ability to *first* observe, compare, and evaluate a number of factors *before* arriving at a final conclusion, based on those observations.

Put another way, inductive reasoning allows you to harness the immense power in the momentary space between a specific stimulus and the response it triggers within you. In this way you have the opportunity to change or neutralise your response to specific stimuli, rather than to react to them automatically in accordance with deeply ingrained, subconscious programs that may not serve you and were, most likely, not consciously chosen to begin with.

Having said this, most people operate, even at the level of the self-conscious mind, with just their deductive reasoning, thereby accepting what they experience and their perception thereof with no critical thinking on their part. But it is the conscious mind's ability to reason inductively and objectively that is the source of its power.

THE ROLE OF THE SELF-CONSCIOUS MIND
Given its capacity to reason inductively, the self-conscious mind has the immensely important role of protecting the sub-conscious mind. The objective mind is the intended guardian of the impressionable subjective mind. It must ensure that only empowering messages or suggestions are allowed through for programming, after careful evaluation of all factors. However, this role is seldom acknowledged and instead, the self-conscious mind is left to operate with the same deductive reasoning that the sub-conscious uses impersonally.

In his 1912 book, The Master Key System, Charles F. Haanel wrote the following in this regard: "The sub-conscious mind does not engage in the process of proving. It relies upon the self-conscious mind to guard it from mistaken impressions. When the watchman is off guard, or when its calm judgment is suspended under a variety of circumstances, then the sub-conscious mind is unguarded and left open to suggestion from all sources."

The Ocean of Your Mind

Think of your mind as a vast ocean. You sub-conscious mind is akin to the deep recesses of the ocean of which you are unaware; and your self-conscious mind is the surface of the ocean, whose activity you are consciously aware of by paying attention to it. Remember that the suggestions that are given to the sub-conscious mind must first pass through the self-conscious mind. In keeping with the metaphor of the ocean, this means that for something to enter the depth of the ocean (subjective mind) from outside, it must first pass through the ocean's surface (objective mind).

This, in turn, means that the less conscious attention you pay to the activity in your physical and mental worlds, then the more unaware you are of the countless suggestions and messages that are indiscriminately entering or 'falling into' your sub-conscious mind. In contrast, the wider your field of conscious attention, then the greater your awareness of your own thoughts about what you are physically or mentally experiencing, which in turn, allows you to intercept them before they enter your sub-conscious for imprinting or programming.

The Automatons of an Unaware Mind

When you were a child, learning to manipulate your environment to get your way, you were not reasoning at the level of self-awareness of the self-conscious mind. Moreover, the chances are that you are most probably still denying your self-conscious mind this fundamental role as an adult. In so doing, you experience life as if you were an unaware automaton directed by the automatic programs of your sub-conscious mind that are based on deep-set beliefs that you are unaware of. Moreover, as long as you are not consciously participating in your life in the present moment with awareness, then messages from the media, society, your environment, friends, family, colleagues and so on, are still indiscriminately being passed down to your sub-conscious where they are either triggering or re-enforcing existing beliefs, or possibly creating new ones.

The Achilles' Heel of the Self-Conscious Mind

The self-conscious mind of the personal self has a weakness of its own. Its Achilles' Heel is that it is wrapped up in the counterfeit ego of your *personality*, which itself comes part and parcel with your perceptions of your memories and related beliefs. Your counterfeit ego is that part of your personality that insists on being right and demands instant gratification or, in other words, getting what it wants, and getting it now.

Moreover, your personality is itself based largely on sub-conscious beliefs about yourself that you did not intelligently choose. This means that since the self-conscious mind is the mind of the personal self, and since your personality has been left largely to the discretion of deeply ingrained programs of which you are unaware of, then your unaware sub-conscious mind rules the day, which is akin to having no advantage over the animal or even plant kingdoms.

Even if you are consciously self-aware at the level of your personality, and even if you do pay attention to your thoughts about what is going on around you, you are more than likely still acting out the *script* held in the sub-conscious mind, albeit unbeknown to you.

The Observer of Your Thoughts

The higher you raise your degree of consciousness, or in other words your degree of self-awareness, then the more aware you become of your automatic thoughts. This, in turn, enables you to intercept and change them accordingly.

To become more aware in this way, however, you must start paying attention to your thoughts, as well as to your automatic physical and mental reactions to whatever circumstances may arise. By doing so, you get to 'catch yourself in the act'. This does not mean to become obsessed with every little thought that enters your mind. On the contrary, it is about becoming their neutral observer without judging them, or yourself, for entertaining them. By increasing your self-awareness in this way, the rate of vibration of your consciousness begins to approach the degree of your super-conscious mind, which is the mind of the I within, and is above the personality of the personal self and the sub-conscious script that keeps it in place.

Incidentally, isn't it somewhat ironic that to be self-conscious, which literally means 'to be aware of oneself', has been negatively distorted to mean being insecure, whereas in truth, without becoming aware of yourself first, you cannot hope to achieve any greater level of awareness, and nor can you harness the mental directive power that comes with it. Nevertheless, let us now look at some further metaphors, this time for the self-conscious mind at the level of the personal self, before moving on to discuss the highest degree of self-aware consciousness, which is the super-conscious mind.

METAPHORS FOR THE SELF-CONSCIOUS MIND

The self-conscious mind can be likened to the actor in the movie, acting out the script. The actor must act out the script. He cannot change the script in any meaningful way in accordance with his will, at least not without risking his acting position as well.

Looked at another way, the self-conscious mind is like the user of the computer, who uses the in-built programs on the computer's hard-drive but whose computing power is limited to the power of those in-built programs.

Finally, the self-conscious mind is analogous to the farmer that indiscriminately sows the seeds, without any critical consideration as to the nature of each seed.

Chapter 5
LEVEL 3: THE SUPER-CONSCIOUS MIND

Your super-conscious mind is also known as higher consciousness or the higher mind. It is the degree of self-aware consciousness at which you find the Real You or Higher Self that is the I within. The super-conscious mind is also referred to as the mind of your Spirit.

Super-consciousness is the highest degree of self-consciousness. The preposition 'super' has its origin in the Latin adverb *super* meaning 'above', and is also the root of the word 'superior', meaning 'higher, upper or situated above'. One can say therefore, that super-consciousness is above and superior to the consciousness of the physical world and of the physical being that experiences it.

It is, however, the least understood and least accessed aspect of mind because it is not directly experienced in the physical or even the mental realms, as its domain is the spiritual realm. In other words, the super-conscious mind of the I is above your physical senses and perceived experiences of the physical world, and is also above your emotions, passions, and even the thoughts of your mental world.

THE REAL EGO

Your super-conscious mind is the seat of your Real Ego, also known as Egohood. This is not to be confused with the counterfeit ego of the personality, that is wrapped up in the sensory feedback provided by the outer world and that insists on being right. You may have been advised to relinquish your ego as you endeavour to better your life experience, but this advice can only apply to the counterfeit ego of the personality. The two are distinguished by using an upper-case 'E' for the Real Ego, which belongs to your Real Self; and a lower-case 'e' for the counterfeit ego, which belongs to the personal self. The two can be distinguished further in that the personality operates at the level of 'me', whereas the Real Self operates at the level of 'I'.

The Real Ego is your Ego in the original sense of the Greek word «ΕΓΩ» (pronounced: *ego with a deep e and o*), meaning I. You can never be rid of the I that is the Real You, because it is the only part of you that is eternally changeless and thus the only part of you that is real. The I that is the Real You says 'I AM' in full authority and since the distinguishing quality of the self-aware mind is the ability to think independently, the I says 'I THINK therefore I AM'. It does not say 'I am this' or 'I am that'. All power resides in 'I AM I' with no constraints or qualification.

The Seat of Your Will

The super-conscious mind is the seat of the full directive potential of your will power. Were it not for the will of your Higher Self, then you could not experience life, because life is the *will* of your Higher Self to experience *itself*. Nothing can be done intentionally in the absence of the will to do so. For instance, you can think about raising your hand and you can even desire it, but you can never do so if you do not will it, no matter how much you try. Try it out for yourself and you will see the truth in this - nothing can be accomplished consciously without your will.

Put simply, your will power is your individual directive power. It must be used to direct your mind and the experiences that it creates, rather than have your mind unconsciously directed for you, as is the 'mind' of everything else in the manifested Universe. By putting your will in the equation, the mantra of the Real You becomes 'I THINK therefore I AM therefore I WILL'.

It is your ability to think that allows you to proclaim the most profound and most powerful statement - 'I AM' - from the highest level of self-awareness. In turn, the Real You that says 'I AM' is completely free to use the full directive power of your will, to direct your mind and hence to create your life in accordance with your heart's desires. This is what it means to say 'I WILL'.

THE ROLE OF THE SUPER-CONSCIOUS MIND

The Real You is above both your personality and the automatic sub-conscious script that keeps it in place. At the degree of consciousness of your super-conscious mind you know that the outside world you experience as your reality, along with your emotional ups and downs and all the qualities of your personality and sub-conscious beliefs, are but passing illusions that are subject to change at will.

The Real You does not distinguish between the opposites of good and bad, right and wrong, happy and sad, success and failure. Not because it is unable to do so but rather, because it has no need to in the knowledge that they are transient and unreal, as you will learn later. Both deductive and inductive reasoning are replaced with the ability to observe things as they are, and say 'it is what it is' in the full knowledge that all is subject to change through the directive power of your will. This is why the Real You is also called the Observer.

The Real You knows you are not your body but rather, your body is the vehicle through which you experience the physical realm. Knowing yourself to be eternal, and knowing that the physical death of your physical body is but the gateway to another realm, you have no need for the fear-based survival programs of your personality. Put simply, the Real You knows, as Albert Einstein said, that "reality is merely an illusion albeit a very persistent one."

Objective Mind - Subjective Reality

As you already know, your self-conscious personal mind is objective in nature. Its objectivity, however, is limited by the 'tunnel-vision' of the personality, which is itself based on the sub-conscious mind's script. Put another way, although your self-conscious mind is objective, objectivity at its level is partial, because it is trapped in the apparent dual nature of 'me' versus 'outside things and people'.

In contrast, complete objectivity belongs to the super-conscious mind. This is because everything and everyone in the manifested Universe, including your body, personal self and mental contents, are objective to the I. At this level of awareness you can observe all things *as they are*, free from the perceptions of the personality.

Unlike the personal self that experiences duality, the I within knows of the non-dual or unified nature of the Universe. At its level you remain undisturbed by outside events, because you do not define yourself by anything in your reality, including your physical experiences and your mental contents of emotions, thoughts, desires, passions, fears, and so on.

Put another way, the Real You is the Observer and everything else, is what is being observed. Observation, however, is distinctly different to perception. The Observer is unaffected by what is being observed, whereas the perceiver is directly affected by what is being perceived, in accordance with his or her perception of it.

At the level of the Observer, reality becomes fully subjective. This means your reality is subject to the direction of your fully objective mind, because you are aware that reality is but a projection of your mind. This is what is meant by 'subjective reality' because reality is taking place *inside* the mind and is hence subject to it. In contrast, objective reality means reality is taking place *outside* the mind and hence is separate from it. The concept of reality being a projection of consciousness is one of the subjects of Part II.

Put simply, your Real Self is fully objective because at its level you observe all things and are undisturbed by them as if you are fully independent of them. At the same time, *your* experience of reality is fully subjective because you are aware of it taking place in accordance with *your* mind. In other words, your reality is subjective to your objective mind, under the direction of your will.

METAPHORS FOR THE SUPER-CONSCIOUS MIND

At the level of awareness of your super-conscious mind, the Real You is both the audience and *intended* director of the movie. You know it is just a movie whose script can be changed at will. You also know that the actor is performing an adopted role based on an assumed script.

The I is the *intended* computer programmer, who intelligently writes the programs to be used, and directs which programs are to be installed in the hard-drive of the computer. The programmer knows that any program can be changed or removed at will, and that no program has any independent power of its own.

The Real You is the farmer who is *intended* to intelligently choose the seeds to be planted in the soil that is your sub-conscious mind, knowing that all growth begins in the inner world of the soil, and ends in an exact replica of the nature of the seed, in the outer world above the soil.

In all three of the above metaphors, the Real You is the Observer. As the Observer you objectively direct your mind with the power of your will. In so doing you choose your thoughts and keep them in place, and hence create your experience of the physical world accordingly. But you never become part of what is being observed and hence, always remain the unchanged and undisturbed Observer.

Having looked at the three levels of your mind, we will now consider consciousness from a different angle. Specifically, we will look at your body associated largely with your sub-conscious mind, your personality at the level of your self-conscious mind of the personal self, and finally the character of the Individual that is associated with your super-conscious mind of the I within.

Chapter 6

THE BODY

Your body is not just your physical body that you can see but also includes a non-visible part that is energetic in nature. Having said this, since everything is energy, then your physical body is itself *part of* your energetic body, with the only difference being its greater density, which makes it visible and tangible to your physical senses.

YOUR PHYSICAL BODY

Since our direct human experience is physical in nature, many people identify themselves with their physical body, believing themselves to be their body and nothing more. This is partly due to mass media's relentless focus on the body, which has created a body-conscious culture whose self-worth is wrapped up in their body-image.

Know, however, that you are not your physical body. Rather, your body is the vehicle or medium through which you can experience yourself as the Real You in the physical realm. To believe you are your body and nothing more denies you access to the limitless power of Universal Consciousness of which your consciousness is a part. Nevertheless, the functions of your physical body are automatic and their respective programs run at very deep, sub-conscious levels.

The Physical Temple that Houses Your Spirit

Do not be misled into thinking that since you are not your physical body, it is unimportant or unnecessary, because without it you could not have a physical experience. On the contrary, it makes your physical body even more important than you may have ever given it credit for, because it really is the temple that houses your Spirit.

Having said this, it does not mean your body should determine your self-worth but rather, you should acknowledge its worth for your Real Self who operates through it. Let these words by CS Lewis be your new understanding of your body. "You do not have a soul. You *are* a soul. You *have* a body."

Your Body Believes Every Word You Say

Each and every one of your body's minute cells that make up all your organs and other physical parts are alive with consciousness and have a mind of their own. The consciousness of your body is subjective, which means it is open to objective direction, as is your overall sub-conscious mind. Your body hears every word you say and think, and being subjective, takes you at your word. Your thoughts can and do have the ability to either harm or heal your body, in accordance with their nature, which is the premise of Mental Healing in Chapter 42.

The mind-body connection is indisputably proven. Perhaps the most widely recognised connection between the two is the so-called placebo effect, a basic example of which is when a sugar pill is given to a person who has a headache but is told it is a specific drug for headaches and so *believes* it will help treat their headache, and it does. It is also well documented that stress has a negative effect on your body whereas enough sleep, relaxation and laughter have an opposite, positive effect.

Is it Sensible to Rely on Your Senses?
The self-conscious mind of your personal self relies heavily on your five physical senses to perceive the physical world, in what essentially is an attempt to keep you safe. In fact, most people rely exclusively on their sight, hearing, touch, taste, and smell to interpret their reality, as these are the five senses that allow human beings to interact with and experience the physical world.

However, just like you should not judge a book by its cover, nor should you judge reality by its appearance. After all, your five physical senses are compelling enough to convince you that you are sitting still while reading these words, when in fact you (and everything on Earth) are rotating at an incredible pace of approximately 66,660 miles per hour (107,278.87 kilometres per hour) around the sun.

Douglas Adams, the author of The Hitch Hiker's Guide to the Galaxy series, had this to say on the subject. "The fact that we live at the bottom of a deep gravity well, on the surface of a gas covered planet going around a nuclear fireball 90 million miles away and think this to be normal, is obviously some indication of how skewed our perspective tends to be."

YOUR NON-PHYSICAL BODY
Your non-physical body is known as the electro-magnetic Human Energy Field that extends energetically and non-visibly beyond the boundary of your physical body while also permeating it. It can be likened to a force-field with attractive and repulsive forces.

Your Aura
The most commonly used term to describe the Human Energy Field is the word 'aura' that has its origin in the exact same Greek word meaning 'breath'. Everything in the manifested Universe is said to have an aura, which is the vehicle of consciousness of that thing. The human aura is ovoid shaped, hence the term 'auric egg'. Your aura

extends outwards from your central spinal column and beyond your body from all sides, to an average of two to three feet, or one meter.

It is imbued by a variety of colours, each having its own meaning. Your auric colours are in constant flux, depending on your physical, emotional, mental, and spiritual states, as well as the state of your immediate environment. In this way, your aura serves as a visual measure of those states, albeit not immediately visible to your physical eyes. Likewise, a disturbance in any one of these states is reflected as a disturbance in your aura.

The Seven Auric Bodies and Chakras
In the same way that there are seven colours in the rainbow and seven notes in a musical scale, your aura has seven major layers with increasingly subtle or less dense rates of vibration. It also has seven major internal chakras or energy centres that are vertically arranged in an upward line from the base of your spinal cord up to the top of your head, and are connected to your aura through an invisible grid of lines within your physical body called the *nadis* or meridian lines.

Chakras are best described as energy vortexes, which look like spinning wheels that receive, radiate, and transfer Universal Life Force or energy throughout your body. In Eastern Philosophy this Life Force is known as *Qi (pronounced: chee)* in Chinese, or *prana* in Sanskrit. Each chakra has its own colour and corresponding organ in your physical body. The more balanced you are emotionally, mentally and spiritually, then the faster your energy vortexes or chakras spin and the brighter their respective light colours. In contrast, the greater the emotional, mental and spiritual disturbances, then the slower the spin and the duller the corresponding colours. While the subject of your chakras is a very interesting one, it is beyond the scope of this book's focus, which is the power of your mind to create the life you intend under the direction of your will.

Nevertheless, understanding your body's physical and energetic nature as described here provides you with a more complete picture of your consciousness and by applying the exercises found in this book, your body's energy will naturally return to greater harmony.

Chapter 7

THE PERSONALITY AND THE INDIVIDUAL

Your personality is the adopted role you play when you interact in the physical world. It identifies with the counterfeit ego of the personal self that knows nothing of the Real Ego of the I. Once again, your counterfeit ego is that part of you that insists on being right and on having what it wants now; not from a place of power or knowledge but more like a child throwing a tantrum.

The hallmark of the counterfeit ego is an inflexibility to change and an insistence on being right, which serves to keep you stuck in your current circumstances. Moreover, your counterfeit ego experiences itself as the 'me' that is separate to everything and everyone else, thereby limiting its own power to the power of the personal self. It knows nothing of the Universal Power that the Real Ego, or the I within, knows it is a part of. Rather, in a misguided effort to be in control, the counterfeit ego usually resorts to fuelling its own power by forcefully taking it away from others, in the false belief that power is limited and finite.

THE ACTOR AND THE ROLE

Your personality can be likened to the role adopted by an actor in a movie. More specifically, the movie is your physical experience and the lead actor is you. Interestingly, the word 'person' has its origin in the Latin word *persona*, meaning 'a role in a drama' or 'the mask used by an actor'. Your personal self has certain idiosyncrasies, traits, likes, dislikes, prejudices, beliefs, strengths, and weaknesses.

Most of these qualities stem from your beliefs or the sub-conscious script from which you are acting, while others you were born with and can be said to be genetic or hereditary in nature, although no less subject to change. Put another way, your personality is always your adopted role that is the 'me' as opposed to the 'I'. It is not the Real You but most people tend to experience life as if the two are one and the same. Indeed, most people identify very closely with their personality, not thinking for one instant that there is a Higher Self that is above it and beyond its specifics.

The reason you are likely to be tied up in your personality is because it is that part of you that is directly experiencing the physical world through your physical senses, and which you have come to depend on almost exclusively to relay your experience of reality to your brain. This really amounts to the actor getting so wrapped up in his acting, that he forgets who he is outside of his adopted role. It can be likened to the actor really believing that he is *only* the role he has adopted to play, whether it is the role of Macbeth, Romeo in Romeo and Juliet or Jack Sparrow in Pirates of the Caribbean. Believing then that your personality is the Real You, is the same as Johnny Depp believing that he actually is Jack Sparrow, which might be fun for a while but does not serve the real Mr Depp in the long-run, as the adopted role itself is limited to its script.

Changing Your Role

When you become conscious of your personality as simply the adopted role of the actor in the movie in which you are acting, you can shake off the illusion that it is the Real You. Change is achieved much easier when you realise that you are more than your assumed role and more than the mask you wear on your life stage, or rather, that you are none of these.

In this way, you can start observing the role you are playing with your specific personality traits, which you have learnt to perform with perfection. This empowers you to choose, change, and transform your role in accordance with the personality traits that you desire to display at any one given moment. To do so you must use the power of your will and apply it intelligently to make the changes in your personality. Auto-suggestion is a very powerful tool for enabling change at the level of the personality, as is discussed in Chapter 41.

Moreover, Albert Einstein told us that "A problem can never be solved at the level at which it was created." What this means, as far as your mind is concerned, is that to solve your problems, be they problems of personality, of circumstance, or of physical health, you must rise above the level of the personality at which they were created. This then brings us to the part of you that is the Individual, which being above your physical body and personality, is associated with your super-conscious mind of the I within.

THE INDIVIDUAL

By setting aside the sensations of the physical body and the mask of the personality you will find the Real You that is above the sensory inputs of the physical world and the script-imposed limits of the personality. At super-conscious awareness you find the Individual with an upper-case I, which is another word for the Real You. As you already know, the role you play is the personality that is the 'me', whereas the Real You is the Individual that is the 'I'. When you take away every last word that you use to describe yourself, or who you *think* you are, what you are left with is the Individual. The word 'individual' has its origin in the Latin word *individuus* meaning 'indivisible'. Unlike modern-day interpretations implying *separateness*, the word 'individual' in its original sense, means that the Individual or I is indivisibly One with All.

The Individual is the Observer. You may hear people saying they are still 'looking to find themselves', without realising it is the eternal Observer within that they are looking for. In the words of Saint Francis of Assisi, "What we are looking for is what is looking." When you stop searching outside of you for 'the one' to love with all your heart, who will love you back, you will find that 'the one' you have been looking for all along, is You – the Real You. You are the *One*.

Your Character

While your personality is the adopted role of the personal self that says 'me' and the Individual is the Real You that says 'I', your character is born out of the balance you strike between the two. The word character differs from personality. 'Personality' means a 'role or mask' whereas the word 'character' has its origin in the Greek word «χαρακτήρα» *(pronounced: haraktira)*, which in its original sense comes from the verb 'to engrave'.

Your character can be likened to the engraving or imprinting of the I within on the personality of the personal self. Your character is built and constantly evolves in accordance with the balance you strike between the counterfeit ego of 'me' and the Real Ego of 'I'. The deeper the imprint of the I, the stronger your character. Put another way, if the weight of the scale bears down in favour of 'me' then one's character is weak, even though one's personality may be strong. Whereas if the scale is tipped in favour of 'I', then one's character is strong even though one's personality may appear subdued.

A strong character uses his personality intelligently whereas a weak character is used by the counterfeit ego of his personality to try to get its way. Strong characters exhibit high degrees of will power and have the ability to influence others as well as their environment through their presence alone, without having to exert physical force or manipulation of any kind. A strong character can walk into a room full of people and, without having to utter a word, everyone seems to turn their head in his or her direction, yet he remains undisturbed. A strong personality, however, is often accompanied by a deeper need for attention. While a strong personality is often over-bearing, a strong character is mesmerising.

PART II
THE ABSOLUTE, UNIVERSAL MIND AND I

Chapter 8
THE ABSOLUTE

Sacred teachings and texts dating back thousands of years tell us of the existence of an Absolute Supreme Power that is the original cause of the Universe, and that unifies everything and everyone, everywhere and eternally. This Absolute Supreme Power goes by several names in esoteric texts, including The Absolute, The All, The Source, The One, The Life Principle, and God. However, irrespective of the name used, humanity's misguided concept of this Absolute Supreme Power has caused much confusion and discord, especially in the case of the name God. For the most part, this is because of an attempt to personify God in the image of man, rather than the other way around, that is man in the image of God.

As an aside at this point, before we consider The Absolute, bear in mind as you read this second part of the book, that it is at times an academic consideration of the underlying nature of the Universe and your place in it, which is intended to provide you with a deeper understanding of your reality and a foundation on which to apply the practical techniques you will gain later on in this book. Having said this, there is no need to be overwhelmed by any of the detail in this part of the book. While my aim was to keep it as simple as possible, some complexity was unavoidable, but the complexity makes no practical difference to your ability to apply the techniques described later in the book.

COMPREHENDING THE ABSOLUTE

Attempting to comprehend the nature of The Absolute offers you a deeper understanding of It, based on reason rather than faith alone. Having said this, something that is Absolute is not readily open to intellectual comprehension. This is because human beings can only represent or describe things by using words and symbols, both of which are finite, whereas The Absolute is infinite and therefore, beyond the finite explanations of words or symbols. Moreover, our physical world experience is constrained by space, time, and constant change and hence, does not lend itself either to understanding the infinite, changeless nature of The Absolute. Nevertheless, an attempt at comprehending The Absolute is still possible and beneficial.

The Empty Circle
While it is arguably not possible to represent the infinite nature of The Absolute by a single finite symbol, the most adequate symbol for it is the empty circle, with the proviso that no matter how wide the circle is drawn, there is always space beyond it to draw it infinitely wider. Indeed, the ancient symbol for The Absolute is the symbol of the empty circle.

In contrast, the more commonly known mathematical symbol for infinity is a side-ways figure of 8. This is the symbol for the infinity of the manifested Universe and suggests by its shape an endless continuation of action and change, both of which presuppose space and time. This symbol therefore, does not apply to The Absolute because It is infinite, changeless, and above both space and time.

Infinite Space
Besides the empty circle as a symbol for The Absolute, the most adequate way to comprehend Its infinite nature intellectually is to think of It in terms of infinite space. Even though physical space is a physical limitation to which The Absolute is not constrained, it does still lend itself well to comprehending something that is infinite. In fact, a deeper consideration of space illustrates how infinite space unifies all things in the Universe, both outwards and inwards.

When you think about infinite space expanding outwards, it will become apparent that no matter how far out you go, beyond the boundaries of the Earth, beyond the Solar System, beyond the Milky Way and other galaxies, and beyond even the boundaries of the observable Universe, you will always find more space beyond that. There is therefore, no end to the outward expansion of infinite space.

The same applies to when you consider space from an inward perspective. While things in the physical Universe may appear to be solid, we know that this is just an illusion produced by our physical senses. The fact is that all ordinary matter, including you, this book, the air you breathe, the planets, the stars, and all the galaxies, are made up of atoms.

An inward look into atoms shows them to be made up of protons, neutrons, and electrons, between which there is mostly space. Indeed, more than 99.9% of an atom is made up of space, and this space continues to expand as we consider sub-atomic particles at the quantum level. Infinite space, therefore, is the most accurate concept available to us to comprehend the infinity of The Absolute.

THE NATURE OF THE ABSOLUTE

We will now consider the inherent nature of The Absolute. In his 1909 book The Arcane Teaching, although written anonymously, William Walker Atkinson describes The Absolute using four major maxims summarised below, and refers to The Absolute as The All.

Maxim 1: "The All Is." This maxim describes the absolute existence of The Absolute, as having always existed and never having come into being. This means that The Absolute was never created, unlike the created Universe. The Absolute has always existed, unconstrained by space and time and is thus infinite and eternal.

Maxim 2: "Beyond, higher, and older than The All, there is not." This maxim tells us that The Absolute is all that is, all that ever was, and all that will ever be. Nothing exists outside of or beyond It, nothing existed before It, and It is superior to everything.

Maxim 3: "The All exists beyond time, space, and change, transcends the Laws, is unconditioned, immutable, self-existent, independent, and abstract." This maxim tells us that The Absolute is All-Present (Omnipresent) and changeless, as in existing everywhere at the same time in Its entirety. 'Transcending the Laws' refers to The Absolute being above the Laws of the Universe, which is why another name for It is The Law. 'Unconditioned' means limitless, including limitless knowledge and power, as in All-Knowing (Omniscient) and All-Powerful (Omnipotent).

'Immutable' means The Absolute is unchanging, unlike the ever-changing things of the Universe. 'Self-existent' and 'independent' mean It needs no cause in order to exist, and nor does It depend on anything for Its existence as nothing is outside of It to depend on. Finally, the word 'abstract' suggests an intangible concept beyond representation by words or symbols.

Maxim 4: "The All is the efficient reason, supreme power, and causeless cause of all things." This maxim tells us that The Absolute is the Original or First Cause of the Universe, but is Itself causeless because it has always existed. 'Efficient reason' suggests Supreme Intelligence and Omniscience because all things in the Universe are created and sustained in perfect order and harmony, with exact patterns that replicate themselves without error in accordance with Universal Laws. 'Supreme power' refers to Omnipotence or the All-Powerful nature of The Absolute.

Bringing these maxims together, the attributes that most concisely describe The Absolute are as follows:

Omnipresence (All-Present): to be present everywhere and in everything eternally, at the same time, and in Its entirety.

Omnipotence (All-Powerful): to have Absolute Power and be the Single Source of All Power. This includes creative power.

Omniscience (All-Knowing): to have Absolute Knowledge and be the Single Source of All Knowledge, known and unknown to humanity, and unconstrained by space and time.

The Absolute as Nothing

The Absolute is sometimes referred to as The Nothing. Although an unlikely term to describe something that is The All, its reasoning is sound. Since the Absolute existed *before* the creation of the Universe of *things*, It cannot be referred to as a thing. Something, therefore, that is not a thing is 'a nothing', with the literal meaning 'No Thing'.

William Walker Atkinson defines the no-thingness of The Absolute as "the possibility of everything, yet without the limitations of thingness." Put another way, The Absolute is the Single Cause of all things but It is unconstrained by the limitation of things. This also underpins the saying 'from nothing, comes everything' and the Latin phrase *creatio ex nihilo*, meaning 'creation out of nothing'.

THE TRUE MEANING OF OMNIPRESENCE

The importance of understanding the true meaning of Omnipresence (All-Present), against the backdrop of infinity and eternity, cannot be over-stated when it comes to identifying the source of your own power. Put simply, being infinite, The Absolute exists outside the constraints of physical space, and being eternal, It existed *before* time.

This means that in order to understand Omnipresence, you must go beyond your conditioned experience of space where one part of The Absolute is present 'here' and another part is present 'there'. You must also go beyond your conditioned experience of time where that part of The Absolute present today is different to what was present yesterday, or what will be present tomorrow. Omnipresence therefore means that The Absolute or God is *changeless* and is present in Its *entirety* in *every* single point in space and time.

In his 1909 book, The Edinburgh Lectures on Mental Science, Judge Thomas Troward drew some astounding conclusions from this concept of the changeless Omnipresent nature of The Absolute, which he referred to as the 'Originating Life-Principle' or 'Spirit'. I can best convey his message by quoting him directly, as follows.

"The great fact to be recognised about unity is that, because it is a single unit, wherever it is, the whole of it must be. The moment we allow our mind to wander off to the idea of extension in space, and say that one part of the unit is here and another there, we have descended from the idea of unity [which is absolute], into that of parts or fractions of a single unit [which is relative]. It is, therefore, a mathematical necessity that, because the Originating Life-Principle is infinite, it is a single unit, and consequently, wherever it is at all, the whole of it must be present. Therefore it follows that the whole of Spirit must be present at every point in space, at the same moment. Spirit is thus Omnipresent in its entirety and it is accordingly logically correct that, at every moment of time, all Spirit is concentrated at any point in space that we may choose to fix our thought upon."

Put simply, this means that The Absolute is present in Its entirety in every point in space and time, in every atom and sub-atomic particle, in everything tangible and intangible from the colossal in size to the minute, including you, and each and every one of your cells. This is the true meaning of Omnipresence and is what underpins the ancient teachings that 'you are one with God'.

Bear in mind, however, that an absolute identification with The Absolute or God is a life-time journey and cannot happen overnight, especially given your perceived experience of separateness to date. Having said this, knowing that The Absolute Supreme Power is by mathematical definition present within you in Its entirety, is the greatest source of inspiration you can ever come to find, and to be inspired is to be In-Spirit. Indeed, the word 'inspiration' has its root in 'to breathe in Spirit and to have Spirit breathe in you'.

EVIDENCE FOR THE ABSOLUTE

You may be justified in asking to see evidence for The Absolute or God. The simplest answer is that the evidence is all around you. You really need look no further than the wonder of nature that surrounds you to conclude that there must be a Supreme Intelligence underlying the Universe. Whether you think about it logically or intuitively, the precision and exactness of the Universal Laws that keep the entire Universe in perfect equilibrium and order cannot be random.

The miracle of life alone, be it the development of a human being from a fertilised human egg or the growth of an oak tree from an acorn that in no way resembles the oak tree, is evidence enough for a Supreme Intelligence.

The briefest of studies of the mathematics and geometry behind the construction of the Universe, from the intricate construction of a flower to that of the most complex organisms, also leaves no room for doubt about the existence of a Supreme Intelligence behind it.

So-called Sacred Geometry reveals that throughout the Universe, at every scale of existence from the sub-atomic to the galactic, there is a continuous repetition of distinct, archetypal patterns, which are the building-blocks of all creation. These patterns range from the simple to the very intricate, and can be likened to the geometric blueprint that forms the basis of all creation and all change. Robert J. Gilbert refers to these patterns as the alphabet or language of creation, that in space are manifested as shapes and in time as rhythms, and that together "create all beings, structures, and processes of the world."

Moreover, Max Planck, who is considered the father of Quantum Physics, had this to say in reference to The Absolute: "Both religion and science require a belief in God. For believers, God is in the beginning, and for physicists He is at the end of all considerations. To the former He is the foundation, to the latter, the crown of the edifice of every generalised world view." The Absolute, therefore, is the Alpha and the Omega.

Finally, it is Nikos Kazantzakis, one of the greatest modern-day Greek authors, who expressed the evidence for God most beautifully with the following words: "I said to the almond tree, 'Sister, speak to me of God.' And the almond tree blossomed."

Chapter 9
UNIVERSAL MIND

The idea of a single Universal Mind, permeating the entire manifested Universe can be traced back to the Greek philosopher Anaxagoras, who taught the cosmological theory of 'Nous' as the ordering force of the Cosmos, where 'Nous' is the Greek word for mind. Since consciousness *is* mind, the terms 'Universal Mind' and 'Universal Consciousness' are used interchangeably. Other names for Universal Mind include The Unified Field, Universal Spirit, and the World Soul.

UNIVERSAL MIND DEFINED

Most modern-day metaphysical teachings equate The Absolute to Universal Mind, with no distinction drawn between the two and they both have the same Omnipresent, Omnipotent, and Omniscient nature. Given that The Absolute is all there is, this definition is in theory correct. Having said this, some older metaphysical texts do draw a distinction, with good reason, although the distinction does not suggest separateness in any way.

In these earlier texts, Universal Mind is said to be the Mind of The Absolute and also Its first manifestation, permeating the entire Universe as pure consciousness or primordial energy. In other words, the countless *ever-changing* forms in the manifested Universe are *created* by the One Mind of The Absolute but The Absolute remains *changeless*. This means the manifested Universe is a projection of The Absolute's Consciousness, or in other words, can be likened to a 'dream' of The Absolute. Think about it this way - the countless creations in the Universe are the reflections of the One Mind of The Absolute, just as the Sun reflects itself in countless raindrops that appear to divide the Sun, but the Sun remains as one. This concept will become much clearer as you progress through the book.

Degrees of Universal Consciousness

Since the underlying substance of the Universe is consciousness, it stands to reason that the Scale of Consciousness *is* Universal Mind or Consciousness. Universal Mind contains the infinite *potential* of *all* things, with an inherent power to transform potential energy into actualised form. Moreover, Universal Mind, being the Mind of The Absolute is Omnipresent and hence is present in everything at the same time in its entirety, and hence is equally present in a tree and in a human being. The difference between the two, however, is that a tree's operations are along unconscious lines, whereas human beings have the *capacity* to raise their degree of awareness from unconscious to conscious operations.

This means everything in the Universe is a centre or hub of Universal Mind, but the degree to which Universal Mind can display Its inherent Omnipotence and Omniscience, depends on the degree of consciousness of Its individual centres, one of which is your mind. In other words, you have the *potential* to share in the inherent All-Powerful and All-Knowing nature of Universal Mind as one of its mind centres, but the degree to which you actualise that potential depends on your degree of self-awareness or positivity.

This is why sacred texts assert that man is created in the image of God, and is also a Divine Spark of God. This is because only human beings, as far as we understand life on Earth at its current point of evolution, have the potential for higher degrees of consciousness and so the capacity to identify their mind with the Mind of The Absolute. Put simply, all of God is in a grain of sand, and all of God is in you. The only difference is that you have the capacity to know so.

To bring what has been written here together, a concise definition for Universal Mind is as follows: Universal Mind is the first creation of The Absolute, present everywhere at the same time and hence, is the underlying substance of All Life in the Universe. As the Mind of The Absolute, It has the inherent *potential* for All-Power and All-Knowledge but the degree to which Its potential is *actualised* depends on Its individual centres. Since everything is mind, everything is a centre of Universal Mind, thus making your mind one of Its centres.

Consciousness Re-Visited
For the sake of continuity, we will now briefly revisit the premise that the underlying substance of the Universe is mind or consciousness, or in other words, that everything *is* mind or consciousness.

Higher degrees of consciousness are marked by higher frequency, self-awareness, intelligence, and directive power or positivity, which is the power to direct change in all those things of a lesser degree of positivity relative to one's own. In contrast, descending levels of self-awareness are marked by an increase in automatic vibrations that operate along unconscious lines. The lowest or densest vibrations are found in so-called 'inanimate' objects that have no self-awareness as we know it, yet are still very much alive with consciousness. In other words, although everything is alive with consciousness, not all things are self-aware of their aliveness, which means that Universal Mind only becomes self-aware through the self-awareness of its individual mind centres, one of which is your mind.

Esoteric texts also assert that all consciousness has substance or body. 'Substance' is not matter but rather, matter is one of the many phases of substance and indeed, the correct scientific word for substance is 'mass' not 'matter'. Albert Einstein's famous Mass-Energy Equivalence equation, expressed as $E=mc^2$, equates energy with mass as follows: Energy (E) is equal to mass (m) multiplied by the square of a constant that is the speed of light (c^2). The equation $E=mc^2$ therefore, affirms that everything in the Universe is energy (consciousness) and that all energy has mass (substance), the only difference being the rate of vibration.

In Him We Live, and Move, and Have Our Being
Since everything is alive with The Absolute's Consciousness, then the aliveness we attribute to living things and the 'deadness' we perceive in matter is an illusion conveyed by our physical senses. Endeavour therefore, to observe the aliveness of consciousness as being present in everything and everyone. Whenever you look at, or interact with, something or someone, endeavour to see that thing, plant, animal, or person as being alive with God's Consciousness because it is.

Wherever you may find yourself, whether relaxing at home, working in your office, or simply walking in nature or on the sidewalk of a busy street, sense how you exist in a vast sea of living energy that is the All-Present Universal Consciousness of The Absolute. When you learn to see God in everything and everyone, and in the infinite space that surrounds you, you will know that "in Him we live, and move, and have our being" (Acts 17:28).

CONSCIOUSNESS IN QUANTUM PHYSICS
Quantum Physics, which is the physics of sub-atomic particles, has granted us the first scientific glimpse of the role of consciousness as the underlying substance of the Universe. In fact, many of the conclusions from Quantum Physics are at the very least beginning to validate metaphysical teachings about the ultimate Unity of the Universe. While Quantum Physics is beyond the scope of this book, I have included some quotes from prominent quantum physicists about the implications of consciousness for the true nature of reality.

Eugene Wigner, who was a recipient of the 1963 Nobel Prize in Physics, had this to say about consciousness: "When the province of physical theory was extended to encompass microscopic phenomena through the creation of quantum mechanics, the concept of consciousness came to the fore again. It was not possible to formulate the laws of quantum mechanics in a fully consistent way, without reference to consciousness." Werner Heisenberg, who was awarded the 1932 Nobel Prize in Physics, said that "atoms or elementary particles themselves are not real. They form a world of potentialities or possibilities rather than one of things or facts."

The theoretical physicist Bernard d'Espagnat said, "The doctrine that the world is made up of objects whose existence is independent of human consciousness turns out to be in conflict with quantum mechanics and with facts established by experiment." Max Planck, who is the originator of Quantum Theory and who received the 1918 Nobel Prize in Physics, said, "I regard consciousness as fundamental. I regard matter as derivative from consciousness. We cannot get behind consciousness. Everything that we talk about, everything that we regard as existing, postulates consciousness."

Max Planck also had this to say in his 1944 speech on the Nature of Matter: "As a man who has devoted his whole life to the most clear headed science, [that is] to the study of matter, I can tell you as a result of my research about atoms this much: There is no matter as such. All matter originates and exists only by virtue of a force which brings the particle of an atom to vibration and holds this most minute solar system of the atom together. We must assume behind this force the existence of a conscious and intelligent mind. This mind is the matrix of all matter."

What we can conclude from these few quotes is that the reality you perceive is an illusion relayed to your brain neurons by your physical senses. Universal Consciousness therefore, is no longer a philosophical idea but is quickly becoming what appears to be an unavoidable conclusion from scientific studies. Niels Bohr, who contributed to the foundations of quantum mechanics and received the 1922 Nobel Prize in Physics, said that "Anyone not shocked by quantum mechanics has not yet understood it."

Conclusions from Quantum Physics therefore, are beginning to support metaphysical teachings from thousands of years ago, that everything in the Universe is energy vibrating at different rates, transforming from one form into another, and that behind this endless transformation of energy one finds consciousness, and more specifically Universal Consciousness.

THE UNIFIED FIELD

If you could see reality for what it is according to the implications of Quantum Theory, rather than what you experience it to be through your physical senses, it would look more like the interference you see on the screen of an un-tuned television. This can be likened to a vast sea of vibrating or pulsating energy, also known as the Unified Field, which itself can be likened to the infinite potentiality of Universal Mind. It is made up of an infinite number of so-called information packets, which can be thought of as containing data, analogous to a mental image or a set of mental instructions, which are actualised into form either unconsciously or under conscious direction.

Universal Mind, through its inherent intelligence and through its mind centres, which includes your mind, processes the information stored in the information packets and transforms it into visible form in the physical Universe. You are part of the Unified Field and are communicating with it mentally at every moment. In fact, you can think of yourself as living in two worlds simultaneously - in the visible world of actualised things and in the invisible world of pure potential information.

Every thought you have, whether consciously or not, sends a specific thought wave into the Unified Field, which resonates with those information packets matching the contents and frequency of your thoughts. In this way, under the right conditions, you direct Universal Mind to transform the data inherent in those invisible information packets that you mentally resonate with, into physical world form. In staying with the metaphor of the underlying nature of reality being akin to an un-tuned channel on your television, we can say that your thoughts determine what channel you tune into, and hence what you see on your screen of reality. The remote control is your mind but, if you do not use it, your experience is then remotely controlled by the unconscious operations of the Universe.

No-Thing, Every-Thing, Some-Thing

Since Universal Mind contains *all* possibilities, it remains unchanged in Its essence. The only thing that changes is the reflections of the One Universal Mind in the physical outer world, in response to the information packets that It is instructed to transform into form through thinking.

One can say therefore, where The Absolute is 'No-Thing', Universal Mind is '*Every*-Thing' and Its countless creations are '*Some*-Thing', as in some things that have been actualised from the potential energy of everything. Think carefully of the following statement: Every-Thing comes from No-Thing, and Some-Thing comes from Every-Thing. This is how, through the medium of 'thinking', the One becomes the many that is experienced as separate things in the physical world, while always remaining the One.

THE CREATIVE NATURE OF UNIVERSAL MIND

Universal Mind is the creative principle behind everything in the manifested Universe. This means that Mind *creates* and since the activity of mind is thought, then thinking is mind's mode or means of creation. Universal Mind therefore, is *undifferentiated* potential energy that through thinking is transformed into *differentiated* or actualised form, and back into energy again.

Unconscious Direction of Universal Mind

Although the Universe is created and sustained by the thinking of Universal Mind, thinking in this sense is not a conscious thought process in the way we are accustomed to the word 'thinking' when we say 'I thought of this or that'. Universal Mind 'thinks' along unconscious or sub-conscious lines, or in other words, below the level of self-aware objective consciousness.

This in turn means that Universal Mind is self-creative through its inherent intelligence, without having to partake in the thinking process at a conscious level. It is impersonal and subjective in nature and so it can be directed in any direction, just as is the case with your sub-conscious, subjective mind.

Looked at another way, throughout the Universe the direction of Universal Mind takes place unconsciously in accordance with the Universal Laws that maintain and sustain the manifested Universe in equilibrium and order. These Universal Laws, discussed in Part III, can be likened to a Universal blueprint or set of instructions that sustain the automatic energy transformation, or thinking process, of Universal Mind. Since these Laws are the Laws of The Absolute, their results or effects reflect Its Supreme Intelligence throughout nature and throughout the Universe in its entirety.

Conscious Direction of Universal Mind

The subjective Universal Mind can be consciously directed by one of its self-aware objective mind centres, albeit still within the parameters of the Universal Laws. By definition, the *conscious* direction of Universal Mind must come from one of its *conscious* mind centres, which includes your mind. Remember that everything in the Universe is a centre of Universal Consciousness but you, as one of Its centres, are objectively *aware* of your consciousness, and so can consciously direct the subjective Universal Mind through thinking. This also means that your mind, as a centre of Universal Mind, is not outside of or separate to It in any way. Rather your mind is one and the same with Universal Mind.

THE CREATIVE PROCESS

Since the subjective Universal Mind is potential energy, it has the *potential* to be differentiated into any specific form that it is directed to. It is only through conscious thought that undifferentiated energy can be *consciously* differentiated. In other words, conscious thinking enables the thinker to *choose* the direction of differentiation, rather than have it unconsciously chosen for him by the impersonal Universal Laws. The creative mode of Universal Mind therefore, is thinking and the *way* It thinks is impersonal, subjective, receptive, intelligent, and without limit, each of which are discussed below.

Impersonal

Universal Mind thinks impersonally. This means that in creating and sustaining the Universe along unconscious lines, Universal Mind is *not personally* aware of Its individual mind centres through which it creates, whether it is a human being, a single cell, a flowing stream, an animal, or a tree. Throughout the Universe therefore, creation, if not consciously directed, is unconscious, impersonal, and in compliance with the equally impersonal Universal Laws.

Subjective

Universal Mind is subjective. This means that Universal Mind is *subject* to being *directed*, and it can be *consciously* directed by one of its self-aware *objective* mind centres. Your subjective mind shares in the subjectivity of Universal Mind, and can also be directed by your own objective mind. Any mental image or message you impress on your subjective mind is impressed on Universal Mind and, under the right conditions, is created in form without any judgement of right or wrong, deserving or undeserving on the part of Universal Mind. This is because there is only *One* Universal Mind, and hence all thoughts are *Its* thoughts, irrespective of the individual mind centre from which the thoughts originate.

Receptive

Universal Mind is receptive. This means that It is able to *receive* impressions through the thinking of its individual mind centres of consciousness. The mental impressions or mental images it receives are, under the right conditions, transformed, reproduced, and created in the physical world of form. This receptive nature of Universal Mind can also be explained by the fact that there is only One Universal Mind, so whatever one of its mind centres thinks, *It* thinks as well, because the two are the *same* mind.

Intelligent

Universal Mind is inherently intelligent. As the Mind of The Absolute, Its inherent intelligence must be the Supreme Intelligence of God. Moreover, since Universal Mind has the ability to receive any thought or mental image and reproduce it exactly to its last detail, irrespective of its complexity, then it must have inherent within it the Supreme Intelligence and Absolute Power of The Absolute.

Without Limit

The creative thinking of Universal Mind is limitless. This is because Universal Mind's inherent potential power is Absolute Power, and hence no creation is too difficult, too complicated, or too big for It, irrespective of whether you believe what you want to create in your life is easy or difficult, simple or complicated, big or small. Such adjectives are relative and have no bearing on something that has the potential of Absolute Power.

This means that what you believe may be difficult for Universal Mind to create, is just as easy as what you believe is easy because there is no distinction between 'easy' and 'difficult' for something that is All-Powerful. In other words, what you consider easy or difficult to create is only ever a reflection of your beliefs and conditioning. One million dollars is as easy to create as a single dollar, an ideal relationship is as easy as a mediocre one, and removing a cancerous growth in its entirety is as easy as removing a single cancer cell. In each case, both outcomes must be equally possible because all possibilities already exist in potential form.

Having said this, your limiting beliefs, thoughts, and fears do not allow for the two equally possible outcomes to be equally probable. Therefore, it is not whether something is possible or not but rather, the question is whether something is probable, and the probability of a possibility depends on your own thinking and beliefs about it. The only thing that limits the power of Universal Mind, is a limitation perceived by one of its mind centres, including your mind. Being impersonal, It then adopts those limitations, even though Its inherent potential power is Absolute Power.

Miracles therefore, are nothing more than the actualised potential of the Absolute Power of the One Universal Mind through The Absolute. If we as human beings, truly knew the potential power of our minds to directly share in God's Absolute Power, then what we call miracles would be as common to us as those daily things that we take for granted.

Chapter 10

THE ABSOLUTE, UNIVERSAL MIND AND I

Understanding the relationship between The Absolute, Universal Mind, and you, is arguably one of the most fundamental mind-shifts that you can come to experience. The greatest metaphysical teachings ever passed down to us tell us that man is created in the image of God, and since an 'image' of God is changeless, infinite, and eternal, then it stands to reason, that the essence of your Real Self is also changeless, infinite, and eternal.

A PROJECTION OF CONSCIOUSNESS

Since Universal Mind is the Mind of The Absolute and everything in the manifested Universe is created *by* Universal Mind, then the entire Universe is a projection of The Absolute's Consciousness. In the same way, since your mind is a centre of Universal Mind and everything in *your* reality is created *through* Universal Mind, then your experience of reality is a projection of your consciousness, which itself is within The Absolute's Consciousness. The 'you' whose reality it is, must be the Real You, since *it* is created in the image of God, not your personal self with its personality.

Having said this, in the same way that we cannot comprehend the concept of infinity within the constraints of space and time, we are also limited in our capacity to understand the idea of our individual reality being a projection of our consciousness. Nevertheless, a helpful analogy is to compare your experience of reality to how you experience your dreams in the physical world.

The Dream and the Dreamer

When you dream, your dream-world is a projection taking place within your consciousness. Everything and everyone in your dream is part of your consciousness, even though you experience them as being both real and separate to the projection of you that is *in* the dream. However, to the you who is the *dreamer* experiencing the dream, it is all just a projection of your consciousness.

No matter what happens to the version of you in your dream, the dreamer remains unchanged. 'Waking up' to the level of self-awareness of the I can be likened to waking up in physical reality from your dream-world and realising it was a dream. Moreover, to *be* the Real You while in the physical world is about realising that it is a dream *while* you are still dreaming. This can be compared to lucid dreaming. A lucid dream is a dream in which the dreamer is *aware* that he is dreaming while he is dreaming and so, can exert varying degrees of control over his participation in the dream-world. This is perhaps one of the reasons why identifying with your Real Self is also called a spiritual *awakening*. This idea of the dream and the dreamer will be discussed in more detail in Part V.

A CENTRE OF DIVINE OPERATION
You already know that your mind is a centre of consciousness in Universal Mind and since there is only One Universal Mind, there is no separation between your mind and It. This means that your mind is a focalised creative hub or centre of the One Universal Mind. Your mind therefore, creates through Universal Mind, and Universal Mind creates through your Mind because the two are the same mind.

Since thinking is the means of creation, what you create depends on your thoughts, which include all your mental activities, such as emotions, mental images, desires, beliefs, fears, and so on. Moreover, whether what you mentally create is along unconscious or conscious lines, depends on your degree of intelligent self-awareness and the use of your will power to direct your mind.

Judge Thomas Troward wrote this powerful affirmation about your mind as a centre of the One Mind, in The Dore Lectures on Mental Science (1909): "My mind is a centre of Divine Operation. Since the Divine cannot change its inherent nature, it must operate in the same manner in me. Consequently in my own special world, of which I am the centre, it will move forward to produce new conditions, always in advance of any that have gone before."

Your Mind is Universal Mind
Since the One Universal Mind is infinite, it means that by definition, it must be present in each of its mind centres in Its *entirety*. This means that Universal Mind is present in *your* mind in Its *entirety*, and so from your point of view, which is all you can ever experience, Universal Mind *is* your mind.

This is a fundamental mind-shift not to be overlooked. Universal Mind is not outside of you, nor is only a part of it within you while another part is somewhere else. Rather, Universal Mind is *your* mind in Its *entirety*, by virtue of it being infinite.

Your mind therefore, may be but one creative centre of Universal Mind, but, at the same time, it is identical to the whole. This then means that you have the capacity to share in the full *potential* of Universal Mind's creative power of limitless possibilities through It.

The Centre of Your Universe

Although it is debatable whether the physical Universe is infinite, Universal Mind *is* infinite. This has a profound implication for your mind's place in Universal Mind because it means that from your own point of reference, your mind must, by definition, be the centre around which the infinity of Universal Mind extends. It can be no other way because in something that is infinite, each of its points must be a centre of that infinity. This is in accordance with the esoteric Arcane maxim that 'The Cosmos is infinite, its circumference is nowhere, its centre is everywhere'.

Your mind therefore, is a centre of Universal Mind in both senses of the word 'centre'. In other words, your mind is a *centre* or hub of creation in the infinite Universal Mind and it is also *at* the centre of Universal Mind by way of location in your experience of reality. From your own point of reference therefore, you are at the very centre of your own personal experience of your infinite Universe.

DEGREES OF IDENTIFICATION

When you are unaware of the creative power of your mind, and of its unity with Universal Mind, then the results in your life appear more random in nature and cannot be said to be self-directed. In contrast, when you intelligently recognise and identify your mind's unity with Universal Mind, you can begin to share in Its potential for limitless creative power and hence, direct your life accordingly.

The degree to which you can create your experience of reality consciously depends on the degree to which you identify your mind as being one and the same with Universal Mind. In other words, the degree of your mental power to create your reality consciously increases in direct proportion to an increase in your identification with Universal Mind.

Moreover, the greater your identification with the Real You rather than with your personal self, then the easier it becomes for you to identify your mind with Universal Mind. Put yet another way, the degree of your power to create your reality through your thinking, is limited to and by your degree of self-awareness or positivity. Remember also that higher degrees of positivity correspond to higher degrees of directive power over all those things of a lesser positivity relative to your own.

Mutual Recognition

You will recall from the previous chapter that the degree to which Universal Consciousness can display Its inherent potential for All-

Power and All-Knowledge depends on the degree of consciousness of Its mind centres, one of which is your mind. Universal Mind therefore, can only become conscious of its own existence to the degree that Its individual centres are conscious of their own. This, in turn, means that by raising your degree of self-aware consciousness, you are raising the degree of self-aware consciousness of Universal Mind in its entirety, by the same degree. It can be no other way because your consciousness is part of Universal Mind, and what happens to any one part of a thing affects the whole.

Moreover, as you begin to identify your mind with Universal Mind, then Universal Mind begins to identify Itself with your Mind. And the degree to which you recognise Universal Mind as being *your* mind in Its entirety, is the degree to which Universal Mind recognises your mind as being one in the same with Itself. Universal Mind therefore, becomes consciously aware of you as one of Its mind centres by virtue of you becoming consciously aware of It first. This is what is known as mutual recognition between your mind and Universal Mind.

In contrast, if you do not recognise your mind's unity with Universal Mind, then it cannot consciously recognise Its unity with your mind. The higher your degree of positivity, then the higher your conscious identification with Universal Mind is, and accordingly Its identification with your mind. A complete identification of your mind with Universal Mind means that your will becomes one with Cosmic Will, and Cosmic Will becomes one with your will, in mutual recognition of each other as being the same thing.

William Walker Atkinson had this to say on the subject and I urge you to pay attention to what is written here. "The Being in whom we are, knows and is conscious of us only when we are conscious of the Being within us. The recognition is mutual in consciousness. And correspondingly, as we advance in the great Scale of Consciousness, we come into a closer recognition and consciousness of the One and the One comes into a closer recognition and consciousness of us. Finally, at the High Noon of Cosmic Consciousness, we come to know that we are the One, and the One comes to know that it is us. Toward this is the aim and goal of Spiritual Evolution." These few words capture the essence of Cosmic Consciousness, of becoming *one* with Universal Mind and It with *you*.

Degree by Degree
By virtue of your existence as a human being, you have the potential to evolve your individual consciousness to the highest level of the I within. There are countless degrees between your current degree of

consciousness and the supremacy of Cosmic Consciousness, but do not let this discourage you. Instead, it should encourage you, because each step you take upwards on the Scale of Consciousness takes you one degree closer to the I. Rising upwards in positivity is a gradual process and even a life-time journey, or one of many lives. Your aim is not to 'climb the ladder' as quickly as possible in a rush to get to the top. Rather, your aim is to raise your positivity degree by degree, knowing that every degree you ascend increases your directive and creative power, and brings you closer to the Real You.

A single glimpse of your Real Self, even if only intellectually, is enough to know in which direction you are heading, and begin your journey. When you elect as your *purpose* to aspire to the I, the relative world of thoughts, things, and circumstances will have less and less power to disturb you. Rest assured it is by no means necessary to reach the supremacy of Cosmic Consciousness in order to direct your mind and create your life, as long as you keep your eye on the I.

Cosmic Consciousness
Ascending the Scale of Consciousness, degree of positivity by degree of positivity, increases your identification with Universal Mind to the same degree. Cosmic Consciousness, however, is not given to you as a gift - it is earned. Your God-given gift is your freedom of choice and power to direct your mind in any direction you will. It is this gift that you can use to raise your degree of positivity towards a greater and greater identification with your Real Ego, with Universal Mind, and ultimately with The Absolute. William Walker Atkinson said, "Every living thing possesses a personal self, but even among men, many fail to reach Egohood. Egohood is earned, not bestowed as a natural gift. Many personalities are born, but few Egos are evolved."

The Secret of the Excluded Middle
As you raise your degree of positivity ever higher, the penultimate degree of Cosmic Consciousness is to sense your unity with It, to float peacefully in the infinite space of utter silence and stillness, and to be *aware* of your mind as being in the very *middle* of The Absolute's Mind until it is the *only* thing you are aware of. And ultimately, in this state of blissful peace, you *exclude* your awareness from the middle, you release it entirely and let it merge with the Consciousness of the infinite Universe, and in this way you *become* the infinite space of utter silence and stillness, and you are no longer aware of anything, for you are *Every*-Thing and you are *No*-Thing. This is the Arcane Secret of the Excluded Middle.

Chapter 11

AS A MAN WILLS, SO HE BECOMES

If you are not *consciously* directing your mind, then you cannot say that you are directing it in any way. This is because if you are not at the helm of your mind, then someone or something else is. This includes your sub-conscious programs and beliefs, the automatic actions and reactions that flow from them, the collective consciousness of your society and even of the planet in which good and evil play out side by side, the actions of others, the will of others, your emotions, desires and whims and those of others, the messages from the media, the impersonal Universal Laws, and so on. All these factors direct your mind and create your life if you do not do so consciously.

Put another way, if you are not *consciously* directing your life, it is being *unconsciously* directed for you, and what shows up can only ever appear to be random arrays of events, some of which are joyful and some of which are painful and even tragic, but most of which are without significance. Having said this, there is no need to fight to overcome any of these aforementioned factors. The only route to consciously directing your life is also the path of least resistance, which is to begin to increase your degree of consciousness upwards on the Scale of Consciousness, degree by degree, towards the I.

THE TRUE MEANING OF BEING POSITIVE

Only by employing the power of your will can you be the director of your mind and hence your experience of reality, because you cannot do something *consciously* in the absence of your will to do so. If therefore, you are not consciously employing your will power, then you are not consciously directing your mind and life either. Anything less than the conscious use of your will power is, to all intents and purposes, unconscious living, even if it feels like choice.

Remember that higher degrees of self-awareness correspond to higher degrees of positivity, or in other words, to higher degrees of directive power to influence all those things in your world of a lower positivity relative to your own. Moreover, the directive power of higher positivity is akin to higher degrees of directive will power, which more specifically, is the power to direct your thoughts at *will*, and hence to choose the reality that is created through your thinking.

Bear in mind, however, that while the highest degree of positivity is the Real You, with each and every degree that you ascend higher in the Scale of Consciousness, you still raise your degree of positivity, and hence your directive power over your life. Once again therefore, the instruction to 'be positive' does not mean to have a happy-go-lucky outlook on life, nor does it mean to be morally good or even to think morally good things or happy thoughts. Rather, to 'be positive' means to raise your consciousness to higher degrees of positivity, and hence, to aspire to the I.

WHEN YOU THINK, UNIVERSAL MIND THINKS

As you already know Universal Mind is impersonal and subjective, and hence does not evaluate the mental images and thoughts that you impress on It through your own mind. This means that Universal Mind receives your mental instructions at face value, just like your subjective sub-conscious mind accepts the messages you impress on it without question or judgement.

Universal Mind does not judge by saying 'John Smith has been a good person, so I will reward him for his good deeds'. Nor does It judge, for instance, that 'John Smith is unkind, so I will punish him for his bad deeds'. Any such judgment is personal not impersonal, and since your mind is not separate from Universal Mind, then It does not deal with your mind or its contents in any personal way. When you think and impress your own subjective mind with your thoughts, then at the same time you impress your thoughts directly on the subjective Universal Mind. More specifically, when *you* think, Universal Mind *also* thinks precisely what you have thought.

As a Man Wills, So He Becomes

Since, Universal Mind *is* your mind, receptive to being directed in any direction, your aim is to think intelligently and consciously and under the direction of your will. What you think counts. What you believe counts. What you relentlessly focus on counts. What you mentally imagine counts. What you fear counts. How you consistently act and re-act counts. Your perception counts. The degree of your self-awareness counts. The degree of your will power counts. The degree to which you allow your will to be directed by others counts. Your understanding of the Universal Laws counts.

All these factors together are the reason behind what shows up in your life. However, since most people operate at an unconscious level when it comes to each of these factors, then what shows up cannot be said to be consciously directed or created in any real way. But God is not to blame. It is you that must raise the degree of your positivity and begin to direct and guard your mind consciously. When all is said and done, what counts most when it comes to creating your experience of reality is your degree of self-awareness. It is the degree to which you employ your will power, and to what end you direct it that counts. When you know your mind is one with Universal Mind and your will is one with Cosmic Will, you are able to say 'as I *will*, so I become'. Indeed, there is great truth in the saying 'where there's a will, there's a way'. It means that your will *directs* the way through Cosmic Will.

Personalising the Impersonal

Your relationship with Universal Mind is your impression of It, and given Its receptive nature, your impression of It is what Universal Mind adopts as Its relationship with you. For instance, if you believe Universal Mind is a guiding, protective, and loving force of Supreme Intelligence, ready to receive any mental image you impress on It and respond by creating precisely that image in your outer world, then that will be your experience of Universal Mind. If on the other hand, you deny the existence of a Universal Mind and instead believe life is a random, chaotic array of circumstances over which you have no direction, then that in turn will be your experience of Universal Mind. Ultimately, when you *know* that Universal Mind *is* your mind then accordingly, It will also know that *It* is your Mind.

Limitless Possibilities

Universal Mind is not subject to any limitations. This means that it is limitless and so there is no limit to the number of mental images you can impress on It through your mind, even more so since it is one and the same with your mind, so anything you think, It thinks too. Moreover, since It is pure undifferentiated energy that can be differentiated into any actualised form, then the potential possibilities held within Universal Mind are also limitless. This means Universal Mind can bring any possibility into actualised form.

Put simply, you cannot exhaust the Limitless because Universal Mind is unconstrained by space and time, and nor is it constrained by your perception of what is difficult or easy. Having said this, your limiting thoughts are adopted by the subjective Universal Mind, and so any limit you experience is a limit imposed by your thinking, or your degree of positivity. In the words of Richard Bach in his 1977 book Illusions, "if you argue for your limitations they are yours."

Leaving Creation to Universal Mind

It is only out of ignorance of the inherent Supreme Intelligence of Universal Mind that you would specify *how* your desired outcome is to be transformed from potential energy into actualised form. There is no need to worry about the specifics, no matter how far removed your desire may be from your current physical world circumstances.

Worrying about or trying to analyse how current obstacles will be reversed or overcome, or trying to impose your own personal 'how' on Universal Mind, amounts to limiting the inherent Omnipotent potential of Universal Mind to your perceived limitations. And being subjective, It once again adopts those limits that you impose on It. This, however, does not imply you do not need to take any action towards your goals. Nor does it mean that you should simply think of your intention and sit back while Universal Mind does all the creative work for you, because remember that your mind *is* Universal Mind.

Learn to see 'leaving the how' up to Universal Mind as leaving the how up to your own mind's shared inherent Supreme Intelligence. This allows it to find the path of least resistance, which is likely to be a way you cannot see as you are personally caught up in a limited view of the world, constrained by time and space. You must learn to trust your own mind to reproduce your desired mental image into form *through* Universal Mind because that is what it does efficiently. At the same time you must be prepared to exert the necessary mental and physical effort in the direction of attaining your desires. In other words, you must be prepared to 'pay the price', as you will learn later.

ABSOLUTE POWER IS THE SOURCE OF YOUR POWER

As you already know, The Absolute is the single Source of All Power. It stands to reason therefore, that the source of Universal Mind's power, and hence your mind's power as well, is The Absolute's Power. This means your creative power is *not* independently yours in the sense that you create and sustain it. Rather, your power to create your reality through your mind's activity originates with God because your mind is a creative centre of The Absolute's Mind. Having said this, your power is limited to and by your level of self-awareness.

If you believe that Absolute Power is 'out there' or that only a part of Absolute Power is within you, then you have descended from the idea of Absolute Power to relative power. Your power is also limited to the degree that you believe it is separately yours. You are never creating your reality independently of Universal Mind, but your results are limited to the degree to which you believe you are.

Here are few words paraphrased from William Walker Atkinson on the subject. The Power of the individual is not something created by him, but in reality is the power of Universal Power in which he lives and moves and has his being. The individual has no power in himself but rather, all the will he manifests must flow through him from

Cosmic Will. The individual is merely the focal point of Cosmic Will, a channel through which the Cosmic Will may act."

This serves as a stark reminder to avoid the sudden rush of arrogance that can be born out of the knowledge of your power being one with Absolute Power. Yes, you have access to Universal Power in its entirety, but it also means that every last iota of your power originates in and depends on Absolute Power.

DELPHIC MAXIM: «ΕΓΓΥΑ ΠΑΡΑ Δ'ΑΤΑ»

One of the three major maxims at the ancient Temple of Apollo, in Delphi, Greece, is «ΕΓΓΥΑ ΠΑΡΑ Δ'ΑΤΑ» *(pronounced: egia para data)*. This maxim, literally means 'guarantee and destruction is nigh', and is a warning against arrogance. Some modern-day interpretations of this maxim suggest that the word 'guarantee' refers to a monetary pledge, but its true message is about arrogance.

This maxim is a warning not to 'guarantee' that your own power, or anything else, is superior to The Absolute, or somehow personally yours in the sense that nothing and no-one can stand in your way. This maxim is today expressed in sayings such as 'pride comes before the greatest fall' and 'today's breakthrough is tomorrow's ego-trip'. Be aware of your counterfeit ego because it thrives on its power-seeking ego-trips, whereas your Real Ego has no need for them because at its level you already know that you are one with the All-Powerful, and there is no greater power that you could ever seek.

Acknowledging Absolute Power as the source of your power does not mean that you have to beg The Absolute or Universal Mind to direct your life in a specific way. In fact, this is ineffective because you are not outside The Absolute or Its Mind in order to plead with It. What it comes down to is gratitude for your God-given power to direct your mind and create your life through Universal Mind. In the face of true gratitude, arrogance stands no chance.

The Absolute Is the Equation

While some people claim that learning to exercise the power of your mind takes The Absolute out of the equation, the truth is that it places It right back into an equation that It was for so long taken out of. Aspiring to the I within does not make The Absolute *part of* the equation, but rather it declares that The Absolute *is* the equation. When you know that The Absolute is *entirely* within you, then all things possible will be yours for creating through God, and you will have discovered that the Kingdom of Heaven truly is within, as the greatest metaphysical masters that ever walked the Earth taught us.

WHO AM I?

You may believe that you must first change or correct some things about yourself in order to get ahead in life and to succeed, as if there is something currently wrong with you. The truth is, however, that there is nothing to change, there is nothing wrong with you, and you are not imperfect in any way. Becoming the master of your life does not come down to changing who you *think* you are but rather, it is about knowing who you *really* are. It is not about first accepting your imperfections but rather, it is about recognising and identifying with your perfection. The Real You is perfect and will be so eternally. Nothing is missing and nothing is in excess.

One of the most misguided things you can say about yourself, and it is often said in resignation, is that 'I am only human'. The truth is, you are a human being created in the image of God. Knowing this, how can you ever say that you are *only* human, as if it were some kind of limitation or excuse when Omnipotence is within you in Its entirety? Thinking you are *only* human limits your potential to your self-imposed limitations, whereas knowing what it really means to *be* human extends your potential to All Power and All Knowledge.

What follows is an excerpt from Walter Russell's 1926 book The Universal One, which perfectly captures the essence of the I. "Just so long as man looks for the God-force outside of nature and outside of himself, just so long as he bows in fear to the personal deity of his early inheritance, he will be the slave of his own imaginings. To know that the universal force is Mind, and that man and all else is Mind, is to inspire man with ecstasy of inner thinking. Ideas and their expression in form have no existences whatsoever. They are unreal. They are but images conjured up by the image making faculty of Mind in the ecstasy of thinking."

Ask yourself this, "Who Am I?" and the answer is "I am I"
"Where God is I am, where I am there God is."
"God is Mind, I am Mind"
"God is Life, I am Life"
"God is Love, I am Love"
"God is Power, I am Power"
"What God is, I am. He gives all to me. He withholds nothing."
"I am the creator of myself. My thinking is self-creating. I am the sum of all my desires. I shall be what I desire to be. I shall know no limitations."

PART III
THE UNIVERSAL LAWS AND PRINCIPLES

Chapter 12
THE SEVEN UNIVERSAL LAWS

According to ancient metaphysical teachings, the Universe exists in perfect order and harmony by virtue of Seven Universal Laws that govern everything in the manifested Universe, including you and everything in your life. Knowledge of the Universal Laws therefore, is fundamental to understanding why your life is the way it is, whether your circumstances are wanted or unwanted. The Universal Laws are fundamental to your existence and to your power to direct your mind and create your life consciously and intelligently.

The Seven Universal Laws can be traced back to mystical texts attributed to Hermes Trismegistus and hence, are also referred to as the Hermetic Laws. Ancient Greek philosophers also made reference to these Laws, most notably Pythagoras and Heraclitus. The most notable modern-day books on the subject are, the 1908 book The Kybalion written by The Three Initiates (William Walker Atkinson writing alone or with another two authors whose identity is not known for sure), William Walker Atkinson's 1909 The Arcane Teaching, Eugene Fersen's 1923 Science of Being, and the 1918 book The Secret Doctrine of the Rosicrucians, again written by William Walker Atkinson under the pseudonym Magus Incognito. This part of the book is based on these and other sources, as well as on my own understanding, insight, and experience.

WHO WAS HERMES TRISMEGISTUS?

Hermes Trismegistus is referred to as The Master of Masters of all the masters of Ancient Greece and Egypt. Trismegistus is a Greek word that literally means 'Three Times Great' or 'Thrice-Great'. While several sacred texts of Hermetic Philosophy are attributed to him, including the Corpus Hermetica and the Emerald Tablet, it is debatable as to whether he ever existed in physical form, and if he did, when. Who Hermes Trismegistus was, and even his teachings, are shrouded in mystery. This mystery is behind the saying 'hermetically sealed' used to refer to something that is airtight, and it also refers to the secret alchemic seal attributed to Trismegistus.

The uncertainty about the existence of Hermes Trismegistus in the physical world is compounded by the fact that he is said to have been the representation of a combination of the Greek god Hermes (the god of communication and writing) and the Egyptian god Thoth (the god of wisdom, astrology, and alchemy).

Irrespective of whether or not he physically existed, the Seven Universal Laws largely attributed to him and which have been passed down to us, are timeless and as applicable to everything in the manifested Universe today as they were thousands of years ago.

THE THREE GREAT PLANES

Before looking at the Universal Laws, the scene will be set by looking at the Three Great Planes of existence of Hermetic Philosophy, namely the Spiritual Plane, the Mental Plane, and the Physical Plane. Since everything is consciousness, each plane has its own frequency or degree of consciousness and together they form the countless degrees of consciousness on the Scale of Consciousness.

Although beyond the scope of this book, there are also Seven Minor Planes within each plane and a further seven divisions within each Minor Plane but it is sufficient to focus on the Three Great Planes for the purposes of conscious creation.

All Planes are One Plane

As is the case with all consciousness, the divisions of the Three Great Planes are arbitrary. All three planes are varying degrees of rates of vibration of consciousness that blend into each other and thus are inseparable and indivisible. Since consciousness is unconstrained by space and time, the Three Great Planes exist simultaneously in the same point in space and time. This means you can mentally access the Mental and Spiritual Planes while *in* the Physical Plane, although they are invisible to your senses owing to their higher frequencies.

The Physical Plane has the lowest or densest rates of vibration, and is the plane of matter in which we have our physical existence. Since there are no major planes below it, the Physical Plane is the least powerful of the planes. It is therefore *negative* in relation to the Mental and Spiritual Planes and they are *positive* to it.

The Mental Plane is the plane of logic, thought, desires, passions, fears, and all other mental activities. Since the Mental Plane is above the Physical Plane in its rate of vibration, it is less dense and hence not visible to our eyes, but it is more powerful than the Physical Plane and so can direct change in it. The Mental Plane is *positive* to the Physical Plane and *negative* to the Spiritual Plane.

The Spiritual Plane is the highest in rate of vibration, and hence also the most subtle and most inaccessible to our physical senses, but it is also the most powerful in directive change. Since the Spiritual Plane is above the Physical Plane and the Mental Plane it is *positive* to both and accordingly, they are both *negative* to it. The essence of the I is that part of you that is Pure Spirit, and so aspiring to its heights of consciousness is analogous to aspiring to the height of the Spiritual Plane. Having said this, the Divine Beings that exist *in* the Spiritual Plane are beyond humanity's greatest imaginings.

The Divine Beings of the Spiritual Plane
Here is a quote from the 1908 book The Kybalion that describes this Plane. "The Great Spiritual Plane comprises Beings possessing Life, Mind, and Form as far above that of Man of today, as the latter is above the earthworm, mineral, or even certain forms of Energy or Matter. The Life of these Beings so far transcends ours that we cannot even think of the details of the same. Their Minds so far transcend ours, that to them we scarcely seem to think, and our mental processes seem almost akin to material processes. The Matter of which their forms are composed is of the highest Planes of Matter, nay, some are even said to be clothed in Pure Energy."

The beings we refer to as Angels, Archangels, and Demi-Gods are said to exist on the highest of the Spiritual Plane's Seven Minor Planes, and the great souls referred to as Masters, Ascended Masters and Adepts, are said to exist in the lower Minor Planes.

These Divine Beings are beyond the heights of our imagination, but we are told they take an interest in and participate in the evolution of humanity and the Universe, and can be turned to by us for help, protection, and guidance.

THE IMMUTABLE AND MUTABLE LAWS
The Seven Universal Laws are divided into three Immutable Laws and four Mutable Laws. The word 'immutable' means something that cannot be changed or transcended and hence, the three Immutable Laws can never be escaped, changed, or risen above. For this reason, they are also known as the Higher Absolute Laws. In contrast, 'mutable' means something that *can* be changed and transcended, and hence the Mutable Laws are also known as the Lower Relative Laws.

While Hermetic Philosophy holds that all the laws operate on all Three Great Planes, Eugene Fersen in his 1923 book The Science of

Being, asserted that the Mutable Laws are transient and operate only on the Mental and Physical Planes, while the Spiritual Plane is above them, governed only by the Immutable Laws. This small discrepancy, however, makes no practical difference to your application of this knowledge in the Physical Plane. Nevertheless, only The Absolute is above all the Laws, which is why It is also called The Law.

Universal Nature and Process
The Immutable Laws (Higher Laws) describe the underlying *nature* of the Three Great Planes of the Universe, which is consciousness or mind vibrating at different rates. In turn, the Mutable Laws (Lower Laws) describe the thinking *process* of Universal Mind by which it creates all things along unconscious lines. As one of Its mind centres, you can use your understanding of the Higher Laws to direct the thinking process of Universal Mind, and also to largely rise above the unconscious operations of the Lower Laws.

Having said this, any unwanted consequences that result from the Universal Laws are not owing to some fault in the nature of the Universe or its Laws. Rather, it is wrong thinking and ignorance of the Universal Laws that create your unwanted circumstances. The Laws themselves in no way seek to punish you for wrong thinking or wrong doing, but nor do they seek to reward you for the opposite.

The next few chapters describe each of the Seven Universal Laws of Hermetic Philosophy, as well as other Universal Principles. At the beginning of each Law's chapter, there are some axioms that express the essence of that Law from The Kybalion and other sources. As an aside, bear in mind, that the descriptions in each Law's chapter outline the essentials of that Law.

How to work with and transcend the Mutable Laws is the subject of Part IV, and just how you can apply your combined knowledge towards consciously creating your reality, is discussed throughout the remainder of the book. Moreover, any repetition of what has already been written earlier in this book, is intended to re-enforce your understanding at a deeper level, and also show you how every aspect fits in with every other.

Chapter 13
LAW 1: THE LAW OF MENTALISM

The first of the Seven Universal Laws is the Law of Mentalism. It is also the first of the three unchangeable, Higher or Immutable Laws.

AXIOMS FOR THE LAW OF MENTALISM
The All is Mind
The Universe is Mental, Held in the Mind of The All

THE LAW OF MENTALISM EXPLAINED
The Law of Mentalism states that All is Mind. It is the Law behind the main premise of this book, that consciousness is the underlying substance of the entire Universe, and that this consciousness is the Mind of The Absolute. Being an Immutable Law, nothing can or ever will change this. This Law therefore tells us that that the very *substance* of the Universe is consciousness or mind. This includes the countless manifestations throughout the Universe in the Physical, Mental, and Spiritual Planes. 'All is Mind' however is not to be taken to mean that everything belongs to the *Mental* Plane. Rather, the Mental Plane is simply that plane of mind associated with mental activities, such as thought and emotion.

Moreover, the Law of Mentalism tells us that the entire Universe is an expression of the One Universal Mind, which in turn means that the entire manifested Universe is 'held in the Mind of The All' or The Absolute. This also underpins the teaching that 'All is One' because, since mind is everything, it is also the *only* thing. Moreover, since All is Mind *your* essence or underlying substance is also mind. This does not mean that you *have* a mind, but rather that your very substance *is* mind or consciousness.

Finally, since everything in the Universe is an expression of mind, then the activity of mind, which is *thinking*, must be *creative*. Likewise, since your mind is a centre of Universal Mind, it stands to reason that your mind is self-creative in response to *your* thinking, which includes your emotions, passions, desires, and mental images. According to Hermetic teachings, if you do not understand the mental nature of the Universe then no real mastery is possible.

The Paradox of the Illusion of Reality
A paradox arises between the mental nature of the Universe and the illusory nature of the physical world that it implies. Since the

manifested Universe is a mental creation held in the Mind of The Absolute, then physical reality must surely be an illusion, as was asserted by Albert Einstein when he said, "reality is an illusion, albeit a very persistent one." Nevertheless, realising that you are a spiritual being, having a physical experience, goes a long way to reconciling this paradox. As long as you exist in the physical world, you cannot deny your experience of reality because it is 'real' to the physical being that is subject to the Laws of Physics and to the constraints of space, time, and change. For instance, if you hit your foot on a wooden table it will hurt, irrespective of the fact that both the table and your foot are made up of countless atoms, which themselves are mostly space. The density or rate of vibration of your physical body corresponds to, and is hence affected by, the density of the Physical Plane.

This explains why you cannot physically walk off the top of a tall building and expect to survive the fall *physically*, no matter how much you believe it, because your physical body and the Physical Plane exist in the same vibrational frequency, and so your physical body is subject to its limitations.

By raising your degree of consciousness *entirely* to the Mental and Spiritual Planes you could arguably control or defy the Laws of Physics as they apply to the physical world. But your aim while here in the Physical Plane is unlikely to be to defy the Laws of Physics. Rather, your aim is to maximise your potential as a spiritual being having a *physical* human experience and to create the life you desire by *directing* your *mind*, which will in turn direct your physical experience.

A Spiritual Being Having a Physical Experience

Denying your physical experience only serves to diminish your power to change it. Once again, to reconcile this paradox of what is real and what is unreal, think of yourself as a spiritual being having a physical experience through your body. In this way, you can strike a balance between the two. Your physical reality is 'real' to you the physical being, but to you the spiritual being, that is the Observer of your experience, your reality is the ever-changing un-real projection of your consciousness. Being a projection, you know it is no more real than the 'reality' of a movie projected on a screen. Moreover, you know that your experience is subject to change through your creative mind, under the direction of your will. You also know that the greater your identification with the One Universal Mind, then the greater the mutual recognition is between you and It as being One, and so the greater your power to actualise the changes you choose.

Chapter 14
LAW 2: THE LAW OF CORRESPONDENCE

The second of the Seven Universal Laws is called the Law of Correspondence. It is also known as the Law of Analogy and is the second of the three unchangeable, Higher or Immutable Laws.

AXIOMS FOR THE LAW OF CORRESPONDENCE
As Above so Below, As Below so Above
As Within so Without, As Without so Within
As it is on the Highest Plane, so It is on the Lowest Plane
To Know One is to Know All
From One know All or *Ex Uno Disce Omnes*

THE LAW OF CORRESPONDENCE EXPLAINED
The Law of Correspondence states there is 'harmony, agreement, and correspondence' between all Three Great Planes of the Universe. The same Laws govern everything in the Universe, and the same identical patterns are expressed on all Planes.

This Law therefore affirms that the underlying substance of consciousness vibrating at different rates, applies to the nature and activity of the amoeba as much as it does to the nature and activity of man, and that of the Divine Beings of the Spiritual Plane.

Piercing the Veil
Since the same patterns govern everything in the Universe, then the Law of Correspondence lends itself to being practically applied in order to understand and discover what you do *not* know or understand, by studying what you *do* know and already understand. It is easy to overlook this Law, yet it is the very Law that allows you to pierce the veil separating the known from the unknown.

Put another way, the correspondence or analogy that is expressed on all Planes enables you, logically and reasonably, to understand the nature of those things beyond your understanding, by studying the nature of those things that you do understand. In other words, you can solve the mysteries of the nature of reality and of the Universe by first studying what you do know about them, and then finding the analogy between the two. It is for this reason that another name for the Law of Correspondence is the Law of Analogy.

For instance, by studying how the atom with its central nucleus and spinning electrons operate, you can understand the operation of the solar system. Likewise, using the principles of Geometry you can accurately measure the movement of distant stars from your seat in an observatory, and by studying the Mutable Laws of the Physical Plane you can understand their operation on the Mental Plane.

Moreover, by understanding the creative aspect of Universal Mind that creates and sustains the entire manifested Universe, you can also precisely understand how your mind creates and sustains your experience of reality. The brilliant inventor, Nikolas Tesla, perfectly expressed this correspondence between all things in the Universe when he said, "If you want to understand the Universe, think of energy, frequency, and vibration."

Your Circumstances Reveal You

The Law of Correspondence enables you to understand the state of your outer physical world by looking to your inner mental world. Similarly your inner mental world can be revealed to you by looking to your outer physical world.

James Allen, the author of the 1902 book As a Man Thinketh, perfectly captured this Law in the statement: "Circumstances do not *make* a man, they *reveal* him." This means that it is not your outer world circumstances that make your inner world, but rather it is your outer physical world that reveals your inner mental world.

DELPHIC MAXIM: «ΓΝΩΘΙ ΣΑΥΤΟΝ»

Importantly, the first of the three major Delphic Maxims inscribed on the Ancient Temple of Apollo in Delphi, Greece, has its basis in the Law of Correspondence.

This most famous of all the maxims is, «ΓΝΩΘΙ ΣΑΥΤΟΝ» *(pronounced: gnothi safton)*, which literally means 'Know Thyself'. The complete maxim is as follows: 'Man, Know Thyself and thou shall know all the mysteries of the gods and of the Universe'.

This is arguably the most powerful instruction ever passed down to humanity. To know yourself is to know the I within. This means that by aspiring to your Real Self, you can begin to *know* in your heart the truth about your real nature, not just intellectually but at a much deeper level of being; as well as to know the nature of the manifested Universe, the One Universal Mind, and The Absolute. Indeed, this is the aim of this book.

Chapter 15
LAW 3: THE LAW OF VIBRATION

The third of the Seven Universal Laws is the Law of Vibration. It is the last of the three unchangeable, Higher or Immutable Laws.

AXIOMS FOR THE LAW OF VIBRATION
Motion is Manifest in Everything in the Universe
Nothing Rests, Everything Moves, Everything Vibrates
The Whole Universe is but a Vibration

THE LAW OF VIBRATION EXPLAINED
The Law of Vibration states that everything in the Universe corresponds to a specific frequency or rate of vibration of mind. This again ties in with the basic premise of this book that everything in the manifested Universe is energy or consciousness vibrating at different frequencies. This is a conclusion that modern science has only recently come to, regardless of the fact that it was first expressed thousands of years ago.

Having said this, while the field of Quantum Physics has begun to consider the idea that consciousness is fundamental to the Universe, the fields of Physics and Metaphysics remain largely un-reconciled, but the gap is narrowing. Nevertheless, while we have already looked at vibrations of consciousness, it is appropriate to re-visit it here in a way that will afford you a much deeper understanding of it.

Rates of Vibration
The only difference between all manifestations of consciousness, be it energy, matter, thoughts, emotions, things or circumstance, is their corresponding rate of vibration. The higher the rate of vibration then the less dense or more subtle that thing is, and the lower the rate of vibration then the more dense or less subtle that thing is.

Everything you experience in the Physical Plane by means of your five physical senses is conveyed through vibrations, which includes everything you see, hear, smell, taste, and touch. These vibrations are interpreted and transmitted by your brain as specific sensations.

In the Mental Plane your thoughts, emotions, desires, fears, and so on, have specific rates of vibration that correspond to their nature. When you think, you emit thought-waves into the atmosphere and each thought-wave has its own signature frequency, albeit invisible to your physical senses.

Since you have your physical experience in the Physical Plane, it only makes sense that you can physically experience those things that are physical or material in nature because your physical senses are attuned to interpreting their frequencies. In contrast, you cannot physically sense what exists in the less dense Mental and Spiritual Planes that are immaterial in comparison, because your physical senses are not attuned to their frequencies.

Incidentally, an example of how humanity is vested in the physical or material world is that the word 'immaterial' has in modern-day language been distorted to mean 'unimportant', whereas it is from the immaterial potential energy that all material, actualised things come.

Your Mental Frequency
The overall frequency of your mental nature is determined by what you persistently think, feel, believe, and perceive, which in turn largely determines the nature of your physical experience. Since you can consciously choose your thoughts, you can also intentionally change and increase the rate of vibration of your overall mental frequency by thinking more positive thoughts of a higher frequency.

Since your physical world experience is a projection of your mental frequency, changing your thoughts changes your experience. This is the metaphysical reason for why you can change your outer world by changing the nature of your inner world. When you consciously choose what you think, under the direction of your will, your moods, emotions, desires, and thoughts have little power to affect your inner world as you will have mastered them.

POSITIVE DOMINATES – NEGATIVE SUBMITS
It cannot be over-stated that one of the most important rules you can ever come to understand about consciousness is that higher degrees of positivity (higher frequency) have directive power over lower degrees of positivity (lower frequency) on *all* planes. The implications of this rule of consciousness will become evidently clear later in this book, but for now let us take a deeper look at what it means.

As an individual, you are *positive* to all those things and people below your degree of positivity, and they are *negative* to you. Likewise, you are *negative* to all those things and people higher in degree of positivity relative to your own, and they are *positive* to you.

In the context of consciousness, another way of saying higher degrees of positivity have higher directive power over lower degrees of positivity, is 'positive *dominates* negative', and 'negative *submits* to positive'. Be very clear that the word 'dominates' does not suggest force or control, although it can be expressed in this way, but rather it means to 'lead or direct', and 'submit' means to 'follow the lead'.

This literally means that all those things in your physical and mental environment that are *negative* to your degree of positivity, can and do submit to your mental direction. The higher your degree of positivity above the Physical Plane, the greater your power to direct all those things and people in your outer world, that have a lower degree of positivity relative to your own, and this works both ways.

It cannot be stressed enough, however, that submission to your direction is not a matter of physical power, mental manipulation, or control in any way. Rather, the force exerted is an invisible mental force of the most subtle nature. At higher degrees of positivity, you do not in fact set out to direct anything or anyone in your physical environment. The only thing you care to direct is your own mind, and the rest follow its lead without need for physical intervention.

THE MALLEABILITY OF THE PLANES

Ascending the Scale of Consciousness in positivity makes your physical reality *appear* more malleable or compliant to your will. This can be likened to decreasing the density of the Physical Plane or else, increasing its flexibility or fluidity. The reason you *experience* your physical reality as being more fluid, is because by raising your rate of vibration of consciousness, you are no longer operating at the degree of the Physical Plane's density, and hence you have more directive power over it.

If, however, you set out to manipulate and control people and circumstances in an attempt to force them into compliance, you are unlikely to succeed, and even if you do, it will be short-lived. This is because this mind-set is operating at the level of positivity of the Physical Plane, looking to outside things and people as separate from you, with no real understanding of the directive power of your mind and the underlying unified consciousness of the Universe.

In fact, when your degree of consciousness is 'stuck' in that of the Physical Plane, then your degree of *positivity* has little, if any directive power over your circumstances, and so you feel you have no choice but to control and manipulate. Think about it this way - it is vastly easier to change something you *know* is an ever-changing projection of your consciousness, even if it appears to be unchanging and solid to the physical you, than it is to change something that you *believe* is real and permanent, even if it is not.

Chapter 16
LAW 4: THE LAW OF POLARITY

The fourth of the Seven Universal Laws is the Law of Polarity. It is the first of the four transmutable Lower or Mutable Laws and is also called the Principle of Duality.

AXIOMS FOR THE LAW OF POLARITY
Everything is Dual, Everything has Poles
Everything has its Pair of Opposites
Like and Unlike are the Same
Opposites are Identical in Nature but Different in Degree
All Paradoxes may be Reconciled
Extremes Meet

THE LAW OF POLARITY EXPLAINED
The Law of Polarity states that everything in the manifested Universe comes in pairs of equal but opposite poles. This means that everything in the Universe has two sides or two poles to it, with many degrees of vibration of that same thing between the two poles. Two things that may appear to be opposites or diametrically opposed to each other, are in fact the two poles of the same thing, with the only difference being their respective rates of vibration.

One pole is not separate from its opposite pole. Rather the two poles of a pair of opposites are relative to each other, the one has the seed or *potential* of the other within it, and the one gives rise to the other along *unconscious* lines. This means that all things, most notably in the Physical and Mental Planes, are relative and not absolute in nature, because something that is absolute does not have an opposite, whereas something that is relative does.

Moreover, one pole has no meaning outside the context of its opposite to which it can be compared. In other words, to be given meaning, one pole must be compared to its opposite pole. Since one opposite comes with its other side and also gives rise to it along *unconscious* lines, the poles of a pair of opposites cannot be separated in any real sense, because they are the same thing, only different in degree. But they can be reconciled or united into a balanced whole.

Everything Comes in Pairs
There is evidence for the Law of Polarity in everything you turn your attention to. The following examples are evidence for the duality of all

things: up and down, top and bottom, high and low, right and left, forward and backward, push and pull, past and future, now and then, before and after, day and night, fast and slow, motion and rest, hot and cold, good and bad, light and darkness, conscious and unconscious, active and inactive, male and female, positive and negative, youth and age, health and disease, birth and death, coming and going, material and immaterial, heavy and light, doing and undoing, broad and narrow, large and small, north and south, east and west, love and hate, courage and fear, faith and doubt, belief and disbelief, right and wrong, true and false.

One of the axioms of the Law of Polarity is that 'extremes meet'. This is easily understood by imagining that you are travelling around the globe. If you travel north to the furthest northern point on Earth, you will reach an extreme point after which you are heading south. Likewise, if you travel in an eastward direction around the Earth, you will reach an extreme point after which you are travelling west, and will return to your original point from the west.

One Pole is the Absence of the Other

It is obvious from the afore-mentioned pairs of opposites that whatever quality you attribute to the one side, then the other side is the *absence* of that quality. For instance, light is the absence of darkness, and darkness is the absence of light. Having said this, what is not so obvious, is that the one pole of a pair of opposites, far from being separate or distinct from its opposite pole, is in fact the same thing expressed in a different way. Remember that one pole is relative to the other, with the only difference being their corresponding rates of vibration or frequencies.

The Basic Example of Hot and Cold

The easiest way to understand the relative aspect of the Law of Polarity is to consider it by way of the example 'hot and cold'. Hot and cold may appear to be distinct from each other as opposites but, according to the Law of Polarity, they are in fact identical in nature. In other words, hot and cold are simply different degrees of rates of vibration of the same thing called temperature.

Think about it this way - at what point on a thermometer would you draw a line that divides hot from cold? For instance, Point A at 30°C on the thermometer may be hotter than Point B at 25°C, yet colder than Point C at 35°C. But Point C may be colder than Point D at 40°C. This simple example illustrates that you cannot tell which point on a thermometer is hot and which is cold, without one above or below it to *compare* it to. This means that the terms hot and cold, as is the case with all the pairs of opposites, are relative and conditional.

Moreover, think of the following examples described in William Walker Atkinson's 1909 The Arcane Teaching. If you go from a cold hallway into a warmer room, you will feel yourself warming up in that room, even if those people already in the room feel cold. Similarly, if you dip your one hand into ice cold water and your other hand into hot water at the same time, and then plunge both hands into a basin of lukewarm water at the same time, then to the 'cold' hand the water will feel warm, while to the 'hot' hand it will feel cool, and yet the temperature of the water in the basin itself is fixed.

One Pole Gives Meaning to Its Opposite

One pole of a pair of opposites cannot exist outside the context of its opposite, because they are the same thing. In other words, one pole *depends* on its opposite pole for meaning. For instance, you cannot speak of north outside the context of 'north and south' otherwise the concept of north by itself has no meaning. In the same way, you cannot mention high tide outside the context of 'high and low tide', or east outside the context of 'east and west'. Put simply, any one opposite is given meaning by its other side, and the meaning it is given is always *relative* to higher and lower degrees of itself.

Positive and Negative Poles

Hermetic teachings refer to the two poles of any pair of opposites as the positive and negative poles. When seen as part of the Scale of Consciousness, as all things are, this means that the positive pole of a thing has a higher rate of vibration than its negative counterpart. This concept of positive and negative may not have much meaning for the opposites of say 'east and west', but it is significant when it comes to your mind's positive and negative emotions and thoughts, as will be discussed shortly.

Bear in mind, however, that positive and negative does not necessarily suggest 'plus and minus' in a mathematical sense. Rather, whether something is positive or negative depends on its relative degree of positivity compared to the degrees above or below it. For instance, take three theoretical points on the Scale of Consciousness, with Point A at 75, Point B at 50, and Point C at 25. Point A is positive to both Point B and C, Point B is positive to Point C but it is negative to Point A, and Point C is negative to both Point A and B, but it is positive to all the degrees beneath its own.

Put simply therefore, the negative pole of a pair of opposites has a lower degree of positivity than its positive counterpart. Drawing on the

Law of Vibration, this means that the positive pole of a pair of opposites has greater directive power over those things of its own nature that have a lower degree of vibration or positivity, which at the opposite extreme, is the negative pole.

OPPOSITES OF MIND

Since everything in the Physical and Mental Plane comes in pairs of opposites, it stands to reason that your emotions, thoughts, and desires come in pairs. This means that every emotion, thought, and desire has its positive and negative poles, with the positive being more powerful than its negative counterpart in directive power. This also means that all your experiences are relative in nature and subject to definition. We will now look at each in turn.

Pairs of Emotions

All emotions come in pairs that are the same in nature, and only different in degree. The pairs of opposite emotions of happiness and sadness, joy and sorrow, love and hate, calm and anger, are all the same in nature and only different in degree or rate of vibration.

The one pole of an emotion *unconsciously* gives rise to its opposite pole, even more so when taken to an extreme, because 'extremes meet'. This is why obsessive love can turn to hate and back again, or when at times you are extremely happy but can quickly feel sad or tearful, or why an over-friendly discussion can quickly turn into a heated argument. The reason is that these pairs of opposites are the same thing, only different in degree, as are all pairs of emotions.

Positive emotions have a higher rate of vibration or degree of positivity, while negative emotions have a lower rate of vibration or degree of positivity. This means that positive emotions are more subtle or 'lighter' while negative emotions are more dense or 'heavier'. Indeed, we refer to positive emotions of say love and courage as the finer or lighter emotions that lift us upwards, whereas their respective opposites of hate and fear are denser or heavier emotions that weigh us down.

This also means that, given their higher rate of vibration, positive emotions have greater directive power over negative emotions, which in turn means, positive emotions can more easily cancel out negative emotions. Put another way, you need a 'lesser amount' of positive emotion to cancel out negative emotion, and a relatively 'greater amount' of negative emotion to cancel out positive emotion. For this to hold true in your experience, however, you must aspire to more positive emotions, otherwise you have nothing with which to cancel out your negative emotions.

Higher and Lower Emotions

The fact that positive emotions have higher positivity does not mean that *extreme* positive emotions have a higher positivity than their more balanced positive counterparts. In fact, all emotions when expressed extremely tend to have a negative undertone. For instance, extreme love is expressed as obsession, extreme confidence as arrogance, and extreme courage as aggression. For this reason, it is more appropriate to refer to emotions as *higher* and *lower* emotions instead of positive and negative. This avoids the confusion that may arise out of extreme positive emotions being considered as higher in positivity, especially since extreme positive emotions can quickly change into their opposite negative extremes.

Moreover, the idea of higher or lower emotions does away with thinking of positive and negative emotions in the sense of good and bad. Rather, any one emotion has its own rate of vibration which is either 'lighter' (finer) or 'heavier' (denser) than any other emotion of its own kind. When distinguishing higher from lower degrees of any one emotion, higher emotions are 'lighter' and impart a feeling of being lifted higher, whereas lower emotions are 'heavier' and impart a feeling of being weighed or pushed down.

For instance, a more balanced expression of love is higher than a more extreme expression of love such as obsessive love, and indeed, balanced love lifts you higher, whereas obsessive love weighs you down. This will be discussed in more detail when we consider optimal emotions. In the same way, extreme negative emotions weigh you down more than their less extreme expressions. For instance, intensely hating someone feels far heavier and hence is a lower emotion than simply disliking someone.

Pairs of Thoughts

All your thoughts come in pairs but ignorance of this can leave you feeling mentally frustrated and confused, as explained by Eugene Fersen in his 1923 book The Science of Being.

Haven't you found that when you really want something and are determined to think positively about it, then when you do, its opposite immediately pops into your head and you become frustrated, thinking 'why am I sabotaging myself' or 'I will never get this right'. Similarly, when you unreservedly decide, '*Yes*, I am going to do this or that', then a voice pops into your head that says, '*No* you're not'. What's more, don't you find when you are determined to be happy about someone else's success that then a part of you insists that you are not? Again, you become frustrated and conclude that there must be something inherently wrong with you.

However, there is *nothing* wrong with you. In each of these cases, the opposite that pops into your head is just the Law of Polarity giving rise to the opposite of the original position you took. It becomes a problem when you fail to recognise this for what it is, and instead fight the opposite thought, rather than simply stay focused on your original intended thought. This usually results in giving your power away to the position that you are fighting against.

Pairs of Desires

All your desires come in pairs. This means that both what you 'desire' and its opposite of what you 'do not desire', are the same thing only different in rate of vibration. For instance, if you desire more money, then 'more money' is the one pole and its opposite pole, which is what you do not desire, is 'financial struggle'. The two poles are an expression of the same desire for monetary wealth, they are relative to each other, and are subject to your definition of wealth.

Moreover, the one pole depends on and gives rise to its opposite pole. This means that if you are currently struggling financially, then your current circumstances give *rise* to your desire for more money, and hence your desire for more money *depends on* your current financial struggles. Likewise if you did not desire more money, then you would not perceive yourself as financially struggling, which means that your desire *not* to struggle financially, in turn *depends* on your desire for more money.

Relative Experiences

All your experiences are relative in nature and subject to definition. This means that one person's negative can be someone else's positive and as the saying goes, 'one man's heaven is another man's hell'.

For instance, your 'poor' may be defined as not being able to go out to an expensive restaurant every night, whereas someone else's definition of 'poor' may be not being able to put food on the table. Similarly, if someone who is homeless, without a cent to his name, is given $100 his personal experience is *perceived* as being positive relative to where he was prior to receiving the $100.

In contrast, if someone earning $50,000 a month gets his salary cut to $25,000, his experience is *perceived* as negative, despite the actual amount of money still being far higher in relation to the homeless person's $100.

The Relative Nature of Good and Bad

Taking this relative nature of experiences further, the Law of Polarity states that one's perception of good and bad is also relative and that the two can be reconciled. This means that your judgment of good or bad depends on your circumstances and on your perception at any given moment, which William Shakespeare expressed as, "Nothing is either good or bad, but thinking makes it so."

For instance, rain is good during a time of drought, but it is equally bad during a time of flooding. A relationship break-up is bad if you want to remain in the relationship, but it is good if you desire to be single. The relative nature of good and bad also underpins the saying 'a blessing in disguise', which refers to an experience that you once considered to be bad and unwanted that then turned out in retrospect, to be to your advantage.

The relative nature of good and bad also explains how the same thing may be good for one person and bad for another person, depending on each person's preference or what side of the fence they are on. For instance, a revolution to overthrow a dictatorship may be good for the people living under such a regime, but bad for the dictators and all those benefiting from the regime.

Moreover, bad depends on good, and good on bad. A simple example is the change in the seasons. Say you prefer summer-time to winter-time and so perceive summer to be pleasant (good) and winter to be unpleasant (bad), yet winter is necessary for summer. Not only does summer's return depend on winter by way of the seasons but also, were it not for your unpleasant experience of winter to compare it to, you could not find or perceive the pleasure in summer.

DISTORTED POLARITY

In your ignorance of the Law of Polarity, you have distorted the natural order of the Universe by failing to see that the two sides of any one thing, be it an emotion, thought, desire, or experience, are the same thing, only different in degree. Instead, you tend to declare the one side as good, desirable, or wanted and the other side as bad, undesirable, or unwanted, yet both sides are the *same* thing.

In this way, you create a mental battlefield on which the opposites are made to fight each other, which is the root cause of your attachment to the side of anything that you declare good, and doubt about ever attaining it or resistance to the side that you declare bad. How to rise above the opposites of attachment and doubt in your desires will be discussed in Chapter 34.

Chapter 17
LAW 5: THE LAW OF RHYTHM

The fifth of the Seven Universal Laws is the Law of Rhythm and it is the second of the four changeable Lower or Mutable Laws.

AXIOMS FOR THE LAW OF RHYTHM
Everything Flows Out and In
Everything has its Tides
All Things Rise and Fall
The Pendulum Swing Manifests in Everything
Rhythm Compensates

THE LAW OF RHYTHM EXPLAINED
The Law of Rhythm states that everything swings between the two poles of a pair of opposites and hence, is closely related to the Law of Polarity. Everything moves forwards and backwards or rises and falls, between its two poles, with the measure of the movement to the one side being equal to the measure of the movement to other side.

Action is followed by an equal but opposite *unconscious* reaction, a forward movement is followed by a backward movement, a rise by a fall, an expansion by a contraction, a swing to the right by a swing to the left. Esoteric texts often use the analogy of a swinging pendulum to describe the backward and forward movement between the two poles of the opposites that is manifested by the Law of Rhythm.

The operative word in the above paragraph is 'unconscious' that means that the equal but opposite reaction to any one action, or the equal but opposite counter-swing of the pendulum, takes place along *unconscious* lines. This means that by consciously becoming aware of the swing of the pendulum in both your physical and mental worlds, you can largely rise above its unconscious operations and once again direct the changes in your own experience of life.

Rhythm is Responsible for Change
The constant change that is observed in everything in the Universe is owing to the swing between the two poles of a pair of opposites, courtesy of the Law of Rhythm. Rhythm is therefore, responsible for change. Put another way, were it not for the compensating swing between the opposite poles in nature, then nothing would change. There is always an out-pouring (giving) and an in-pouring (receiving) between the two poles and the one balances and counter-balances the

other for any work to be done or change to take place. There is great metaphysical truth in Isaac Newton's Third Law of Motion that 'every action has an equal but opposite reaction'. Therefore, nothing is at absolute rest in the *manifested* Universe because everything changes rhythmically between the two poles of a pair of opposites. This is the basis of the Principle of Balance discussed in Chapter 20.

Evidence for the Law of Rhythm

Evidence for the changes produced by the Law of Rhythm is everywhere in the Universe. It is seen in the rise and fall of the waves of the ocean, in the cyclical change of the seasons from winter to summer and back again, in day-time followed by night-time, in the waxing and waning of the moon, in the rise and fall of the greatest empires, in business cycles from boom to bust and back again, and even in technical trading rules in financial markets. You can also find evidence for the Law of Rhythm in your mental nature by way of your mood swings, the swaying of your thoughts from being constructive to being destructive, the swaying of your emotions between their respective poles and, in your general outlook on life from being optimistic to pessimistic.

The Forward and Backward Swing

As Eugene Fersen explained in his 1923 book The Science Being, when anything reaches a point of culmination, by reason of its own weight or force having peaked, the backward swing or movement begins almost unnoticeably. The speed of the backward movement increases continuously, until such time that the forward movement has been *almost* completely reversed.

Thereafter, by reason of an equal but opposite force, the forward movement begins again and the process is repeated. The complete movement from one pole back to the other is circular, or more accurately elliptical in shape. This gives rise to the cyclical nature of life, or the tendency for your experiences to appear to go around in circles, as we will discuss later in the Law of Rhythm's derivate, the Principle of Cyclicity.

According to Eugene Fersen, it is nature's inherent tendency towards evolution that allows for any progress to take place, as he explained with the following words: "The backward movement is so strong as to bring Humanity *almost* to the same point from which it started, and the little gain still made is due exclusively to the operation of another law called the Law of Evolution, which in some measure counteracts the operation of the Law of Rhythm."

The Law of Rhythm is therefore responsible for the very slow pace of evolution, whether it be on a planetary scale or at the level of your personal life. Put another way, for every four steps you metaphorically take forwards, if you are unaware of the Law of Rhythm, then it will reverse your progress by three steps back. In other words, 'four steps forward, three steps back' is how the Law of Rhythm operates in your life, along *unconscious* lines.

Everything Changes, Everything is Becoming

As we saw in the Law of Polarity, each pole of a pair of opposites has the seed or potential of its opposite within it. When one pole of a pair of opposites manifests, mentally or physically, then the seed of its opposite pole *unconsciously* begins to grow, and so the opposite pole is *becoming*. In the same way, when the opposite pole in time manifests, then the seed of the original pole is sown, and so *it* is becoming, and the cycle of continuous change is created.

In the words of the philosopher of Ancient Greece, Heraclitus, 'everything changes, everything is becoming'. With this in mind, since everything unconsciously changes and becomes its opposite, only to change back again, then being attached to anything is as futile as fearing its opposite, all the more so when you learn how to rise above the unconscious operations of the Law of Rhythm in Chapter 25.

The Relative Extremes of a Relative World

The Law of Rhythm's metaphorical pendulum does not necessarily swing to the extreme poles of the opposites. It swings *towards* one pole and then *towards* the other. In fact, it is difficult to establish absolute extremes in a relative Universe, as extremes are themselves relative. For instance, the extremes to which the pendulum swings that manifest as the four seasons of a country in the upper Northern Hemisphere are different to those of a country nearer the Equator.

Moreover, it is difficult to establish common extreme polar opposites in the mental world of emotions and thoughts. In other words, your emotional extremes depend on your mental nature and can be significantly different from someone else's extremes. Similarly, you can be extreme in one emotion but not in another, and someone else may be extreme in your moderate emotion while being moderate in your extreme emotion.

Swinging Between Degrees of Vibration

As is the case with the Law of Polarity, while the pendulum swings between the opposite poles labelled 'positive' and 'negative', this is not to be taken literally to necessarily mean 'plus and minus' in a mathematical sense, nor does it mean 'good and bad'.

Rather the swing is always from one degree of rate of vibration towards another degree of rate of vibration of the same thing. The labels of 'positive' and 'negative' is for the purposes of distinguishing between the degrees of vibration. For this reason, the swing between the two opposite poles of positive and negative, is perhaps more accurately illustrated directionally, as in a wheel rotating or moving in one direction and then in the other direction.

DELPHIC MAXIM: «MHΔEN AΓAN»

The Law of Rhythm's compensating backward movement of any forward movement means that the more extreme your emotions are then the further apart the poles of your emotions, and hence the greater the swing of the pendulum between your emotional extremes.

This means that by allowing for extremes in your overall mental nature, emotions, and thoughts, you effectively set yourself up for something of a recurring emotional roller-coaster ride of 'heaven and hell'. Having said this, if a person thrives on mental extremes in their temperament, they are compensated for it by way of the Principle of Compensation, discussed later.

Nevertheless, one of the three major maxims inscribed on the ancient Temple of Apollo in Delphi, Greece, is «MHΔEN AΓAN» *(pronounced: miden agan)*. It means 'nothing in excess' and advises us to avoid extremes. Put another way, since everything has something set opposite to it in order to balance or counter-balance it, then the more extreme the action, be it mental or physical, the more extreme the reaction that it gives rise to in order to compensate it.

Rhythm in Your Desires

The Law of Rhythm also manifests itself in the way you hold your desires. Desperately wanting or desiring something is accompanied with an equally desperate desire not to have its opposite, as the one pole gives rise to the other, courtesy of the Law of Polarity.

The Law of Rhythm then keeps you swinging between the two extremes, which are experienced as a vicious cycle of attachment to the desired outcome on the one hand, and doubt that it will ever happen for you on the other hand. In this way, you land up either never getting what you want or losing it soon after you get it.

Once again, how to rise above attachment and doubt in your desires is the subject of Chapter 34.

THE PRINCIPLE OF COMPENSATION

The Principle of Compensation is a derivative of the Laws of Polarity and Rhythm and hence, is closely related to both.

The Principle of Compensation Explained

This Principle states that everything has its compensation or in other words, the degree of the swing of the pendulum in one direction determines the degree of the swing in the opposite direction. If the swing in one direction is short, then it will be *compensated* by an equally short swing in the opposite direction. In contrast, a more extreme swing is followed by an equally extreme swing to the other pole. To illustrate this, if an object is thrown upwards in a straight line, then the distance it must travel back downwards to return to the original point from which it was thrown upwards, always equals the distance it reached in height above that point.

Compensation in Temperament

According to Hermetic Philosophy, man is always compensated for his capacity to feel emotions, whether he is extreme or moderate in his temperament. Those who have the capacity to feel intense or extreme suffering, also have the capacity to feel intense or extreme joy. In contrast, those who permit for only small degrees of pain in their temperament are capable of equally small degrees of enjoyment.

Both are equally compensated for their respective temperaments, especially if their experience of life is along unconscious lines. Having said this, Hermetic Philosophy also tells us that joy need not be followed by pain, as the swing of the pendulum between the opposite poles can be transcended.

More specifically, joy can either be experienced as a state of being, or it can be expressed as an emotional reaction to something in your life. In the first instance, joy as a state of being, irrespective of what is going on in your life, is not counter-balanced by the Law of Rhythm because there has been no *action* which led to that joy, and hence no re-action will follow which could take it away. In contrast, if you allow your circumstances to determine your joy, then you are equally allowing them to deny it.

Everything has its Cosmic Price

The Principle of Compensation also states that everything has its cosmic price, meaning that you cannot get something for nothing. There is always a price to be paid in attaining anything. The saying that 'you cannot have your cake and eat it too' has its origin in this Principle. It means that that you cannot both *eat* your cake and *keep* it at the same time, or in other words, to *gain* the enjoyment of eating your cake you must *lose* your cake by actually eating it.

This tells us therefore, that in order to gain something, you must lose or give up something else because 'nothing is given for nothing'. But likewise, if you lose something, you are compensated for your loss by gaining something else. Think about it this way - when you do not have what you want, you cannot lose it either, whereas having everything you want, comes with the possibility of losing it all.

Put another way, for everything a person *has*, he does not have or he *lacks* something else, and so the balance is struck. Once again, the more a person has, be it in the way of possessions or anything else, the more afraid he is of losing it and the greater the blow if he does. In contrast, a man who has little also has little to lose, and so does not fear loss. Similarly, a financial crisis makes the rich man fear for his fortune, whereas it passes unnoticed over the poor man. And a person that is ill appreciates being alive, whereas a person who has his health does not appreciate it.

Everything has its pleasant and unpleasant sides. There is some good in every bad, and some bad in every good. The cosmic price is paid or received to maintain balance, which means that the grass only *seems* greener on the other side. Bear in mind these words from the Greek philosopher Socrates: "If all misfortunes were laid in a common heap whence everyone must take an equal portion, most people would be content to take their own and depart."

Paying the Price for Attainment
In the context of your desires, the Principle of Compensation means that you must pay the price for attainment. What you lose or 'give up' in the way of paying for what you want to attain is not to be seen as bad, but rather as the compensation necessary for you to attain your desire and maintain balance. The cosmic price that is to be paid can be likened to the necessary effort that must be exerted in the specific direction of attaining your desire, as well as the effort that is required to sustain it, once you have attained it.

For instance, you cannot attain an athletic physique if you do not 'pay for it' through physical exercise and healthier eating, whereas what you lose is your previous, unchecked freedom of unhealthy eating habits and lounging around for hours on end. Likewise, you cannot attain a loving balanced relationship if you do not 'pay for it' by committing time and effort to your relationship and being willing to compromise with your partner, whereas what you lose is your previous freedom of no personal or intimate commitment to anyone.

Similarly, you cannot hope to consciously change your experience of reality in any meaningful way if you do not 'pay for it' by applying the knowledge you gain in that direction, whereas what you lose is the previous misguided freedom of not taking any responsibility for your life and leaving it up to 'chance' and statistical probabilities.

Put simply therefore, the Principle of Compensation tells us that to attain your desire you must be willing to 'pay the price' for it in the way of making the necessary physical, mental, and spiritual effort in its direction. It should be obvious therefore, that to desire something alone is not enough. To attain your desire and keep it, you must find the discipline to take the necessary mental, physical, and spiritual actions, and that discipline can only ever be achieved under the direction of your will power.

Having said this, it does not suggest 'hard work' in the sense of a constant struggle. In fact, when you are truly at the helm of your will power, then anything you do *feels* effortless because there is no internal mental resistance to fight or overcome.

THE PRINCIPLE OF CYCLICITY

The Principle of Cyclicity is also a derivative of the Laws of Polarity and Rhythm. It states that all things and events in the manifested Universe tend to move in a cyclical trend. Put another way, there is 'a universal tendency for things to swing in circles'.

The Principle of Cyclicity Explained

This Principle is evidenced throughout nature, for instance by the circular movement of electrons around a central nucleus, and by the planets' revolutions around the central sun, as well as by the cyclical movement of the four seasons. At the level of society, we see fashion coming around in circles, as well as interest in certain subjects in literature. Even the present day revival of interest in metaphysics and mind power is a result of this tendency for things to go around in circles. The saying 'history repeats itself' has its basis in this Principle.

Cyclicity in Your Life

The Principle of Cyclicity also applies to your life. By looking at the big picture of your life to date, you will notice the tendency for the nature of your experiences to be repeated whether it is in your career, finances, relationships, and so on. Each experience may be different by way of location, duration, and the people involved, but the general nature of your recurring experiences tend to be similar to the nature of similar experiences that have gone before them.

Lessons from the Past

This tendency for things to go around in circles underpins the saying by George Santayana that "those who cannot remember the past are condemned to repeat it". Indeed, remembering your past mistakes and successes, comparing them, and learning from them, goes a long way in understanding how the unconscious operations of the Mutable Laws may have affected your past experiences to date.

Moreover, a simple yet life-changing secret passed down to us in metaphysical texts, is how to convert the cyclical nature of your own life experiences into an upward rising spiral. In this way, instead of your life going around in circles, at each return of the cycle you find yourself at higher degrees of positivity. Converting the cycle into an upward spiral is one of the subjects of Chapter 25.

Chapter 18

LAW 6: THE LAW OF CAUSE AND EFFECT

The sixth of the Seven Universal Laws is the Law of Cause and Effect. It is the third of the four changeable Lower or Mutable Laws.

AXIOMS FOR THE LAW OF CAUSE AND EFFECT

Every Cause has Its Effect, Every Effect has Its Cause
Everything Happens According to Law
Chance is but a Name for Law not Recognised

THE LAW OF CAUSE AND EFFECT EXPLAINED

The Law of Cause and Effect states everything happens for a reason. The reason, however, is not some deeper unknown reason, but rather the reason is the *cause* of the effect. In other words, for every effect there is a cause, and that cause is the reason behind the effect.

More specifically, every effect is the result of a sequential chain of causes. This means that nothing happens in the absence of a preceding sequence of causes leading up to an event, or in other words, effect. Moreover, each cause in the chain of causes is a consequence of the cause that preceded it. Looking at all the causes and all the effects together, one finds a chain of events in which every event leads to the next one and to the next one, and so on.

The simplest interpretation of this Law is that the same cause will always yield the same effect. Just like an acorn can only yield an oak tree, and in the same way, you cannot plant tomato seeds and expect potatoes to emerge above the ground. This is humorously expressed in the saying, 'madness is doing the same thing over and over again and expecting a different result'.

A Question of Chance

This Law takes chance or luck out of the equation and renders them words used by humanity in ignorance of the Law of Cause and Effect. There is no such thing as chance or luck. A person may *appear* to be lucky, but behind this appearance, you more often than not find a person of an overall positive mental nature or higher positivity.

Even the throwing of a dice and the number on which it lands is in accordance with the Law of Cause and Effect. While the fall of the dice may appear random, behind it there is a string of causes, including the original position of the dice when it was picked up, the amount of force used in throwing it, the angle of the throw, the condition of the surface on which it was thrown, and so on.

Similarly, you may think it chance that you were born, but again there was a long chain of events that led to your birth. Since you came from two parents, and your parents came from another two parents each, and each of those from another two, then going back just twenty one generations connects you to more than one million direct ancestors that set in motion the causes that you are the effect of today.

A Question of Fate

Fate suggests that there is an influence outside the Law of Cause and Effect. Were fate to exist, it would render man's power to direct his mind useless. Fate also lays the burden of responsibility on the shoulders of an outside influence, because no one can be responsible for their own actions, good or evil, if they were fated to take them.

Fate also implies that the end is predetermined, irrespective of the means, whereas it is the means (cause) that determines the end (effect). Finally, fate would also render all Universal Laws ineffective because they work in accordance with very specific rules that leave no room for fate. Therefore, while the cause may be obscured, behind every effect there is a string of sequential causes.

Karma is Cause and Effect

Another word for cause and effect is 'Karma'. Karma is not a form of deliberate reward or punishment of a Higher Power. Rather it is just cause and effect in action. Incidentally, the original Sanskrit meaning of the word Karma is 'action'.

This means that nothing happens in your life as a result of some higher deity outside of you, punishing or even rewarding you. Rather every effect has its cause, and every cause has its effect. 'As a man sows so shall he reap' means that you can only ever reap what you have sown, and what you sow has much more to do with what you think, than with what you do.

TIME IN THE PLANES

The next subject we will consider is the Law of Cause and Effect in the context of time. In his 1923 book The Science of Being, Eugene Fersen wrote that the experience of time as a function of cause and effect differs on the Three Great Planes. Put simply, metaphysical texts assert that the elapse or passage of time is experienced differently in accordance with the Plane of existence in which the experience is taking place.

Physical Time

The constraint of time in the Physical Plane means that there is a time lag between any one cause and its physical effect. It is easy to see the immediate effects of your physical actions, such as placing one leg in front of the other to walk. However, it is not easy to see the whole chain of events between the physical actions taken, say a year ago or even just a few days ago, and their physical world effects or effective outcomes today. Looked at in the broadest sense, every action, whether mental or physical, that you have taken from the day you were born has led you to precisely where you are at this very moment, reading these words. Similarly, every action you take from now on will lead you to where you will be in your future.

Mental Time

The immediate effects of your mental actions are the thought-waves they emit and the thought atmosphere you create around you. If you could see your mental world as you do your physical world, you would become just as careful and selective about your mental actions as you are about the physical actions you take. In the same way that you *look* twice when crossing a road, you would *think* twice before entertaining any thought. Thought power and its effects will be considered in Chapter 22 on The Principle of Thought Power.

The Mental Plane is not constrained by time in the same way as the Physical Plane, but its physical effects are. This means there is a time lag between your mental causes and their physical world effects. This time lag dilutes the creative power of your thoughts, either because a thought was fleeting and hence did not have enough energy to be created, or it was 'overwritten' by a conflicting thought. Given the sheer number of negative thoughts people entertain, this time lag and thought power dilution is to our benefit. Having said this, it also explains why you must consistently focus on your goal without concern for your current conflicting circumstances.

Spiritual Time

The Spiritual Plane is wholly unconstrained by time. This means that in the Spiritual Plane, every cause has an instantaneous or immediate effect, so cause and effect appear to be inseparable. The *final* effects of your thoughts are *automatically* created in the Spiritual Plane. Put another way, the mental causes you set in motion by way of a mental image, whether positive or negative, and the final outcome are created simultaneously in the Spiritual Plane without the need for the chain of events between the two. From that point on, the longer you hold a mental image in mind and exclusively concentrate on it without contradictory mental images, the sooner it is created in the denser Mental Plane. And then, it is usually only a matter of time before it manifests in the densest Physical Plane.

Moreover, the instantaneous manifestation of your thoughts on the Spiritual Plane also means that the higher you raise your degree of positivity, the more you are able to 'sense' the instant creation of your mental images and so, the easier it becomes for you to focus on them without doubt.

COLLECTIVE CONSCIOUSNESS

You are likely to have had experiences that appeared to be random and unpredictable, which seem to contradict the Law of Cause and Effect. This seeming contradiction can be reconciled by considering collective consciousness and its effects on the life of a person who is living largely along sub-conscious or unconscious lines.

As long as you are operating at the level of your personal self alone while looking at your outer physical world as the basis for what is real, and with little or no consideration for your inner mental world, then you are effectively trapping yourself in a closed system with no outside influence. Since everything is consciousness, a closed system such as the society you live in, has its own consciousness.

This is called collective consciousness because its frequency is determined by the sum or collection of the consciousness of the individuals that live in that society. Therefore, by denying or failing to direct your own individual consciousness, you allow for the possible outcomes in your life to be directed by the collective consciousness in which you live. Moreover, the possibility of negative outcomes in your life could arguably outweigh the possibility of positive outcomes because the collective consciousness is made up of mostly destructive messages, courtesy of the negatively-biased focus of the media and other news sources. These messages then pass unchecked down to your sub-conscious mind for programming.

Since most human beings largely live their lives unconsciously, the multitude of factors inherent in the collective consciousness of their society, make their outcomes appear disordered and unpredictable. One *cannot* say therefore, that someone specifically attracts a tragedy or accident into their lives. Rather, the tragedy was one of the many possible outcomes of the actions they unconsciously took in the past, which was also influenced by the nature of their society's collective consciousness, over which they had no conscious say.

Chapter 19
LAW 7: THE LAW OF GENDER

The seventh Universal Law is the Law of Gender and it is the fourth and last of the four Mutable Laws.

AXIOMS FOR THE LAW OF GENDER
Gender is in Everything
Everything has Its Masculine and Feminine Principles
Nothing is Created Outside of Gender

THE LAW OF GENDER EXPLAINED
The Law of Gender states there are two opposing or dual forces in the One Universal Mind, and all creation on all Planes is the result of the actions and re-actions between these dual forces. These two forces are the masculine and feminine principles. For creation to take place both the masculine and feminine principles must be present. For this reason, the word 'gender' in this sense is a verb with its origin in the Latin word *generare*, which means to 'bring forth or generate'. The purpose therefore of The Law of Gender, is creation.

The Masculine and Feminine Principles
According to the Law of Gender, the masculine principle is positive and the feminine principle is negative. Having said this it cannot be emphasised enough that the terms positive and negative, do not in any way imply good and bad, and nor do they suggest a mathematical plus and minus. Moreover, in the context of the Law of Gender, positive in no way means strong or better, and negative does not mean weak or worse. Both principles are equally powerful and equally necessary to each other, as well as to creation, although their respective powers are in opposing directions. To avoid therefore, the tendency to think of the word 'negative' as meaning 'bad', it is more useful to refer to the principles of gender as the masculine and feminine principles, or alternatively, the Father and Mother Principles

What's more, although a derivative of the Law of Polarity, it is not useful to think of the masculine and feminine principles as being the opposite poles of Polarity. This is because the pairs of opposites, for instance, east and west or long and short, do not lend themselves to the idea of a masculine and feminine principle in any meaningful way, at least not in so far as conscious creation is concerned. For the purpose of distinguishing between Polarity and Gender, we can generally say Polarity's two opposite poles of positive and negative are on the right and the left of balance and the pendulum's swing between the two opposite poles causes change. In contrast, Gender's masculine and feminine principles are above and below respectively, and together they generate creation.

This is perfectly depicted in the cover design of this book. The male face above the mirror represents the masculine principle or Father God, and the female face below the mirror, represents the feminine principle or Mother Earth. The two smaller faces, on either side of the mirror look the same but are looking in *opposite* directions and are found opposite each other, and represent Polarity's equal but opposite poles of the same thing. Finally, staying with the cover of this book, all creation between the masculine and feminine principles and all activity or change between the positive and negative poles take place within The Absolute's Mind, which is represented by the mirror in the image.

The Role of the Masculine and Feminine Principles

To understand the workings of creation one must first understand the respective roles of the masculine and feminine principles in the creation process. Put simply, the role of the masculine principle is to *direct* its inherent energy toward the feminine principle, which triggers the creation process and in turn, the feminine principle *receives* the energy and carries out the creation with it. This emphasises the fact that the feminine principle is in no way weak or less powerful, as it is the principle that always creates.

Put another way, the masculine principle energises and incites activity while the feminine principle conceives and brings forth creation, making both equally necessary to creation. The best-known expression of the Law of Gender is between man and woman whereby both sexes are necessary for creation or reproduction. In fact, another esoteric term for the Law of Gender is Sex Polarity. Sex in this context is the action and re-action between the masculine and feminine principles, and applies to all creation on all Planes.

THE MASCULINE AND FEMININE QUALITIES

To understand the respective roles of the masculine and feminine principles, you must understand the qualities inherent in them. This is of paramount importance to understanding the creative nature of your mind and is the foundation of practical conscious creation. The respective qualities inherent in the masculine and feminine principles oppose each other. This does not mean that they fight each other, but rather they work together in opposite directions and towards the same purpose of creation.

The key masculine and feminine qualities are listed below. In each of these pairs, the quality on the left is inherent in the masculine principle and the quality on the right in the feminine principle.

MASCULINE - FEMININE
FATHER - MOTHER
DIRECTIVE - CREATIVE
LEADING - FOLLOWING
PROJECTIVE - RECEPTIVE
PROTECTIVE - NURTURING
ACTIVE - PASSIVE

By bringing the first four pairs together, one can say the following about the creative process between the masculine and feminine principles throughout the Universe. The masculine *father* principle is *directive* and so *directs* what the *creative* feminine *mother* principle is to *create*. The feminine principle *follows* the masculine's direction and creates what it is directed to create. With this aim in mind, the masculine principle *projects* its energy towards the feminine principle, which *receives* it.

MENTAL GENDER
Before we look at what the qualities together mean for conscious reality creation, we must first understand the Law of Gender on the Mental Plane. Your mind has masculine and feminine principles that work together for mental creation to take place, which determines what is manifested in your physical world. There are three main pairs of masculine and feminine principles of mind that are fundamental to your understanding of mental creation and hence, to your success in directing your mind to create the life you intend. These pairs are listed below with the masculine principle (Mental Man) on the left and the feminine principle (Mental Woman) on the right.

MENTAL MAN – MENTAL WOMAN
OBJECTIVE MIND - SUBJECTIVE MIND
WILL - DESIRE
REASON - EMOTION

In accordance with the three mental pairs, the masculine principles of mind are your objective mind (conscious mind), your will, and your reason. The respective feminine principles are your subjective mind (sub-conscious mind), desire, and emotion. Bear in mind however that the objective conscious mind, in this context, is *not* the mind of the personality. Rather, it refers to those degrees of consciousness *above* sub-consciousness, which at higher degrees of positivity is the mind of intelligent self-awareness and directive power.

Moreover, the most important feminine principle of mind is your intuition, which will be discussed in detail later. In fact you can say that where your will is the masculine principle of the I within, your intuition is its equally important feminine partner. The only reason it has not been mentioned here is because it does not play as direct a role in the creation *process* itself as do the other principles, and nor is it directed by the will. Rather, in the context of conscious creation, your intuition's role is paramount to *knowing* in your heart what you truly desire, and so can be said to be the starting point of the creation process itself.

MENTAL CREATION

Mental creation is a metaphysical term for consciously creating your reality through the power of your mind. Put simply, mental creation involves you using the *directive* power of your masculine *will* to persistently hold the mental image of your feminine *desire* in your *objective* mind until such time that it is impressed on your feminine *subjective* mind where all creation takes place through its *creative* power. This is the basic premise of conscious reality creation based on Mental Gender and it will be re-visited in detail throughout the book.

In closing this introduction to Mental Gender, it must be stressed that you must never do yourself the disservice of believing that the masculine principles of your mind are more powerful than their respective feminine counterparts just because they are directive and the feminine are receptive. After all, there is little use for the directive power of the masculine principles in the absence of the creative power of the feminine principles.

It is the feminine principles that do *all* the *creating* while the masculine principles *direct* the creation, and hence both are *equally* necessary to each other and to creating the reality you desire.

Chapter 20
THE PRINCIPLE OF BALANCE

The Principle of Balance underpins the harmony and order that is present throughout the manifested Universe. Although not expressly one of the Seven Universal Laws, The Principle of Balance can be traced back, in western philosophy, to Pythagoras of Ancient Greece and is closely related to the Laws of Polarity, Rhythm, and Gender. My inspiration for this chapter is based largely on William Walker Atkinson's 1909 book The Arcane Teaching, and Walter Russell's 1926 book The Universal One and his 1950 Home Study Course.

AXIOMS FOR THE PRINCIPLE OF BALANCE
There is Always Check and Counter-Check in Every Manifestation
There is Always Something Opposed To Something Else
Everything is Set-Off and Off-Set by Other Things

THE PRINCIPLE OF BALANCE EXPLAINED
The Principle of Balance states that nature always seeks balance and hence everything in the Universe is balanced and counter-balanced by something else that is set opposite to it. It is obvious from this description that the Principle of Balance is derived from the Laws of Polarity and Rhythm because balance and counter-balance occurs between the positive and negative poles of Polarity for work to be done and be sustained.

The Principle of Balance is again expressed by Isaac Newton's Third Law of Motion that 'for every action there is an equal but opposite reaction', and the Greek philosopher Plato also expressed it, in the context of extremes, as follows: "The excessive increase of anything causes a reaction in the opposite direction."

Balance Drives Change
Walter Russell expressed the Principle of Balance in his writings with the following statement: "Action and reaction are equal and opposite. Sequentially they are repeated in reverse, the reaction becoming the action, and the action the reaction."

This means that the one pole of a pair of opposites is balanced, counter-balanced, and balanced again, by its opposite pole in an ongoing and rhythmic cycle. In other words, no change can occur anywhere in the Universe in the absence of the continuous search for balance between the opposite poles of Polarity.

The Balance of Breathing

The mechanics of breathing lend themselves to understanding the Principle of Balance by way of analogy. Breathing requires a rhythmic interchange between inhaling, and its opposite pole of exhaling. Both inhaling and exhaling are equally imbalanced states and the one seeks to balance and counter-balance the other in order for life to be sustained through breathing. Let us see how this works.

When you begin to inhale an imbalance is created and when you have inhaled fully, it is momentarily balanced. This balance cannot be maintained because the force of inhaling gives rise to its opposite force of exhaling. Upon exhaling, another imbalance is created, and when the air is completely exhaled, momentary balance is achieved. But once again, it cannot be maintained because the force of exhaling gives rise to its opposite force of inhaling, and the cycle is repeated in a rhythmic continuous interchange of balance - imbalance - balance - imbalance, and back again

Giving, Receiving, and Re-Giving

Nature's search for balance is a process of giving, receiving, and re-giving between the two poles. The one pole gives to the other, and the pole that receives then re-gives to the original pole, which in turn receives and re-gives, so that the cycle can continue. To give only is like trying to exhale all the time without ever taking an inward breath. In contrast, to receive only can be likened to breathing in and trying to hold your breath without exhaling.

Giving and receiving therefore, are both equally necessary for the balanced expression of all life. Neither is better or worse than the other. Both are equally necessary to each other and the one gives rise to the other.

Balance Drives Creation

In his 1950 Home Study Course, Walter Russell expressed nature's search for balance in the context of creation. Bear in mind that Walter Russell did not draw a direct distinction between the opposite poles of Polarity and the masculine and feminine principles of Gender, and indeed as you already know, the latter are a derivative of the former.

Nevertheless, here is what Walter Russell said: "Without desire for creative expression through thinking there could be no sex division [imbalanced opposite poles]. Without desire for balance there could be no sex desire [desire to create]. Without attainment of balance, there could be no repetition. Without repetition, there could be no continuity."

The Necessity of Balance and Imbalance

Balance and imbalance are equally necessary for change or creation to occur. Let us see how this conclusion is reached. One pole of a pair of opposites alone is in a state of imbalance. This means that in search for balance, its opposite pole is necessary to counter-balance it. But balance is only *momentarily* attained before another imbalance arises and so the cycle continues.

This suggests that the natural order of the Universe is imbalance *seeking* balance. It stands to reason therefore, that nature's search for balance drives the counter-balancing of an imbalance, and since everything in the Universe is always changing, then balance is also a changing condition. Moreover, if nature did not seek balance then no change would occur, and if there were no opposing imbalanced poles, then nature could not seek balance. This brings us full-circle back to the original premise, that balance and imbalance are equally necessary for change or creation to occur.

EVIDENCE FOR BALANCE IN NATURE

Balance and counter-balance is also evidenced throughout nature. For instance, everything in nature has its natural predator, which keeps its population in check, be it an animal, plant, or insect. Without natural predators, the overpopulation of a specific species would create an imbalance in the world's ecosystem, which in most cases would be detrimental to the planet.

It is because man has rid himself of his natural predators that our imbalanced actions have given rise to the imbalances we are currently experiencing in nature. Man has created a cycle of events which if not balanced by him, will in time be counter-balanced by nature in a way that could cause his ultimate destruction. Man's destructive actions are in ignorance of the fact that he is part of nature, and hence part of the imbalances that he is creating and also part of the counter-balancing effects that will follow.

Similarly, when anything in nature is excessive in its imbalance, it is counter-balanced by its equal but opposite, excessive imbalance. This of course is the Law of Rhythm in action. For instance, very hot weather creates an imbalance that is followed by a downpour, in search of balance. A build up of pressure in the earth's crust creates an imbalance that is counter-balanced by an earthquake or volcanic eruption, in search of balance. Floods, earthquakes, eruptions, and all other natural disasters, are nature's way of correcting imbalances. Nature's extreme counter-balances therefore, may be perceived as disastrous but they are essential to the Earth's survival because without them, the planet would descend into chaos, and on a larger scale, so would the Universe.

DESIRE IS A SEARCH FOR BALANCE

The motivating force behind your desires is balance. This is because a desire is to want something that is absent in your life. From the Law of Polarity you know that if something is absent, then its opposite is present. This means you desire something because you perceive its opposite in your current circumstances, otherwise you would not desire it. Put another way, you can only desire what is absent from your life, and what is absent from your life is an imbalance, by virtue of its opposite being present.

Desire therefore, is a desire to balance what you perceive to be missing in your life, or in other words to counter-balance its opposite that is present in your life. Having said this, what you consider to be absent is always relative and subject to your own definition, but as long as you perceive an imbalance, then you will desire to balance it by desiring its opposite. When your desire is satisfied then balance is momentarily restored, and you then go on to desire something else and the cycle of personal creation continues.

In the same way that nature's search for balance is the force that drives creation in the Universe, your desires are the force that drives creation in your life. Similarly, the imbalances present in your life are the force behind your desires. Put simply, if there were no *perceived* imbalances in your life, you would have no desires, and if you had no desires, you would *perceive* no imbalances. Both are equally necessary to motivate you to create what you want to experience.

Chapter 21
THE LAW OF ATTRACTION

The Law of Attraction is the most famous of all the Universal Laws written about in the last twenty to thirty years. Even though it is not one of the Seven Universal Laws of Hermetic Philosophy, Eugene Fersen referred to the Law of Attraction as 'the basic Law of the Universe', and both Hermetic and Arcane texts refer to this Law as being the greatest attractive force in the Universe.

AXIOMS FOR THE LAW OF ATTRACTION
Like Attracts Like
Like Vibration Resonates with Like Vibration

THE LAW OF ATTRACTION EXPLAINED

The basic premise of the Law of Attraction is that 'like attracts like'. The word 'attraction', however, has given rise to much confusion because it automatically triggers the notion that 'opposites attract' and that 'likes repel', as is the case for instance with what appears to happen between the two opposite poles of a magnet. To overcome this contradiction, it is helpful to think of the Law of Attraction in terms of resonance *and* attraction. In this context, the Law of Attraction states that you attract into your reality those things and circumstances that resonate with or correspond to the rate of vibration of your mental contents.

Lessons from a Magnet

To reconcile 'like attracts like' in the context of a magnet, one can say that a magnet *attracts* another magnet or another object that can resonate with its magnetic field (like attracts like), whereas it does not attract something that is unlike itself. 'Opposites attract' can also be reconciled with 'like attracts like' by looking at the direction of the magnetic field of a magnet. The following explanation is for the purpose of illustration, so do not get caught up in its detail.

In a bar magnet the magnetic field emerges from the north pole and re-enters the south pole. Now imagine bringing two magnets together. If you bring the *same* poles of two magnets together, their magnetic fields flow in *opposite* directions because you have turned the two *same* poles of the magnets around to face each other. Their magnetic fields therefore flow in *opposite* directions and hence they oppose each other, and the two magnets are *repelled*.

But if you bring the *opposite* poles of two magnets together, then their magnetic fields flow in the *same* direction and the two magnets *attract* each other. Put simply, this illustrates that magnetic field lines that flow in the *same* direction *attract* each other (like attracts like) and magnetic field lines that flow in the opposite direction *repel* each other (opposites repel). Therefore, even though it *appears* that 'likes repel' and 'opposites attract' at the point of two magnets' respective poles, a look at the direction of their magnetic fields reveals that the reason opposite poles *appear* to attract is because their magnetic fields are flowing in the *same* direction.

You can also think about it this way - if opposites do attract, then surely the opposite poles of a magnet, or any other pair of opposites, would be in the centre and not at *opposite* ends. Considering how magnets work at a more fundamental level therefore, supports the Law of Attraction's premise that 'like attracts like' or more accurately, 'like vibrations resonate with like vibrations'.

MENTAL MAGNETICS

Your mental world can be likened to a mental magnet that attracts to you outer world experiences matching your mental frequency, which itself is determined by your thoughts. And the more concentrated a particular thought is, the greater its attractive power. In ignorance of the Law of Rhythm, however, you leave your mind undirected and hence your thoughts tend to be scattered not concentrated, and your emotions swing between their higher and lower counterparts.

Put another way, by leaving your mind undirected, the contents of your mind are like puppets hanging off the swinging pendulum, one moment being positive, and the next negative. The conflicting nature of your thoughts then cancel each other out and your experiences tend to stay the same, or appear to repeat themselves in cycles, with your overall experience matching your *overall* mental frequency. Once again, if you are not *directing* your mind, you cannot say you are creating your life in any real way. Instead the Universal Laws are directing your mind along unconscious lines, and creating your life accordingly. How to direct your mind to attract to yourself what you desire is covered throughout the remainder of this book.

Another way to look at the Law of Attraction is in the context of the Unified Field. Remember that the Unified Field is the field of the infinite potential energy of Universal Mind, containing all possibilities in *potential* form, which are in turn transformed into *actualised* form through thinking. Your thoughts resonate with and attract to you in physical form those possibilities that match their frequency.

Chapter 22

THE PRINCIPLE OF THOUGHT POWER

The Principle of Thought Power works along the lines of the Laws of Vibration and Attraction. For the purposes of this chapter, unless otherwise stated, 'thoughts' include all your mental activities from emotional thoughts to thoughts of reason.

AXIOMS FOR THE PRINCIPLE OF THOUGHT POWER

Thoughts are Things
Like Thoughts Attract Like Thoughts
Mental Attraction is Thought Resonance
Mind Power is Thought Power

THE PRINCIPLE OF THOUGHT POWER EXPLAINED

Thoughts are *things - invisible* things with *visible* effects. The difference between the substance of your thoughts and that of solid matter is that you cannot physically see thought substance, because it is of a much higher rate of vibration compared to physical world things. But just because you cannot see, hear, or measure something does not mean it does not exist.

For instance, there are many degrees of light and sound vibrations that no human eye or ear can detect, yet we know they exist because we have invented scientific instruments that can detect them. In the same way, we cannot see the vibrations of the forces of electricity or magnetism, but for the same reason we know they exist.

Learning how the invisible vibrations of electricity and magnetism are produced and transmitted has enabled man to direct and make use of them for his benefit. But, just because we are *aware* of and can direct these forces today does not mean they did not exist *before* we became aware of them. When you understand that thoughts produce a force as real as the force of magnetism and electricity, you will guard your mind just as you do your body from being electrocuted.

We will now consider why and how thought power works along the lines of thought vibrations. This is a fundamental principle of the Mental Plane, and is reason enough to keep your overall mental state and thoughts at higher levels of positivity.

Knowing how thought force is produced, transmitted, and received enables you to make immediate and correct use of its incredible potential power for your greatest benefit.

THOUGHT FORCE

Thoughts are produced when you think - that is stating the obvious. But what is not so obvious is just *what* is being *produced*. Put another way, what is meant by the word 'thought'? The answer is thought is a force or power, just as real as the forces of magnetism and electricity. Thinking generates mental energy that powers the thought. And, as is the case with any power, the power of thought has the capacity to be immeasurably constructive or equally destructive depending on how it is used. But ignorance of the power does not make you immune to the consequences of its use.

Thought Power Emission

When you think you emit mental energy in the form of thought-waves in the Mental Plane, just like the Sun emits light energy in the form of light-waves in the Physical Plane. Thought-waves are made up of a fine ethereal substance vibrating at such high frequencies that they are inaccessible to our five senses.

Thought-waves spread outwards in widening circles in the Mental Plane, in the same way a pebble thrown into a body of water creates circular ripples on the water's surface in the Physical Plane. The difference between thought-waves and the ripples produced by a pebble in the water, is that ripples spread out in widening circles on a level plane that is the water's surface, whereas thought-waves spread out from a common centre in all directions in the Mental Plane, just as the Sun's rays radiate outwards in all directions from it.

The Medium of Thought-Waves

The medium through which thought-waves travel is the Mental Plane but remember that the Mental Plane is not *above* the Physical Plane in location - only in degree of vibration. The Mental Plane exists in the same space and time as the Physical Plane, only you cannot see it because of its much higher frequency.

The atmosphere of the Mental Plane is comprised of a substance referred to as ether in metaphysical texts. This mental atmosphere of ether is all around you, just as is the physical atmosphere of air. You exist *in* it and move *through* it, in the same way you exist in and move through the physical atmosphere with its multitude of vibrations that you cannot see, such as light-waves, radio-waves, and sound-waves.

Thought-Wave Transmission

The transmission of thought-waves in the Mental Plane is analogous to the transmission of radio-waves in the Physical Plane. Radio-waves radiate outwards from their central point of origin that is the broadcasting station, with a frequency corresponding to that of the station. In the same way, thought-waves radiate outwards in all directions from their central point of origin that is the thinker, with a frequency that matches the mental frequency of the thinker.

Thought-Wave Reception

Taking the radio-wave analogy further, you can also understand how your thoughts are received by others and how you receive their thoughts in the Mental Plane. In the case of radio-waves, on the one end the broadcasting station transmits radio-waves with a frequency corresponding to it. On the other end your radio antenna picks up the broadcasting station's frequency and you then tune into it, *provided* its frequency is available on your radio.

If the station's frequency, however, is *not* available on your radio, you *cannot* pick it up and nor can you tune into it, and hence you cannot experience its effects, which in this case is listening to what has been broadcast. Herein lies the whole truth about thought-wave reception in the Mental Plane. Let us see what this means.

In the Mental Plane you are the mental broadcasting station that emits thought-waves of a specific rate of vibration that matches your mental frequency at the time of thinking. Your thought-waves are transmitted through the ether or atmosphere and are tuned into by all those people who have a mental frequency that matches your own. If someone does not have your mental frequency available in their own mind, then they cannot tune into your thought-waves. Thought-wave transmission and reception works in both directions. There are countless thought-waves in the mental atmosphere constantly being transmitted by others in your environment, far and near. Which of those countless thought-waves you mentally tune into, can only ever be the ones that resonate with your mental frequency.

Thought-Wave Propagation

The distance a specific thought-wave travels, or in other words how far it is propagated, depends on how *intensely* you or someone else holds that thought. A weak or passing thought with little emotion travels only a short distance and has little if any effect. Its signal is weak and also, it does not have enough energy to be propagated any significant distance.

In contrast, a thought held with enough emotion, intensity and concentration, emits a thought-wave of far greater energy and so travels much longer distances. It also has a very definite mental effect on those people tuning into it, albeit at a sub-conscious level.

For the most part, however, people produce weak thoughts. Not weak as in negative, but weak in intensity. This is because few people recognise the inherent power of their thoughts and hence scatter their thought power in the form of thousands of pointless thoughts on a daily basis. On the other hand, however, it is also most often the case that intense thoughts for most people are mostly negative in nature rather than positive. In so far as your success and happiness is concerned, there is no greater waste than the waste and scattering of thought power on trivial and negative thoughts.

Thought-Wave Amplification

When your mind tunes into an external thought-wave, your matching thought is amplified by the energy inherent in the incoming thought-wave. This once again works both ways and hence applies to those people tuning into your thoughts-waves as well. The amplification of your own thoughts by the thought-waves of others is on its own reason enough to maintain an overall positive mental frequency, and to limit any negative thinking and stop it in its tracks should it arise. Think about it this way - the more you think the same thoughts of the same nature, the stronger and more vital those thoughts become, and the greater their attractive force will be.

Thought-Wave Interference

When two thought-waves of the *opposite* nature meet there is what is called interference between the two thought-waves. Each thought-wave *loses* power in proportion to its *own* weakness. What this means is that thoughts of opposite nature do not change one another's nature but neutralise each other if they are of equal strength. If one thought-wave is stronger than the other, the less powerful one will be neutralised, but the more powerful one will have also lost some of its strength in proportion to the less powerful one's weaker strength.

This means you cannot *tune into* a thought-wave that is unlike in nature to your own, but the power of your own thoughts can be reduced or neutralised by those of an opposite nature. Bear in mind that since positive thoughts have a higher frequency and so are more powerful than negative thoughts, then positive thought-waves are proportionately less affected when coming into contact with negative thought-waves, and the reverse also holds true. But even so, the more intense a thought, the more powerful is its thought-wave and hence, a very intense negative thought-wave can 'at worst' neutralise your less intense positive thought-wave.

This neutralisation of thought-waves, 'at worst' when negative thought-waves neutralise positive thought-waves, or 'at best' when the reverse is the case, is nature's in-built safety mechanism. This is because if one thought-wave was able to change the *nature* of the other, then we could have no meaningful direction over our own thoughts.

Nevertheless, the neutralisation or reduction of your own thought power by conflicting thought-waves is also reason enough to maintain intense positive thoughts. You can take comfort in the fact, however, that most thought-waves in the ether are weak or not intense, and hence their power to reduce your own more intense thoughts is limited. Having said this, you can actually protect your energy field from negative thoughts and negative energy wherever you may find yourself, as will be discussed in Chapter 39.

Targeted Thought-Waves

The thought-waves of thoughts targeted towards a specific person, intentionally or otherwise, do not only travel in your immediate environment, but can and do travel rapidly and across any distance to a person that may be many miles away from your location. This is because the Mental Plane is unconstrained by space in the way that we experience physical distance.

The greater the intensity of a targeted thought and the longer you hold it for, the more you strengthen its transmission. This explains instances of mental telepathy when you may be thinking of a certain person intensely and they suddenly but unexpectedly contact you.

Moreover, transmitting thought-waves unconstrained by distance is behind the mental phenomenon of distant healing. In distant healing, a person objectively sends mental instructions *via* thought-waves to another person's subjective mind, irrespective of the physical distance separating the one person from the other. Provided the intended recipient is open to receiving the healing thought-waves, meaning he is not otherwise mentally engaged, then they are received sub-consciously. Mental Healing is discussed in detail in Chapter 42.

Objective Sender - Subjective Receiver

As you already know from Part I, the subjective sub-conscious mind is that part of your mind that receives impressions and suggestions irrespective of their source. In the context of thoughts, it means you tune into thought-waves *sub-consciously* and hence are not consciously aware of picking them up, even if they are amplifying, reducing, or neutralising the power of your own thoughts.

The thinker therefore, is the *objective* sender of a thought-wave and the person tuning into it, is the *subjective* receiver. Sending is *active*, while receiving is *passive*. The objective-to-subjective mode of thought-wave transmission is known as Mental Induction, and holds within it a vital lesson. Even if you are *not* actively thinking something, you can still resonate with an incoming thought-wave at a sub-conscious level in accordance with its nature, more so if your objective mind is off guard. This explains why you must maintain an overall positive mental nature. If you try to think positively *only* every now and then but without much concern for your *overall* thoughts, then your thoughts will still swing between positive and negative, or even worse, bear down towards the negative.

THOUGHTS OF ATTRACTION

To bring what has been said here together, thought-waves resonate with other thought-waves that match their frequency, and can also subjectively induce mental states of their own kind in others. This is 'like attracts like'. Thought-waves of opposite nature can neutralise or weaken each other but do not change each other's nature and so, you cannot tune into a thought-wave that is unlike your own in nature. The stronger and more intense a thought is, the greater its power, the farther the distance it travels, and the more definite its effect is.

Like Resonates with Like

In accordance with the Law of Attraction, you are attracted to and by those people whose mental frequency resonates with your own. And the more your thoughts find resonance in theirs and theirs in yours, the more you will be attracted to each other. Put another way, thoughts are alive with consciousness and seek their own kind just like 'birds of a feather flock together'.

In contrast, thoughts of unlike frequency do not resonate with each other and hence are not attracted to each other, and are said to be repelled. But repulsion in this sense is not so much the opposite of attraction. Rather, it means that one thought-wave has not found anything to resonate with in the other, although bear in mind that the one can reduce the strength of, or neutralise, the other.

In accordance with the Law of Attraction therefore, you attract to yourself those people whose mental nature matches your own. Think positively, and you attract positive people, because your thoughts resonate, and you also mutually raise each others' positivity. Think courageously and you attract people of courage who boost your own. Think thoughts of success and you will attract people who inspire you and assist you in achieving the success you desire.

It works both ways, however. Think negatively, without an inner desire to change and you will attract people with whom you can wallow in your shared negativity. Positive people with a mind-set of courage, strong resolve, and success will pass you by. And even if they do 'stop' for a while, you will be unable to develop or maintain a rapport with them, and so meeting each other will prove fruitless.

Moreover, bear in mind that since you attract people with whom you have a similar mental nature, those people mirror or reflect your inner self back to you. This means that some people in your life may be reflecting a part of your mental nature you are not acknowledging. If you see desirable or undesirable mental qualities in another person that encourage or frustrate you respectively, the chances are they are reflecting something in your nature that you are not acknowledging, want to change, or want to develop.

THOUGHT POWER AND MENTAL IMAGERY

The power of thought produced through focused mental imagery is known as visualisation. The mind 'thinks' in images and visualisation is the *intentional* concentration of your Life Force or energy on a very clear mental image of your desire, as you would like it to be in the present moment, and with no concern for outer world things and conditions. No matter how fanciful this may sound at first, be very certain that visualisation is not idle daydreaming, which itself does little more than scatter your thought power. Under the right mental conditions, visualisation is one of the most powerful ways to apply your thought power to attaining your desires, and it will be discussed in detail in Chapter 40.

PART IV
MASTERING THE MUTABLE LAWS

Chapter 23
TRANSMUTE AND TRANSCEND

Having looked at the Universal Laws and Principles, we can now turn our attention to how you can correct your mental activities in light of these Laws, and also how to use your understanding of the Higher Immutable Laws to work with, transmute and transcend the Lower ones. To transmute something is to change it, and to transcend is to rise above. We will now consider each Law and Principle in turn.

As you already know, all Universe Laws, whether they are Laws of Physics or of Metaphysics, operate along *unconscious* lines. This means there is no personal consideration or judgement in their operations. For instance, the misuse or abuse of the Laws of Electricity will have the same effect on every person, irrespective of whether the person is good or evil, kind or unkind, deserving or not, and irrespective of whether they intended to misuse it or not. Your *potential* for higher degrees of positivity through conscious *thinking*, is the key with which you can escape the impersonal operations of the Lower Laws, and instead use them to your advantage.

THE PRICE OF THINKING

The higher the value of something, the higher its price, and there are few things more valuable than the freedom of choice in thinking. This means the freedom to choose your thoughts comes at a high cosmic price, and indeed wrong thinking is the single most 'costly' or destructive force in your life. Wrong thinking leads to wrong choices and wrong actions, and ultimately to unwanted outcomes, from the trivial to the more serious. Having said this, the price you pay for your *freedom* to choose what you think is only owing to ignorance because the gift is free. Wrong thinking can be corrected under the intelligent direction of your will to choose what you think, feel, and say, and also to choose how you act and re-act.

RE-CAPPING THE UNIVERSAL LAWS

To set the scene for correcting your mental activities, we will briefly re-cap how the Universal Laws and Principles work together along impersonal lines. Everything in the manifested Universe is energy vibrating at varying rates. Universal Mind therefore, is the matrix of the Universe. And the activity of mind, which is thinking, is what transforms undifferentiated potential energy into actualised form. All energy transformation, all change, and all creation is carried out in accordance with Universal Laws and Principles that maintain the balance and harmony of the Universe. If not consciously directed, energy transformation occurs along unconscious lines in accordance with the Universal Laws and Principles.

Change is the only constant in the Universe. Everything changes courtesy of the pendulum's rhythmic swing between the two equal and opposite poles of the countless pairs of opposites. Moreover, every change has its cause and every cause has its effect. Everything is becoming and everything *unconsciously* becomes its opposite. All *creation* everywhere in the Universe is generated by the opposing dual forces of Universal Mind, which are the masculine and feminine principles of Gender. They are equally powerful principles with opposite qualities and work in opposing directions for the same purpose, which is creation.

The driving force behind all change and all creation is nature's Universal search for balance between the two imbalanced poles of a pair of opposites and between the masculine and feminine principles. In turn, the imbalances are what drive the search for balance, making both balance and imbalance equally necessary for creation or change to be generated and sustained.

In accordance with the Law of Attraction, like vibrations resonate with like vibrations, which means 'like attracts like' in all planes. The frequency of your overall mental nature is determined by what you think and how you feel, whether consciously or not. You tune into those thought-waves in the mental atmosphere that resonate in tune with your own, and weaken or neutralise those thought-waves whose nature is opposite to your own. And this works in both directions. Moreover, you attract those things, people, and circumstances that resonate at your mental frequency. Finally, your mental frequency is your degree of positivity. Throughout nature, higher degrees of positivity have directive power over lower degrees of positivity. Any one degree of positivity is *positive* to those degrees that are beneath it, and *negative* to those degrees that are above it.

The next few chapters explain how to correct mental activities that create unwanted circumstances and keep you from experiencing the life you desire as a result of your ignorance of the impersonal operations of the Universal Laws.

Chapter 24
TRANSMUTING THE OPPOSITES

This chapter is about transmuting the opposites of Polarity. The definition of the verb 'transmute' is 'to *change* or *transform* from one form, nature, substance or state, into another'. Interestingly, the word 'transmutation' was originally associated with the ancient Hermetic knowledge of the transmutation of base metals into gold, and is also referred to as alchemy or *alchemical* transmutation that hints at it being a mystical knowledge of *chemistry*. The Kybalion (1908) refers to transmutation as a Mental Art by which "mind may be transmuted, from state to state, degree to degree, condition to condition, pole to pole, vibration to vibration." Put simply, by understanding that all opposites are the same thing only different in degree, you can learn to transmute or transform an undesirable pole of a pair of opposites into its desirable opposite pole by raising its rate of vibration.

THE ART OF MENTAL TRANSMUTATION

Since everything in the Universe is *mind* or consciousness, *Mental Transmutation* applies on all Planes, and the Mental Plane is just one of the Three Great Planes of consciousness. Mental Transmutation therefore includes the transmutation or transformation of physical, mental, and spiritual conditions along lines of vibration.

Transmutation in the Physical Plane for instance, is the way by which ice is transmuted into steam by raising its rate of vibration or in other words, by increasing its temperature. In the Mental Plane, an example is the transmutation of hate into love by way of increasing the rate of vibration of hate to its positive pole love, or of cowardice to courage. Finally, little if anything is known about transmutation in the Spiritual Plane but one could speculate that it has to do with attaining Cosmic Consciousness.

Nevertheless, it is Mental Transmutation in the Mental Plane that enables you to raise your degree of positivity upwards on the Scale of Consciousness from your current degree. For this reason, we will focus on transmutation in the Mental Plane, which is the ability to transform mental states, thoughts, and emotions, which will in turn transform your outer world circumstances.

Transmutation in the Mental Plane will direct change in the lower Physical Plane by virtue of the Mental Plane's higher positivity over it. In other words, your outer physical world will yield to the changes created in your dominant inner world of the Mental Plane without having to physically force or manipulate anything or anyone in the Physical Plane. Bringing together what has been said here, Mental Transmutation is akin to becoming a Mental Chemist, whereby you transform your mind's elements through the power of your will.

Transmutation Along the Same Lines

Transmutation always takes place along the same lines. As is written in The Kybalion, "things belonging to different classes cannot be transmuted into each other, but things of the same class may be changed, that is may have their *polarity* changed."

In the context of emotions for instance, this means you can only transmute a negative emotion into higher degrees of its own kind. You cannot transmute hate into happiness, or laziness into courage because each of these two sets of emotions are not in the same pair of opposites. Rather, you can only transmute hate into love, sadness into happiness, laziness into activity, and cowardice into courage. Think about it this way - just as you cannot transmute ice into paper in the Physical Plane, nor can you transmute emotions that are not alike in nature into each other in the Mental Plane.

Energy Can Never be Destroyed

Mental Transmutation is not about destroying energy. Energy or consciousness cannot be created or destroyed, but rather it can *only* be transformed from one state into another, degree by degree. So, you can only change the rate of vibration of any one emotion into something higher or lower of its own kind.

For instance, you can never destroy or fight the emotion of hate, and hope to win the fight. To fight an emotion, or anything else in the Mental Plane, is analogous to going into battle totally unarmed in the Physical Plane. Think about it this way - if you set out to resist or fight an emotion, or anything else for that matter, you do little more than focus on whatever it is you are resisting or fighting, which then strengthens it in proportion to your focus. This is why, 'what you resist, persists'.

TRANSMUTING EMOTIONS

As you already know, the Law of Polarity states all emotions come in pairs of inseparable opposites. The most common pairs of emotions are happiness and sadness, love and hate, calm and anger, courage and cowardice, and faith and doubt. Even though they may appear to be different to your mind's counterfeit ego, both sides of each pair of emotions are the same in nature only different in degree. The transmutation of emotions therefore, is about changing negative emotions into their positive equivalents, and the *only* reason you can do this is because they are the *same* thing, only different in degree. To transmute a negative emotion into its positive equivalent, you simply focus your mind's attention on the *pole* of the desired emotion. In Hermetic teachings, this is known as Mental *Polarisation*.

Focus on *Higher* Emotions Not *Extremes*

It is not advisable to go to an opposite positive *extreme* of the negative emotion you want to transmute, because this creates an equal but opposite imbalance which in time is likely to be counter-balanced. Moreover, since 'extremes meet', going to emotional extremes and staying there, will swing you back to the opposite extreme and so set you up for an emotional roller-coaster ride.

When positive emotions are expressed extremely, they tend to be negative in their expression just like obsession is a negative expression of love. It is preferable therefore, to transmute any one emotion by simply focusing on a higher emotion of its own kind rather than an extreme. For instance you can transmute a feeling of being 'scared' into a feeling of 'courage'. But you do not want to go from feeling scared to extreme aggression or foolish recklessness.

Remember, the rule of thumb to use as your yardstick is that higher emotions impart a *calm* feeling of being lifted higher with a sense of motivation and love for life, while lower emotions weigh you down, and extreme emotions tend to make you lose your sense of objectivity. Losing your objectivity means leaving your objective conscious mind off guard and hence also leaving your subjective sub-conscious mind exposed to any message from any source.

Emotional Transmutation in Practice

There are a number of simple but effective ways in which you can transform any lower emotion into its opposite *higher* equivalent. Let us look at the example of feeling 'scared to do something you know would benefit you', and how you can transmute that feeling, into a feeling of 'courage' with simple mental and physical exercises.

Mental Plane: You can focus on the word 'courage' and repeat it over and over again in your mind while giving it your full attention, but not in a parrot-like fashion (Power Words Ch. 38). You can use auto-suggestion by mentally telling yourself that you are a person of courage and strength, and really feeling it (Auto-Suggestion Ch. 41). You can visualise yourself taking bold and courageous steps and successfully doing whatever it is you are scared to do. You can also think of a person whose courage you admire, and imagine what he or she feels like and then focus on that feeling as if it were your own, which it is (Visualisation Ch. 40). Finally, there is immense power in asserting the I by saying 'I AM' or 'I CAN and I WILL' with a calm, authoritative voice.

Physical Plane: Here are some things you can do physically rather than mentally. Listen to powerful songs that fill you with a sense of courage, strength, and motivation, and even dance to them. A song I personally recommend is the 1984 song 'Live is Life' by Opus. Find quotes on the subject of courage. Read them, write them down, and put them somewhere you can see them often. Think of someone you admire who is courageous and take on the posture of their body. For instance stand with your back straight, shoulders back, arms uncrossed, head facing forward, looking life 'in the eye', and with a smile of confidence on your face. Changing your body posture goes a long way to transmuting most emotions from their lower to their higher counterparts. This is because your body is part of your subjective mind, and so adjusting your posture produces automatic changes in your mood.

The Directive Power of Higher Emotions
As you already know, higher emotions have a higher positivity on the Scale of Consciousness than their negative counterparts, so lower emotions are *negative* to them. In other words, higher emotions have directive power over lower emotions by virtue of their higher rate of vibration. The more you transmute lower emotions into their higher equivalents, the higher you raise your degree of positivity. In so doing, higher emotions will feel more natural to you because your own degree of consciousness will be vibrating at their higher rate, while lower emotions will feel more foreign to you, as your rate of vibration of consciousness gets further and further away from them in degree. Put another way, the higher you raise your degree of positivity, the more you will find yourself naturally being positive, and all those negative emotions that once plagued you without your consent will yield to your command 'to be gone', until such time that their visits become few and far between.

Finally, as you allow your higher emotions their natural role of directive power in any circumstance, you will find yourself becoming a calmer, lighter, and happier person. And rest assured, your physical world will in time 'catch up' to match the resonance of the higher positivity of your Mental Plane. In other words, the Physical Plane being *negative* to the Mental Plane will follow its direction. Bear in mind also, that whatever you do repeatedly becomes a habit. Your emotions are a habit. How you feel is a habit. How and what you think is habit. Mental Transmutation cultivates positivity, and there is no habit more powerful than the habit of positivity.

TRANSMUTING THOUGHTS

The Mental Transmutation of thoughts works along the same lines as transmuting emotions. To transmute a negative thought, simply focus your mind's attention on its opposite and equivalent positive thought. To do so effectively, however, you must first become aware of your thoughts, especially your habitual thoughts. And to become aware of your thoughts, you must pay *attention* to what you are thinking, rather than let your thoughts wander aimlessly and idly from positive to negative and back again courtesy of Rhythm's pendulum, or in reaction to ever-changing external world stimuli.

Bearing in mind what was said about the attractive power of thought-waves in Chapter 22, train yourself to hold strong positive thoughts with conviction and *purpose*, and deny yourself the mental laziness of idle and purposeless thinking. As you do, you will once again find negative thoughts yielding to your command 'to be gone' by virtue of their lower rate of vibration and without having to consciously transmute them. In time, your outer world circumstances will once again follow suit, as they transform to match your higher positivity by attracting more positive circumstances and people into your life that can assist you on your journey, and you on theirs.

Having said this, if a negative thought is all consuming, and trying to think of an opposite positive equivalent feels beyond your own power at the time, then simply change your thought entirely. Think of something completely unrelated to the negative thought, or physically do something that will positively engage your objective mind in another way until the negative thought dissipates. If and when it arises again, deal with it then, but do not shy away from it too often. Be prepared to face it and transmute it lest you give it so much power over you that it becomes a tyrant. Indeed, thoughts are either faithful servants or tyrannical masters. But under the directive power of your will, which is a centre of the All-Powerful Cosmic Will, no negative thought or emotion stands a chance.

Chapter 25
TRANSCENDING RHYTHM

Transcending rhythm is about *rising above* the swing of the pendulum in your inner mental world and outer physical world, and is based largely on the Hermetic teachings of Mental Polarisation. When you are consciously aware of the impersonal swing of the pendulum you can largely rise above its continuous swing between the positive and negative poles of your mental world, or else you can work with it.

Transcending rhythm enables you to direct and sustain the changes you intend to create in your experience under the direction of your will, rather than have change imposed on you. Ultimately, transcending rhythm is to mount your mind at the top of the pendulum's pivot, rather than let it hang like a puppet off its rod, which swings back and forth beneath it.

MOUNTING THE PENDULUM

To transcend rhythm you must polarise your mind on the positive mental pole. The term *'to polarise'* is a metaphysical term that means to focus your mind on one pole of any mental pair of opposites and to hold your focus there with your will. To transcend rhythm you must focus your mind on the *positive* pole of your emotions and thoughts and *intentionally* keep your mental contents positive rather than allow for them to be automatically swung about by Rhythm's pendulum.

Moreover, to transcend rhythm in your desires, you must find the resolve to focus persistently on a mental image of your desire, free of doubt and attachment to the outcome of your desire, and without concern for outer world circumstances, other than as a yardstick for what you want to create, what you want to uproot, and what you want to develop further in your life.

To be able to transcend rhythm you must begin to pay *attention* to your mental thoughts and emotions, and to the physical actions and re-actions that stem from them. If you fail to pay attention *consciously*, then the Law of Rhythm will continue to work unconsciously in your life to undo and unwind your positive mental actions, as well the positive outer world circumstances that flow from them. In contrast, if you pay attention you can polarise your mind on the pole you *choose* and let the swing of the pendulum pass unnoticed *beneath* you.

According to Hermetic teachings, the Law of Rhythm operates on two planes of consciousness. The first is the lower unconscious plane and the second is the higher conscious plane. On the lower plane there is nothing you can do to escape the swing of the pendulum, as is the case throughout nature where the unconscious swing ensures the cycle of the seasons for instance, and the rising and setting of the sun. But on the higher plane of consciousness, you can rise above the swing and *neutralise* it by polarising or focusing your mind.

MENTAL POLARISATION

The word 'polarisation' generally means to 'induce polarity' and in Physics it means 'to restrict vibrations wholly or partially to one direction'. Mental Polarisation therefore is to cause, or will your mind to focus on one of two conflicting mental polar positions and *restrict* your mental vibrations to that pole, and of course the position of choice is the positive pole.

Lessons from Polarised Sunglasses

Polarisation is a scientific term used in the polarisation of light, as is used in the technology of polarised sunglasses. Let us see how this works and then draw the analogy with Mental Polarisation. Light-waves travel outwards in both a horizontal and vertical direction. When light hits a reflective surface the light is said to be polarised when the reflected light vibrates parallel to the surface (horizontal vibrations) while the rest of the light (vertical vibrations) is absorbed.

The result of the horizontal-only vibrations of light is experienced as glare. Polarised sunglasses prevent the horizontal vibrations of light from passing through the filters of its lenses. This is achieved by slots in the lenses set in a vertical-only direction that only allow vertical light vibrations through and block out the horizontal light vibrations that cause glare. Let us now draw the analogy.

Thought-waves also radiate outwards in all directions. In keeping with this analogy, positive thought-waves are akin to the vertical vibrations, negative thought-waves are the unwanted glare caused by horizontal vibrations, and your mind is the pair of sunglasses.

If you do not polarise the filters of your mind, both positive and negative thought vibrations will pass through to your subjective mind. But by focusing on positive thoughts and emotions, you create a positive-only polarised mental filter which only permits entry to positive vibrations, while negative vibrations are blocked out. This does not mean negative thought vibrations are destroyed. But rather, they have been blocked from entering your mind because it does not resonate with them, as explained in Chapter 22 on thought power.

Mental Polarisation works both ways. If you wallow in negative thoughts, you create a mainly negative-only polarised mental filter, which permits entry to negative thought vibrations and largely blocks out their positive counterparts. Polarising your mind therefore, is to endeavour to set your mental filter at *positive-only* by focusing on higher degrees of positivity in thoughts and emotions, and in so doing you only allow positive thought vibrations to pass through. Once again, your outer world circumstances will in time be transformed to match the higher positivity of your mental world.

DEALING WITH THE RETURN SWING

While Hermetic teachings assert Rhythm can be *neutralised*, bear in mind that being a Law of the Universe, albeit a Lower Law, its force is extremely powerful. This means even as you raise your positivity degree by degree, you may still encounter the backward swing in your life, the difference being you are now prepared for it.

With this in mind, *becoming aware* of the subtle start of the backward movement of the pendulum in your physical and mental worlds is the first step to transcending it entirely. This includes being aware of the start of the backward swing in the already existing circumstances that you intend to keep in your life. Once again, to do so effectively you must live consciously and pay attention to what is going on in your inner mental world and outer physical world.

Evidence of the Backward Swing

Here are some tell-tale signs that the return swing has begun. Your previous motivation, commitment, and drive for an important goal begin to wane. You start to 'slip up' or return to your old ways and habits, after much effort to change them. You start to 'take your eye off the ball' with a sense of arrogance that what you want to attain is a done deal before you have attained it. You may feel unmotivated about life for no particular reason, and perhaps even discouraged. The backward swing can be experienced in a period of a few hours, days, months, or years, and a combination of these.

Dealing with the Backward Swing

If and when you feel the start of the return swing, relax, do not panic, re-group, and remind yourself it is *only* the Law of Rhythm 'doing its thing'. When you *know* it's just Rhythm and nothing inherent within you, it is far easier to deal with or even deny the pendulum's swing.

Without necessarily doing anything goal-orientated, simply remain positive. Make an effort to keep your overall mental state positive, but also bear in mind it will be more difficult to do so than when the pendulum was working in a positive direction. This will become easier the more you practice Mental Transmutation on a daily basis.

Find the resolve to remain committed to your desire or goal with the power of your will. Keep the outcome you intend at the forefront of your mind. Do not permit doubt or fear to trespass. Use positive auto-suggestions (Ch. 41), tailor-made to reverse whatever negativity you may be feeling.

Above all, assert the I within by saying 'I AM I' and 'I CAN and I WILL'. Remind yourself that your mind is a centre of Universal Mind, that your will is a centre of Cosmic Will for which nothing is impossible, and that you are created in the image of The Absolute that is entirely *above* the swing of the pendulum.

Mentally place the All-Powerful in front of and behind your thoughts, words, actions, and desires, in the knowledge that no power is greater than the Single Source of All Power that is within you in Its entirety. When you know, this how can you fear the return swing of the pendulum? In fact, how can you ever fear anything?

Lessons from a Strong Swimmer

In his 1923 book The Science of Being, Eugene Fersen compared mentally responding to the return swing of the pendulum to the strength of a swimmer, swimming against a strong current. When a swimmer swims against the current, he prevents himself from being swept backwards, while the strength of the backward current will in time propel him forwards when it also reverses its motion.

This does not mean to fight life. Rather, it means to be in favour of a fuller expression of the life you intend for yourself. It is about mentally holding your position with self-discipline, despite the swing of the pendulum, while knowing the backward swing is what will in time propel you forward even further and with greater motivation, when the forward swing resumes, which it will.

However, even if all your previous efforts are reversed and you find yourself right back where you started, remember by virtue of the very same Law, the upward motion will start again and progress will resume. In contrast, if you fall into a 'woe is me' trap you will delay the return swing, and the full potential of its inherent energy.

The Law of Rhythm is not to be feared at all. Rather, it is to be worked with intelligently. Be cautious of it by paying attention but do not become suspicious of every mood swing. Learn to sense the pendulum's backward movement and hold your position with strength, rather than allow yourself to be swept backwards as if you were a log floating on a stormy sea.

Do Not Start Anything New

Eugene Fersen recommended that you *not* start any *new* projects or endeavours when you feel the backward swing of the pendulum because you will lack the natural energy to get them off the ground and to propel you forward. Rather, use the time to focus your energy on staying focused on already existing goals and on higher degrees of positivity, until the backward swing has stopped and the forward swing has resumed.

CONVERTING THE CYCLE INTO AN UPWARD SPIRAL

As you already know, the Law of Rhythm, together with the Principle of Cyclicity, state that the pendulum swings between the positive and negative poles of a pair of opposites, thereby creating a tendency for your life to appear to go around in circles with recurring outcomes, emotions, and experiences. Transcending cyclicity is to convert the on-going cyclical experience of life into an upward spiral, so that the changes manifested by the Law of Rhythm tend upwards in degree of positivity, instead of back and forth at the same degree. The Secret of the Upward Spiral is one of the great secrets passed down to us in esoteric teachings. Its beauty is in its simplicity.

Your Mental Point of Equilibrium

The point of equilibrium around which your life's personal pendulum swings, is determined by the frequency of your Mental Plane, and the pendulum swings between your mental extremes. As long as you do not change the rate of vibration of your overall mental nature, the nature of your experiences will tend to be similar to those that have gone before them, and you will experience life as if going around in circles. Incidentally, if you want to know where your degree of positivity is now, just look at your current inner world thoughts and outer world circumstances. Remember these wise words by James Allen that "circumstances do not make a man, they reveal him."

Raising Your Point of Equilibrium

Converting the cycle into an upward spiral is achieved by increasing the frequency of the point of equilibrium around which your mental pendulum swings. To do so effectively you must change the polarity of your mental contents. The more you focus on positive thoughts and the fewer negative thoughts you permit, the higher the rise in frequency of your central point of equilibrium. Since your experience of reality is largely the making of your overall mental frequency, then the more positive your point of equilibrium is, the more positive the physical experiences that follow will be.

Bear in mind that the pendulum's swing between the positive and negative poles is not a swing between a mathematical plus and minus or between good and bad. Rather, it is a swing between *degrees* of positivity of the same nature. In other words, *your* negative pole is simply a lower degree of positivity relative to *your* positive pole, but your *negative* may be higher than someone else's positive.

As you raise your central point of equilibrium, the pendulum will still swing between the positive and negative poles, the only difference being at each return swing, both *your* positive and negative poles will have increased in degree of positivity, and hence so will your experience. When you continue to raise the positivity of your overall mental frequency, then the result is an upward spiral of increasingly positive experiences, rather than a repetitive cycle of similar experiences over and over again in your physical world. All progress is achieved in this way but most people advance 'by accident' or not consciously, which makes it a long and winding road, which usually also involves a lot of pain.

Throwing the Ball of Positivity Upwards

To understand The Secret of the Upward Spiral, imagine yourself throwing a ball up in the air, and then raising yourself onto a higher platform to catch it when it comes back down and hence preventing it from returning to its original lower platform as it would have, had you remained stationary. Thereafter you throw the ball upwards again and repeat the process by raising yourself onto an even higher platform, and again catching the ball on its way down.

The ball is analogous to your focus and throwing the ball upwards is akin to focusing on higher degrees of positivity above your current degree. Lifting yourself onto a higher platform is analogous to staying positive and keeping your eye on the ball above. Catching the ball on its return while on the higher platform is to have succeeded in raising your degree of positivity and to have denied the full counter-swing of the pendulum by holding your focus.

Since everything is relative, raising your degree of positivity in an upward spiral means what once was 'as *good* as it gets' may become 'as *bad* as it gets', and the 'good' you experience may be beyond anything you have experienced. This works both ways. If you let your point of equilibrium slide downwards by getting caught up in a negative rut, what once left you unfazed, may just become 'as good as it gets'.

Dealing with Emotions

Stop identifying yourself too closely with your emotional world. In other words, do not let your changing emotions alter your positivity, but rather let your positivity define your emotions. Emotions are a creative feminine principle of mind, but emotional *overwhelm* creates much nervous energy and does not serve you or your desires.

When you know that according to the Law of Rhythm, a low *will* be followed by a high, you refuse to take the low too seriously and so it passes you by. Likewise, by refusing to allow your emotional highs to define your mental state, your positivity remains unaffected by fluctuations in your positive emotions.

Not taking your emotions too seriously makes them less serious, and also easier to transmute and direct. Moreover, learn to temper *extreme* emotions that cause you to lose *objectivity*. Avoiding emotional extremes keeps your pendulum's bandwidth short. The shorter the bandwidth, the shorter the swing of the pendulum, and the faster you rise upwards, degree by degree.

Dealing with Difficult Days

Transmuting polarity and transcending rhythm does not mean you will never again face any challenges or have difficult days. In fact, the bigger the goals you set in life, the higher the price you must pay for their attainment, and hence the more resistance you are likely to face, as you will learn in Chapter 36 on taking action and dealing with reaction. What matters is how you perceive and deal with difficult days and resistance. Whenever possible, refuse to take difficult days too seriously; deny yourself the misguided comfort of self-pity; learn to trust Life no matter what is going on; banish doubt and don't forget that nothing stays the same forever - everything changes.

EXTERNAL PENDULUMS

You must also be cautious of so-called external pendulums. These are pendulums created and sustained by collective consciousness whether it is at the level of your immediate environment or that of the entire planet. In other words, external pendulums *originate* in your *outer* physical world, whereas internal pendulums originate in your *inner* mental world of thoughts and emotions.

For instance, say the country you live in is experiencing a financial crisis. If you do not remain alert and positive in your mental vibration in this regard, then your personal experience will be swept up in the financial crisis. You, however, have the option not to climb on the bandwagon by guarding your mind, and hence your experience, from the negative thought vibrations in the atmosphere. This can be likened to letting the external pendulum largely play itself out while not making it one of your internal pendulums. Once again, the answer lies in polarising your mental world on all that is higher in positivity by way of vibration, and thereby literally denying the rest entry into your mental and hence physical experience.

TRANSCENDING COMPENSATION

Remember, according to the Principle of Compensation everything is compensated, and everything has a 'cosmic price' that you must be willing to pay for its attainment.

Mental Transmutation and Polarisation enable you to rise above the swing of the pendulum between joy and sorrow. By polarising yourself on higher thoughts, you attract things into your life that match your higher mental frequency, rather than have your joy be followed by sorrow in time. Moreover, if you define your own mental state, and resolve to 'be positive' no matter what, rather than let your outer world determine the state of your inner world, then even if the pendulum continues to swing in your experiences, it will leave you less disturbed in both directions.

What's more, paying the 'cosmic price' for attainment is not about exhausting yourself, although you must be prepared to be exhausted if that is what it costs. Having said this, once you have exerted the mental effort to bring your mind under the direction of your will, all other effort will *appear* effortless. This is because when at the helm of your will, anything you do, you do because you *choose* to and you *want* your desire enough without having to fight sub-conscious habits.

The physical effort exerted to attain your goals is still the same. But when you desire something enough under the direction of your will, physical effort is never 'hard work'. When effort comes from directive power and pure desire, it is expressed as a deeper love for life and feels effortless. In the words of Kahlil Gibran in his 1923 book The Prophet, "work is love made visible."

Chapter 26
REVERSING CAUSATION

Reversing causation is about reversing the feedback loop that exists between your mental world and your physical world, which keeps your circumstances little changed. In other words, it is correcting the Law of Cause and Effect's *flow* of causation, which will in turn enable you to create the changes you want in your life.

To set the scene for understanding this, bear in mind that the Mental Plane is *above* the Physical Plane in positivity, and hence has directive power over it. Within your inner mental world, your creative sub-conscious mind is *subjective*, and is hence *subject* to the direction of your objective conscious mind. But whatever messages pass down to your subjective mind must first pass through your objective mind, whether you are conscious of the messages going through or not.

REVERSING THE FEEDBACK LOOP

Your objective mind is that part of your mind that deals with the outer physical world. By interacting with your physical world, you send mental images of its current condition down to your subjective mind. The same applies when you think of the past over and over again. Given the receptive quality of the subjective mind, it receives and accepts those mental images without question. And given its creative nature, it then reproduces those images in form in your outer world which serves to keep your circumstances little changed.

This in turn re-enforces the misguided belief that your outer world is real, while your inner mental world is fanciful. But this of course is out of not knowing that it is your inner mental world that is in fact creating your outer physical world courtesy of a feedback loop between the two that you have set up in the *wrong* direction. Put simply, since your inner mental world (both subjective and objective minds) determines your outer physical world, then your *inner* mental world should be given directive power over your *outer* physical world.

Correcting the Feedback Loop

When you give directive power to your inner mental world it *reverses* the feedback loop between your inner and outer worlds and hence makes the inner world the *cause*, and the outer world the *effect*. Bear in mind though, irrespective of the direction of the feedback loop, the inner mental world is always the *cause*, the only difference is that in the *wrong* direction, physical *effects* determine the new mental causes set in motion, whereas in a feedback loop set up in the *right* direction, the new mental causes set in motion are not limited to or by outer world circumstances or effects.

CONSTRAINED VS UNCONSTRAINED CAUSES

A mental cause set in motion in response to your physical world is constrained by the limitations present in your current circumstances, and hence is a *constrained* cause. Constrained mental causes create a sequential chain of causes and effects, based on the misguided belief that the outer world is a solid permanent thing over which you have no meaningful direction.

In contrast, by understanding that your inner mental world is the cause and has directive power, then you stop looking to your outer world circumstances for what is possible. In turn, the new mental causes you set in motion are *not* constrained by the physical world. Mental causes set in motion without concern for what you perceive in your outer world are *unconstrained* causes.

Lessons from Photography
Attempting to modify your physical world by trying to force change on the Physical Plane, can be likened to manipulating an already printed photo, and expecting that the next time you print it out from its original negative, the changes will be reflected.

Just as the same photographic negative will always produce the same photograph, so it is that your unchanged mental conditions will also produce the same results. There is no need, or even any real use in trying to manipulate, convince, trick, or force anything or anyone to change in your outer world. Rather, you must come to understand the *mental* nature of the Universe and realise that to change your experience, it is your mind you must change, not its projections.

BECOMING THE CAUSER

To be at the helm of your outer physical world experience, you must *first* be at the helm of your inner mental world. In other words, to direct your outer world, you must first direct your inner world. To become the director of your mind, you must use the power of your will, which is discussed in detail in Part V.

Ultimately, the higher you raise your degree of positivity, the greater your directive power over your inner world and hence also over the outer world it creates. In this way you become the *Causer* of your experience of reality, rather than being one of many constrained causes. In so doing, your self-*directed* mind becomes the dominant cause in your experience with no concern for what is going on in your circumstances, other than as a yardstick for what you want to create, what you want to change, and what you want to keep. Once your outer physical world catches up to your *new* inner mental world, then the feedback loop will work to your benefit in both directions because the conditions of your outer world will then be reflecting your positive mental state.

As you already know, consciously transmuting or changing your negative thoughts and emotions into their positive equivalents, and being prepared for the backward swing of the pendulum, go a long way in raising your degree of positivity and your directive power. By becoming the director of your mind, you can then begin to impress your subjective mind with mental images of your desires through visualisation and other techniques, as is discussed in Part VI.

Not All Desires or Fears Come to Pass

While every effect, whether physical or mental, has its own cause, not every mental cause will have a physical world effect. In other words, not everything you think of, desire or fear will necessarily manifest. It depends on the intensity of your thought, how often you focus on it, how much you want it, how emotional you are about it, what mental and physical actions you take, and so on.

In fact, more often than not, what you simply fear or desire does not come to pass. This is because the aforementioned *wrong* direction of the feedback loop means your current circumstances determine your outcomes, because you interact with them more than you think about your fears and desires. And because your fears and desires are *not* part of those circumstances, they more often than not do not come to pass.

For a desire to be consciously created in your physical world, you must desire it under the *correct* mental conditions, and to be able to do so, you must first correct the feedback loop direction, by giving your inner world directive power over your outer world. On the other hand, due to the fact that what you may fear is something you anticipate happening in the *future*, it has actually nothing to do with your *present* circumstances. This is reason enough for you to forget your fears because chances are they will not materialise since you are not thinking about them under the correct mental conditions. But even if something you fear does come to pass, you probably already know from experience that it is never quite as bad as you imagined it would be. Forget your fears therefore, and they will forget you.

Chapter 27

MENTAL GENDER IN CREATION

All creation everywhere in the Universe is generated as a result of the interaction between the masculine and feminine principles of the Universe. As you already know, both the masculine and feminine principles are equally powerful and equally important to creation and no creation can take place without both principles being present. The Law of Gender also applies on the Mental Plane and hence to mental creation. In order to create what you desire, you must come to know and awaken both the masculine and feminine principles of your mind, and enable them to interact with each other in accordance with their inherent qualities listed here.

MASCULINE - FEMININE
FATHER - MOTHER
DIRECTIVE - CREATIVE
LEADING - FOLLOWING
PROJECTIVE - RECEPTIVE
PROTECTIVE - NURTURING
ACTIVE - PASSIVE

Below is a reminder of the feminine and masculine mental pairs. The 'Mental Man' principles on the left are the three major masculine principles of your mind, and the 'Mental Woman' principles on the right are the respective feminine principles. It is very important to bear in mind that all human beings have *both* the masculine and feminine principles of mind equally available to them, irrespective of their physical sex being that of male or female.

MENTAL MAN - MENTAL WOMAN
OBJECTIVE MIND - SUBJECTIVE MIND
WILL - DESIRE
REASON - EMOTION

Remember also, the objective mind in this context is not the mind of the personality but rather that part of your mind that is above subconsciousness and hence is objectively self-aware. Bringing what has been said together, the three main directive masculine principles of your mind are your objective mind, your will power, and your reasoning or rational mind. And the three main creative feminine principles of your mind are your subjective mind, your desires, and your emotions. Throughout the Universe, the masculine principle is proactive. It incites activity and initiates creation by *directing* its inherent energy toward the feminine principle. In turn, the nurturing feminine principle responds to the actions of the masculine principle. It receives the energy directed towards it and uses it for creation. Let us now consider what this means when it comes to creating your desires by looking at each of the three mental pairs in turn.

OBJECTIVE MIND - SUBJECTIVE MIND

Your objective mind is the masculine principle and your subjective mind is the feminine principle. As you already know, your subjective mind receives mental impressions at face value and from any source, and sets out to create what is inherent in the messages that are given to it. But remember also, that all messages must first pass through your objective mind. This means that you must objectively protect your sub-conscious mind from unwanted messages by paying keen attention to what messages you give it. Most people, however, live their lives with little objective self-awareness, which essentially makes a mockery out of the truly immense creative and receptive power of their subjective mind.

You must bear in mind that your subjective mind by definition, must be *subjected* to your *objective* direction and protection. If you leave it undirected, you essentially leave it open to being directed by the will of others and to creating anything that passes through your unprotected mental filters.

Your subjective and objective minds are equally important to the creation process. But unless you honour the inherent creative power of your subjective mind, and stand guard at its door to protect and guide it then you cannot say you are consciously creating anything.

WILL - DESIRE

Will power is a masculine principle and desire is a feminine principle of mind. Understanding what this means for conscious creation is fundamental to effectively applying the power of your mind to create your desires. To create something consciously, you must first desire it. That is stating the obvious but the reason I do so, is because most people stop right there - at desire. It is not enough just to desire.

To desire something alone is like holding the seed of a flower you desire to see grow, but never planting the seed in the soil. Your desire is a creative feminine principle of mind but without its masculine counterpart, which is your will, the chances are you do not focus on it correctly and hence, it will not be 'planted' in your subjective mind and thus will not be created. You must employ the power of your will to hold a mental image of your desire in mind persistently. By failing to use your will power to focus on your desire, you more often than not idly think of many arbitrary desires, and scatter your thought power amongst them.

Moreover, if you do not use the power of your will to focus on your desire exclusively, then the mental image of your desire is left to fight it out with conflicting images in the form of feedback from your current circumstances. Your must therefore, also protect your desire from any external influence. Moreover, when you are at the helm of your will power, you can use all your other mental faculties to assist you in attaining your desire, including your imagination, intellect, concentration, and so on. What is not so obvious from what is written here is that to *incite* or rouse the directive power of your will into action you must desire what you want *enough*. Most people, however, are mentally lazy and desire half-heartedly, which amounts to little more than wishful thinking. Behind every person who attains his or her desires, you will find a strong will and an equally strong desire. Successful people are not lucky people. They are people who know what they want, desire it enough, and use the power of their will to direct their mind in order to attain it.

The Power of Your Intuition

Once again, the highest feminine principle of mind is your intuition. The power of intuition is seldom covered in esoteric teachings on Mental Gender because it is not as obviously or directly involved in the creation process as much as the other principles of mind are. This, however, does not mean that your intuition is not important and in fact, its power should never be overlooked.

Your intuition empowers you to *know* that you *can* indeed create what you desire. Moreover, it helps you know what *you* want to create in your life, rather than what you *should* want to create, based on society's expectations of you. And it also lets you know if your desire serves your greatest good or not, or if it is just your counterfeit ego trying to satisfy itself. The power of your intuition and of your desires will be discussed in detail in Chapters 33 and 34.

REASON - EMOTION

Your reasoning mind is a masculine principle and your emotions are a feminine principle. This means reason is directive but *not* creative and explains why just thinking about something rationally is not a motivating force in the same way emotions are. Emotions are a very powerful creative principle of mind and for this reason, how and what you *feel* counts far more than what you *logically think* when it comes to creating your desires. Moreover, without your emotions you could not express your feelings towards anything or anyone, which would leave your experience in the hands of cold logic.

Emotions are to the mental image of your desire what water is to the seed in the soil. At first glance this may suggest the more emotion the better because of course, seeds need water to grow. But just like too much water will drown a seed, too much emotion can and does overwhelm your mind and 'drown' your desires.

In failing to realise the directive power of reason over emotions, most people live their lives in an overly emotional world, in which their emotional reactions to external stimuli determine their mental state. And the more extreme the emotions you permit in your mental nature, the more extreme the counter-balancing that follows.

Moreover, when overwhelmed by emotions, your objectivity tends to go flying out the window and you become a puppet whose strings are pulled by your emotions, one day feeling positive and the next negative. Making matters worse, when you are emotionally overwhelmed, you stand little chance of effectively using your will power, let alone your reason and other mental faculties - at least not in a productive way that best serves you.

You must therefore employ the directive power of your reasoning or rational mind to *guide* your emotions and keep them at optimal levels. This is *not* about denying your emotions their rightful place but rather granting it to them, so that you can use and express them to your advantage, rather than have them use you and express you to your disadvantage. Moreover, by guiding your emotions and keeping them at optimal levels, you create a powerhouse of creative energy that you can access at any time to motivate you in pursuing your desires. Optimal emotions are discussed in the next chapter.

Lessons from a River

A good analogy for the relationship between your emotions and your reasoning mind is a river and its banks, where your emotions are the ever-changing flowing river, and your logic is its still and stable banks on either side. In the absence of its banks, the river would flood and drown all the surrounding area, whereas in their presence the river creates, nurtures, and sustains life around it. The banks of the river do not stop the river from flowing, but rather allow it to flow by guiding, directing, and ultimately protecting it. On the other hand, were the banks of the river over-sized, which is akin to denying your emotions and living only on the plane of cold logic, then the banks would hinder the flow of the river and it could no longer create, nurture, or sustain the life around it. The one complements and balances the other, and both are equally important to each other. By allowing reason to guide your emotions, you will find life flourishing in areas that previously overwhelmed you, and the same will be the case in areas that previously seemed lifeless.

THE MENTAL COUPLE

When you awaken both the masculine and feminine principles of your mind, and allow them to work in harmony with each other and in accordance with their inherent qualities, then what you get is The Relationship of the Mental Couple.

The Relationship of the Mental Couple

The mental creation process starts with a desire. As long as you desire something *enough*, your masculine objective mind is attracted by the desire which then incites your will into action. In other words, your desires stir your will into activity and you use your will to *direct* your *feminine subjective* mind to *create* your desire by holding a mental image of it persistently. You *project* your energy to your desire by *actively* focusing on it, and your subjective mind *passively receives* the energy and uses it to create.

You objectively take action in your outer world to pay the 'cosmic price' for your desire, whatever its price, as long as it is worth it to you. With your *reasoning* mind you direct your *emotions* and *protect* yourself from emotional overwhelm. You also *protect* your subjective mind from negative messages and conflicting images by paying attention. And in return your subjective mind *nurtures* your outer world experience by *creating* your desire in form.

Your mind is *both* the Mental Man (objective) and Mental Woman (subjective) and your outer world creations are your Mental Children. By understanding what has been written here, you can understand how your subjective mind can create what you truly desire under the direction of your will, the guidance of your reason, the creative power of your emotions, and its firm protection by your objective mind.

The aspects of Mental Gender are discussed in more detail in Part V in the context of Top-Down-Living. And just how to practically apply the directive and creative aspects of your mind to create what you desire is the subject of Part VI.

Chapter 28
OPTIMAL BALANCE

Since nature seeks balance, it only makes sense for you to balance your inner and outer worlds intentionally, rather than have balance imposed on you by the impersonal operations of the Universal Laws. Having said this, since everything in the Universe changes, nothing is perpetually balanced. Balance therefore, is dynamic not permanent. If you were permanently balanced, you could not desire anything, you could not create anything, and nothing would change. Remember, it is the imbalances in your life that drive your search for balance, and your search for balance is what drives your desire to create.

GIVING AND RECEIVING

The Principle of Balance states that balance is momentarily born out of the counter-balancing between giving and receiving. It is the result of a rhythmic out-pouring and in-pouring between the two poles of a thing. And for a cycle to continue, balance is followed by imbalance, imbalance is then followed by balance, and back again in rhythmic repetition. Balance therefore, is not an equal measure of good and bad. Rather it is the rhythmic continuous interchange between the two poles of the same thing, where one pole gives to the other, the receiving pole re-gives to the pole that originally gave, and so the roles are reversed. In this way, the giver becomes the receiver, the receiver becomes the giver, and the cycle continues.

This is evidenced by science and nature, for instance, in the cycle of giving, receiving, and re-giving between the anode and cathode poles of a battery for electricity to be generated. In nature, human beings and animals give off carbon dioxide by exhaling, which is received by plants and used for photosynthesis. Plants then re-give in the way of oxygen, which is in turn received by humans and animals inhaling, only to be re-given as carbon dioxide, and so the cycle continues.

Your aim therefore, is to balance your imbalances consciously, so that whatever you want to create can be created and sustained. This is what I call *optimal* balance, and we will now consider what this means in the context of your desires, actions, and emotions.

OPTIMAL BALANCE IN DESIRES

As you already know, your desires are creative and seek to balance an imbalance you perceive in your life by virtue of your desire's absence. Balancing your desires is simply a case of giving and receiving what you desire to experience. Think about it this way - everything you want to experience in your life comes down to something of value to you that you desire to *receive*, whether it is more love, more money, more health, or more spiritual awareness. Since the opposite pole of 'to receive' is 'to give', it stands to reason you must give what you value in order to receive it. In other words, you must be willing to give something of value in exchange for attaining your desire, which is another way of saying you must be willing to pay the 'cosmic price' in exchange for your desire. Everything you desire to experience has its own currency of exchange. Money is the currency of exchange for material and other outer world things, but it is not the only currency.

Balanced Desires in Action
Most people are familiar with money as a currency of exchange. By understanding how a desire for money is dynamically balanced, we can draw the analogy for other desires. Since money is the exchange of value of one thing for another, you must find something of *value* to give to the world, so that you can receive the money you desire in compensation for the value you have given.

Giving something of value creates an imbalance, which in order to be balanced attracts in your outer world people and circumstances set up to 'receive' the value you are offering, and in turn give you the money you desire in exchange for your value, which momentarily balances the cycle. To maintain the cycle, which means to continue to receive the money you desire, you continue to give something of value, which creates a further imbalance, and so the cycle is repeated.

This example highlights that giving value in exchange for what you desire to receive does not necessarily mean exchanging the same thing. In other words, you do not give money to receive money, just as plants do not give off carbon dioxide to receive it, but instead give off oxygen. It is a case of giving something of *value* that creates an imbalance, which is then balanced by you receiving your desire, which is what you value. And to keep the desires you attain, you continue to re-give, receive, and re-give. Let the *value* you *give* be your focus, and rest assured that what you value in return, will come.

The Cosmic Currency of Exchange
The cosmic currency of exchange for anything you desire is value. The more valuable a desire is to you, the more you are willing to pay by giving value in exchange for it. If for instance it is more love you want to receive, you give something of 'love-value'. This creates an imbalance that is balanced by receiving love, which you then re-give, and the cycle continues. The currency of love for instance, is being

truly grateful for the love you already have in your life, loving all life including yourself, and acting on your love. Giving love therefore, is love in action. If, however, you are exclusively focused on receiving love without appreciating and giving love, no love will be ever be enough for you and even if you receive it, you might as well not have.

In the context of your health, if you desire to experience more health in your life, you give something of value in the way of health, and so you receive health. The currency of health includes taking healthier actions, thinking thoughts of health, and appreciating the health you already have. In this way you receive more health and to maintain it, you continue to re-give in the same way. If, however, you are exclusively focused on receiving health, but take no action in its direction, you cannot expect to receive it.

In the context of your mind, if you desire to receive all that the power of your mind can give you, you must pay the price by applying the knowledge you gain. The currency of exchange for mind power includes self-discipline, persistence, paying attention, using your will power, staying positive, protecting your sub-conscious mind, refusing doubt or fear, and so on. If, however, you focus only on receiving the benefits of mind power but give nothing in return for its rewards, you cannot expect to receive them.

Imbalanced Desires in Action

Most people exclusively focus on receiving what they desire, with little or no consideration for giving. And the more attached you are to your desire, the more you are exclusively focused on receiving it, which is in turn compounded by the fear that you will never get it.

Without giving and receiving in the name of balance, then even if you attain your desire, you are unlikely to keep it. If you fail to give of what you receive, it either stops coming to you, or anything you do receive never feels enough, so you might as well not have it. This is true for instance, of people who hoard money. Their bank accounts may reflect a large number but they live their life as if money is the scarcest commodity and so never get to enjoy what they have received. This also applies to people for whom nothing ever seems to be enough, whether it is love, affection, possessions and so on. You usually find that such people are more focused on receiving rather than giving what they want, and while from the outside it may *appear* they have everything, from their perspective they have very little.

A Word for the Givers

You may have been advised of the moral good in giving, but it is only one side of the equation. If you give without allowing yourself to receive, you exhaust yourself and the reserves of whatever it is you are giving. More often than not, you attract relentless 'takers' in your life, who when you have nothing left to give, usually already have one foot out the door.

When you understand the nature of balance by way of giving, receiving and re-giving, then and only then, will you be able to give, but not out of some moral obligation to 'be good' but rather, out of a deeper understanding of balance. At the same time, you will be open to receiving what you desire without any sense of guilt, unworthiness, shame, or any other misguided moral standards of this kind. Samuel M. Jones (1846-1904), a past mayor of Toledo Ohio, in the U.S. had this to say about desires. "What I want for myself, I want for everybody else." This is a very powerful attitude to have as it frees you from any sense of competing with, or comparing yourself to others, and from any misguided guilt for desiring what you want.

Universal Mind is the Single Giver
Since Universal Mind is the single creative source of all things, It is also the single giver of all things in Life through its countless life centres. Knowing this enables you to shift your attitude from giving to someone in order to receive from that specific person, and instead you give to All Life abundantly, and open yourself up to receiving abundance from the Universe in all ways. To trust in the continuous cycle of giving and receiving between you and Universal Mind, affords you with a sense of inner freedom, knowledge and joy that giving with the expectation to receive cannot grant you.

Remember that what *you* desire and think is also what Universal *Mind* desires and thinks because Universal Mind *is* your mind; and the greater your identification with Universal Mind, the greater Its identification is with you, in mutual recognition of each other. Also bear in mind that since Universal Mind includes *all* possibilities, your desire already exists in potential form, and is waiting to be actualised. Put another way, depending on or expecting others to give to you, limits what you receive to what you believe they can give. And being impersonal, Universal Mind adopts those limitations. In contrast, trusting in the abundance of the limitless Universal Mind opens you up to unlimited receiving, free of the constraints of what you may have believed was possible for you to receive until now.

OPTIMAL BALANCE IN ACTIONS
The dynamic balance of giving and receiving applies to the physical world actions you take, as much as it does to attaining desires.

Optimal balance in your actions is achieved by not being one-sided in the actions you take. The one side of the pole is active, which is the pole of giving. The other side is passive and is the pole of receiving, which is the opposite of the action you have taken and will, in turn, allow you to continue taking the actions you want to take.

Balanced Actions in Action

Giving is not only giving to others. Rather, giving can be defined as any outward action, just like exhaling is giving outwards and inhaling is receiving inwards. A one-sided action therefore, is doing the same action over and over again without counter-balancing it with its opposite. This amounts to squandering or even wasting what you have, without replenishing its reserves.

This applies to anything you give away without replenishing by its opposite, whether it is expending physical energy, studying for exams, pursuing your objectives, and so on. The opposite of expending your physical energy is physical rest, and only if you rest physically can you continue to expend your physical energy. The opposite of studying with your full concentration, is taking a break to clear your mind, and only if you do so can you continue studying with concentration. The opposite of pursuing your goals is playful relaxation, and only if you relax, can you maintain your motivation to pursue your goals.

In accordance with the Law of Rhythm, if your actions are one-sided and extreme, the pendulum will swing to the opposite one-sided extreme, and you will find yourself without the necessary energy to continue with the actions you want to take. By balancing your actions and allowing room for their opposite in your life, you get to counter-balance the swing of the pendulum yourself, and so it does not swing you impersonally to the extreme opposite side.

The Balance of a Positive Life

Living a positive life is not about always living on the edge with a 'go, go, go' attitude of all work no play. This is an extreme that by its own force will in time burn you out. And it, in turn, makes it difficult to deny the counter-balancing swing of the pendulum when it arises, because you will have exhausted all your energy. In fact, this attitude hastens the return swing of the pendulum because it is triggered by the peaking of *your* own energy that was driving you forward.

Make sure therefore, to balance work-time and play-time. Partake in more passive activities that boost your energy, read books, listen to relaxing music, go for walks in nature, meditate, and get adequate sleep. You can take action and take time out to relax in both directions of the pendulum's swing. But be wise and use the forward swing of the pendulum to pursue your desires with determination and overcome any obstacles. And the backward swing to relax more, play more, and sleep more, which in turn enables you to resume the pursuit of your desires with determination and a renewed sense of energy when the forward swing resumes, which by Law it will.

Let Action Direct In-Action

In the context of the Law of Gender, taking action is a quality of the masculine principle of Gender, and its opposite that is passivity is a quality of the feminine principle. This means being active and passive are both equally necessary to creation. But it also means it is your actions that are directive and hence, they must determine or direct your passivity, and not the other way around.

In other words, take action first and then relax. If however you relax aimlessly waiting to be motivated into action, you will seldom if ever find the motivation to do so. This is because being passive does not have directive power over being active, and so you leave the directive power of action untapped.

You must be the one who intelligently strikes a balance between your action and in-action. Doing so becomes easier the more you act first and then take the time to relax and replenish your reserves. This also provides you with a continuous stream of achievement, rather than achieving much in one year and then nothing else for the next couple of years just because you ran out of energy to carry on.

It also maximises your mental clarity, because taking a step back from your actions helps to clear your mind and decide on your next step intelligently, which in turn increases your productivity. Optimal balance in your actions also builds up great inner reserves of mental and physical energy that you can then use to power through those days where continuous action is required, without losing your drive and concentration.

Do not, however, permit your mind to become lazy by letting negative thoughts and emotions run free. Insist on mental positivity. When you are mentally positive, the actions you take are inherently positive and so is your in-action, because your relaxation is not born out of idleness or an 'I couldn't be bothered' attitude. Instead, you *relax* because you *know* to relax is just as important as taking action.

OPTIMAL BALANCE IN EMOTIONS

Optimal balance in the context of your emotions is not so much an equal balance of giving and receiving emotions, as it is maintaining an optimal emotional mental state. As you already know, however, this has nothing to do with extreme emotions. The word 'optimal' means 'most favourable' and has its origin in the Latin word *optimus* meaning 'best'. Therefore, the most accurate definition for optimal emotions, in the context of conscious self-aware living is 'the most favourable emotions for living the best possible life'.

Higher Emotions and Extremes
Optimal emotions are the higher emotions that promote a love for life. In contrast, as has already been said, extreme emotions cause you to lose your sense of objectivity and work you up into frenzied emotional states which overwhelm you and usually lead you to make reckless decisions, or leave you spinning your wheels while thinking you are making progress.

In fact, positive emotions when taken to an extreme are more negative in their expression than they are positive, because 'extremes meet' as the Law of Polarity tells us. The emotions and other mental states listed here give you an idea of what is optimal and hence to be aspired to on the left, and their extreme expressions to be avoided on the right. You can add to the list below by thinking of your own dominant emotions and mental states. And bear in mind that the extreme expressions listed here are intended for you to get a feel for the difference between optimal and extreme, but there are other ways that mental states and emotions can be expressed extremely.

OPTIMAL - EXTREME
Courage - Aggression
Noble - Self-Righteous
Confidence - Arrogance
Active - Hyperactive
Ambitious - Ruthless
Love - Obsession
Joy - Frenzy
Trust - Naivety
Nurturing - Smothering
Connection - Attachment
Sensitive - Petty
Compassionate - Pitying
Kind - Pushover

Optimal Emotions as a State of Mind
Since your reasoning mind is a masculine directive principle of mind, it is up to you to direct your emotional world with optimal emotions and avoid their extreme expressions and negative counterparts. Once

again, optimal emotions do not cause you to lose objectivity and nor do they overwhelm you or weigh you down. They mentally lift you higher, fill you with a calm, unshakeable love for life, and motivate you to pursue your desires with confidence and enthusiasm.

Endeavour therefore, to be a kind and joyful person. Pursue your goals with courage and confidence. Stay calm and trust Life to lead you where you desire to go. And wherever you may be on your journey, endeavour to love all life and be grateful for your own.

Moreover, adopt these optimal emotions and mental states as a way of being, rather than as a way of re-acting to outer world stimuli. In this way, your experiences, whether positive or negative, will have far less influence over your overall mental state. In time, what you create or attract in your life will serve to add to your inner sense of courage, confidence, love, and joy, because they will have been your points of attraction. In fact, there is great power in denying yourself emotional reactions to outer world stimuli. Think about it this way - by depending on outer world circumstances to feel 'good', you give them the power to make you feel 'bad' if and when they change.

Forgive and Forget
One of the most extreme emotional imbalances you can experience is resentment towards others for their unkind and hurtful actions or words towards you. Resentment and revenge can only deny you inner emotional balance and they also keep you imprisoned in the past. Forgiving the people who have hurt you and forgetting their actions is fundamental to your mental freedom. In contrast, holding onto anger, as Siddhartha Gautama Buddha said, "is like grasping a hot coal with the intent of throwing it at someone else - you are the one getting burned."

Forgiveness is a divine quality. Mark Twain captured its essence, most poignantly, when he said "forgiveness is the fragrance that the violet sheds on the heel that has crushed it." Moreover, while to be able to forgive is a sign of strength, to forget is a sign of wisdom. To forget, however, does not imply 'to go back for more' and indeed you must learn from your past, and be willing to walk away from hurtful people or situations in your life, if you so choose. To forget means to *know* that the I within is undisturbed and that nothing that anyone else does or says to you can ever change the *unchanging* I.

I like to think that to for-*give* is to *give*, and to for-*get* is to *receive*. It is only in for-giving someone that you can give them their freedom from your mental grasp, and it is only in for-getting their indiscretion that you can rise above your resentment and get free of their hold over your mind. If you endeavour to forgive but do not forget, then sooner or later something will happen to trigger the pendulum's swing back to resenting the person you wanted to forgive. Similarly, if you forget someone's indiscretion without forgiving them, then too you will find yourself being reminded of their indiscretion as you have not removed it from your mental contents.

This is not about taking responsibility or condoning others' actions. Instead, it is about granting yourself the freedom to walk away, if you choose, and to deny others any say in your mental world, in the knowledge that nothing and no-one can disturb the Real You. In the words of Philip Yancey, "To forgive is to set a prisoner free and discover that the prisoner was you." And to forget is to throw away the prison key. To forgive *and* to forget affords you with an inner balance and peace that neither one alone can grant you. In the same breath, forgive yourself and, where you cannot make amends, forget your indiscretions towards others, lest you repeat them.

THE OPTIMIST'S CREED

The following excerpt from Christian D. Larson's 1912 book Your Forces and How to Use Them, was adopted as the creed of Optimist International in 1922, and is generally known as the Optimist's Creed. Read it carefully with your full attention and make what is written here a promise to yourself, every day and in every way.

Promise Yourself

"Promise Yourself to be so strong that nothing can disturb your peace of mind. To talk health, happiness, and prosperity to every person you meet. To make all your friends feel that there is something worthwhile in them. To look at the sunny side of everything, and make your optimism come true. To think only of the best, to work only for the best, and to expect only the best. To be just as enthusiastic about the success of others as you are about your own. To forget the mistakes of the past and press on to the greater achievements of the future. To wear a cheerful expression at all times and give a smile to every living creature you meet. To give so much time to improving yourself that you have no time to criticize others. To be too large for worry, too noble for anger, too strong for fear, and too happy to permit the presence of trouble. To think well of yourself and to proclaim this fact to the world, not in loud word, but in great deeds. To live in the faith that the whole world is on your side, so long as you are true to the best that is in you."

Chapter 29
MAGNETIC THINKING

Combining positive thinking and higher degrees of positivity with the Law of Attraction is what is called magnetic thinking, and a person of magnetic thinking is called a Magnetic Person.

POSITIVE THINKING

Thinking refers to all your mental activity. And positive thinking is to think *positively*. It is to transmute and replace negative thoughts and emotions into their higher positive equivalents without a moment's hesitation. It is to deny your mental pendulum any room to sway in your moods. It is to discipline yourself to maintain a calm mental state of courage and confidence, fortified by a love for life. It is to deny entry to doubt in your mind by trusting Life.

Your Mental Centre of Mass

In Physics, the point of equilibrium between two things is called the centre of mass or centre of balance. If two things have an equal mass, then the centre of balance is exactly between the two. In contrast, if one thing has more mass than the other, then the centre of balance is closer to the one with the greater mass, by the same proportion.

As you already know, everything in the Universe, including your thoughts, has mass by virtue of having substance. When you permit your mind to operate along unconscious lines, your *mental* centre of balance approximates somewhere between your positive and negative thoughts because your mental pendulum swings more or less equally between them. Having said this, your mental centre of balance along unconscious lines may arguably be closer to your negative thoughts because of society's relentless focus on all that is evil and upsetting in the world, played direct to your front room courtesy of the media.

Alongside Mental Transmutation and Polarisation, you can also effectively neutralise a negative thought as it arises by mentally saying 'cancel, cancel', and immediately replacing it with a positive thought, or by thinking of something entirely different that has nothing to do with the unwanted thought. By focusing on positive thoughts and by transmuting, replacing, and cancelling negative thoughts, you shift your mental centre of balance towards the positive pole of thought and away from the negative pole, because you have given greater mass to the positive by way of your focus. In so doing you create a positive mental nature for yourself and hence, find more positive people entering your life and more positive things happening for you.

You will also find you no longer partake in negativity, whether in the way of idle gossip, moaning about life, or watching negatively-skewed news broadcasts. This is not accompanied by any resistance towards all that is negative. But rather, all that is negative no longer comes home to roost in your mind, because you do not resonate with it anymore. In other words, negative thought-waves do not find anything to resonate with when they cross your mental path. And, while they may to some degree weaken your positive thoughts, if you keep your positive thoughts strong then *you* neutralise them, or else send them on their not-so-merry way, reduced in their own power.

HIGHER POSITIVITY

Higher positivity is to *be* positive. And once again, to be positive means to be self-aware and pay attention to what is going on in your mental and physical world. It is to use your objective thinking mind to guard and protect the messages and mental images passed down to your subjective receptive mind. It is to use the directive power of your reasoning mind to keep your emotions at optimal levels.

Above all, the more you use the power of your will to direct every aspect of your mind, from the thoughts you think, to the emotions you permit, and the mental images you imagine, then the higher your degree of positivity rises. Ultimately, to be positive is to aspire to the higher vantage point of the I within, to identify your mind as being a creative centre of Universal Mind yet one in the same with It, and to know your will is a centre of Cosmic Will that is All-Powerful.

Positive Dominates Negative

It is well worth repeating that one of the most important things you can ever come to understand about the varying degrees of mind or consciousness is higher degrees of positivity (higher frequency) are positive to, and have directive power over, lower degrees of positivity (lower frequency) on *all* planes. Since this is premised in the Laws of Mentalism and Vibration that are both Immutable Laws, you cannot change or escape it in any way, period. But you can use it wisely to your greatest advantage. Let us re-cap just what this means, using what was written in the Law of Vibration (Ch. 15). You are *positive* to all those things and people in your environment below your degree of positivity, and they are *negative* to you. Likewise, you are *negative* to all those things and people higher in degree of positivity relative to your own, and they are *positive* to you. The higher your degree of positivity above the vibrations of the Physical Plane, the greater your power to direct and influence your circumstances. But, it cannot be stressed enough, this is *never* a matter of physical power, mental manipulation, passive aggressiveness, or any such kind of controlling behaviour in any way. Any such behaviour is a tell-tale sign of the counterfeit ego and belongs to a person who has little power to influence his own mind, let alone his environment.

Mental directive power is an invisible magnetic force that is as real as are the forces of electricity and magnetism. At higher degrees of positivity therefore, your intention is *not* to physically change *anything* or *anyone*. The *only* thing you are concerned with is directing your own mind and its images, emotions, and thoughts, with the power of your will. And your physical world will follow the lead of your mental world by virtue of the former's lower degree of positivity, without any physical intervention other than to take all the necessary physical actions to attain your desire, and to do so gladly.

THE MAGNETIC PERSON

By combining positive thinking with higher degrees of positivity of will power, you become what metaphysical teachings call a Magnetic Person. Magnetic people have varying degrees of power to attract and influence others in their environment with their presence alone, without force, actions, or even words. They appear to have luck on their side and are 'in the right place, at the right time' far more often than statistical probabilities would predict. But there is no luck or 'magic' involved. What it does come down to is their degree of positivity, their ability to direct their mind and all its contents with the power of their will, and also their willingness to focus their energy on their desires with laser-like precision and concentration. To become a person of such directive influence over your environment, it is *your* mind you must direct, *not* the minds of others.

Once again, your aim is to raise your positivity degree by degree, upwards towards the I. And every degree by which you ascend higher on the Scale of Consciousness is one degree closer to the I, which in turn makes your Mental Plane increasingly *positive* to the degree of consciousness of the Physical Plane. But even so, the greatest reward of higher degrees of positivity is not the ability to influence others or your environment, or even to attain your heart's desires. They pale in comparison to the real reward, which is becoming the master of your mind. And nothing is more mentally rewarding than a calm, positive, and strong mind, always ready to be directed at your command.

PART V
TOP-DOWN-LIVING

Chapter 30
A REALITY OF TWO WORLDS

The first four parts of this book have set the scene for conscious living and conscious reality creation. You now have an understanding of consciousness, the creative nature of your subjective mind and directive nature of your objective mind, The Absolute, Universal Mind, and the Real You, as well as the impersonal Universal Laws, and how to work with the Lower Laws.

This part of the book is about Top-Down-Living, which is living life from the vantage point of the Real You while using the power of your will and intuition to direct your mind and attain your desires. And finally, Part VI focuses on practical techniques for conscious reality creation. To get started let us take a look at the nature of reality against the backdrop of your now more *complete* understanding of consciousness.

THE VISIBLE AND INVISIBLE WORLDS

Although you have your physical experience of reality in the Physical Plane, the truth is that you live in two worlds. The one is an invisible world of *limitless* potential and the other is a visible world of *limited* actualisations. The substance that underlies both worlds is energy or consciousness. The rate of vibration of consciousness of the visible world is much lower and hence it is a world of greater density, which is why it is visible to our physical senses. In contrast, the frequency or rate of vibration of consciousness of the invisible world is much higher and hence it is a more subtle world of finer substance, which is why it is invisible to our physical senses that are attuned to the visible world.

The only difference in your experience of the two worlds is that the one is visible to your physical senses while the other is not. Both worlds, however, are taking place in the same point in space and time. The invisible world is not above or below the visible world in any physical way. But it is 'above' the visible world in frequency, which means it has a higher positivity and hence, has directive power to influence the experience of the visible world. Since the underlying substance of both worlds is consciousness or mind, and the activity of mind is thinking, the mode of communication between the two is thought, whether it is conscious or unconscious. In this way, the visible and invisible worlds are in constant communication with each other *via* a feedback loop.

The visible world experience is constrained by time and space, while the invisible world is wholly unconstrained. Since the invisible world is that of limitless potentiality, then every *possible* combination of everything that has ever been or could have been, and every possible combination of everything that will ever be or could be, exists in *potential* form in the invisible world. Moreover, since the invisible world is not subject to time and space, every possible past and future possibility is present in potential form, *at the same time* in the invisible world.

In contrast, your visible world is the sum of the potentialities that have been actualised into physical form by way of your thinking and mental focus, whether along conscious or unconscious lines. If you do not consciously participate in directing your mind and its contents then for all intents and purposes, your experience of reality can only ever be a reflection of the collective consciousness in which you live, because it is what you have allowed to determine your thinking.

Put another way, if you are not directing your mind, someone or something else is. And if you do not think for yourself consciously, then your visible reality is simply a projection of your sub-conscious mind, which itself is just a collection of assumed beliefs based largely on the beliefs of the collective consciousness in which you live.

It stands to reason therefore, that the bottom-line definition of conscious creation is conscious thinking. And to think consciously you must be the director of your mind. And to direct your mind, you must employ the power of your will. And to employ your will at its *highest* degree of power, you must come to know the I within, even if just theoretically or intellectually at first.

YOUR MAGIC MIRROR

Both worlds make up your single reality. In esoteric texts, your single reality is called your Magic Mirror reflecting your consciousness back to you in visible form. The invisible world of limitless possibilities is what is *outside* the mirror and the visible world of your limited actualisations is what is reflected *in* the mirror. Indeed, this is what is meant by the esoteric teachings that the world is your mirror, as is also depicted on the cover of this book.

Your magic mirror can be likened to a three-way system, where your physical world of actualised form is the visible world, Universal

Mind is the invisible world of undifferentiated potential energy, and your mind is the means by which you communicate with Universal Mind. Since Universal Mind is infinite, it is one and the same with *your* mind in Its entirety. This means that communication between your mind and Universal Mind happens *instantaneously* because what *you* think, *It* thinks. You direct Universal Mind when *you* think. And what you think determines what is to be transformed from *potential* form in the invisible world, into *actualised* form in the visible world.

In the analogy of the mirror, what is projected *onto* your Magic Mirror, and hence what you experience in the visible world, is the sum of the *possibilities* you have given your attention to by thinking, which were in turn actualised. And the more attention you give to something, the stronger and clearer its reflection in your mirror is, and hence also your experience of it.

This is analogous to mentally placing specific possibilities in front of the mirror by focusing on them. Whatever you place in front of the mirror is what is reflected in it. To change what is reflected *in* the mirror therefore, change what you place in front of it by changing what you focus on. In so doing, the reflection is changed and your visible world experience, taking place *in* the mirror, also changes accordingly. As the Buddha said, "since everything is a reflection of our minds, everything can be changed by our minds."

The Observer is Not In the Mirror
To see your face in the physical world you must look in a mirror or reflective surface. In the same way, to see your consciousness you must look at your physical world. But you are not what you see in the mirror of your physical world, just like your face in the mirror is just its *reflection* and not your real face.

The Real You is the Observer looking at the mirror from outside of it, but you remain *unchanged* and undisturbed by the reflections in the mirror. Think about it this way - for any change to be observed, there must be something *changeless* doing the observing, otherwise it would be unable to discern the change being part of it. Moreover, you can not directly observe the Observer because you *are* the Observer doing the observing. Put simply, you cannot *see* your consciousness without looking in the mirror of your visible world, but what you see in the mirror is *not* the Real You. Rather, it is just a *reflection* of a small selection of the limitless possibilities that you have actualised through your thinking to date. By changing your thinking, you can actualise new possibilities that will be reflected in your mirror, but the Observer never changes.

Mirror, Mirror on the Wall

Everything and everyone in your visible world is *your* mirror. In other words, your world is but a reflection of your consciousness. Your underlying beliefs about yourself, about others, and about life are always staring you in the face.

Learn therefore, to recognise your mind's contents and your expectations in your experiences. And also learn to recognise yourself in other people. In so doing, you rise above blame, judgement, and feeling like a victim of circumstance or of other people's actions or words. Learning to see yourself in your visible reality is not about blaming yourself or taking responsibility for others' actions towards you or anyone else, especially since you are likely to have left your mind unguarded and undirected up until now. It is, however, about taking responsibility for your mind and about learning the lessons inherent in your unwanted circumstances. If you do not learn a lesson, you continue to get the same lesson until you do. For instance, even if people and things in your life change, your *experience* of them is repeated until you learn the lesson. "You must be the change you want to see in the world" as Mahatma Gandhi said.

Once you understand your circumstances to be but a reflection of your consciousness, your focus shifts to directing your mind instead of trying to manipulate anyone or anything in the physical world to change. Any attempt to change someone or something in your life without first changing your mind yields temporary results at best, because your consciousness reflected back to you has not changed.

Things change when you *mentally* enable and allow change, not when you force change in the physical outer world. To see your physical world change in response to your mental changes alone will astound you as if it were magic. But for the person who truly understands the nature of reality it is no more magical than the sun rising over the horizon.

THE DREAM AND THE DREAMER

The idea that your physical world experience of reality is a reflection of your own consciousness is admittedly a significant mind-shift. To aid you in this direction, you can once again draw on your experience of dreaming. In so doing you can begin to entertain the idea of your physical reality being akin to a 'dream' of the Real You. To re-cap what was written earlier, when you dream, you play the central role in your dream. A friend or colleague may also appear in your dream, together with other people, animals, buildings, places, and the whole Universe as you know or may imagine it to be. While you are dreaming, everything outside of *your* role in the dream is perceived as being separate to you, and you experience all other people as having a consciousness independent of your own.

Your dream, however, is captured *within* your consciousness and is a projection of it. The role you play in your dream is a projection of your consciousness just as much as everything and everyone else that appears in your dream. Yet not even when you wake up do you truly realise that everything in your dream was but a projection of your consciousness as the dreamer. Instead you relay your dream in a relative way by saying, for instance, 'I saw so and so in my dream' and refer to people, places and things as being separate to you.

Realising the 'dreamer' in your physical world is the Real You, can be likened to lucid dreaming. In lucid dreaming, the actual dreamer knows, while *in* the dream, that he is dreaming. In this way, he has varying degrees of conscious directive power in the dream, and hence over his experience within it, while also being aware it is a dream. Interestingly, research into lucid dreaming shows it is a conscious process, unlike normal dreaming that is an unconscious process. This is because brain activity during lucid dreaming is at the Beta Level of brainwaves (Ch. 37) associated with wide-awake consciousness.

Consider these words by Don Miguel Ruiz. "What you are seeing and hearing right now is nothing but a dream. You are dreaming right now in this moment. You are dreaming with the brain awake. Dreaming is the main function of the mind, and the mind dreams twenty-four hours a day. It dreams when the brain is awake, and it also dreams when the brain is asleep. The difference is that when the brain is awake, there is a material frame that makes us perceive things in a linear way. When we go to sleep we do not have the frame, and the dream has the tendency to change constantly. Humans are dreaming all the time."

Learning to observe your physical reality as a dream in which you are lucid, is a fundamental mind-shift. Your life is still experienced as a physical experience of solid things, by the *physical* you, in the visible world. And your physical body is still limited by the Laws of Physics. But reminding yourself of your outer world's dream-like nature enables you simultaneously to *observe* your world instead of being wrapped up and overwhelmed by its specifics.

Having said this, it is best to strike a balance between these two views of your world, rather than adopt any one view exclusively or extremely. The more balanced you are in your view, the more you will sense the fluidity and malleability of your physical world and the directive power your mind has over it. This is what 'living your dream' is really all about.

WHAT IS REAL DOES NOT CHANGE

Another mind-shifting esoteric teaching is that 'what is real does not change, what changes is not real'. Only something that is *changeless* is real, because if it changed then it would no longer be the same thing it was prior to the change, and so it was not real to begin with. Moreover, something that is changeless is also eternal because since it never changes, it always stays the same and hence is eternal. Given this definition of 'real', something that changes is *not* real and hence, is unreal or impermanent.

Since The Absolute is changeless and eternal then the Absolute is real. And since the Real You is created in the image of The Absolute, then the I within is real, which is why it is the *Real* You. Universal Mind is real because it contains *all* possibilities infinitely and hence does not change. But Its countless creations or manifestations are not real because they are always changing. By observing the activity of your mind, you will notice nothing stays the same. Your thoughts, emotions, and desires are always changing, which means they are by this definition not real. Your circumstances, whether wanted or unwanted, are also always changing, and hence are not real either.

A New View of Reality

Only that part of you that is observing is real. You can easily prove this to yourself by following your thoughts for a few moments. Your thoughts change at lightning speed and you may even find it difficult to recall a train of thought. Yet that someone within you who is *doing* the thinking remains unchanged, irrespective of how many thoughts your have or the nature thereof. The Observer within therefore is real, but what is being observed is not.

Learn to perceive your reality for what it really is - a projection of your mind's ever-changing contents. This is not to say your reality does not *feel* real to the physical you having the experience, but rather that it is not real to the I *observing* it. Instead of thinking in terms of 'in my reality' shift to 'in my *experience* of reality', which serves as a reminder that what you are experiencing is just an experience and even if it *feels* real, it is not permanent in any real sense. By declaring your problems unreal or impermanent, you assert that they are subject to change under the direction of your will, and so deny them power over you. Likewise, by refusing to see your good times as real or ever-lasting, you take away their power to determine your happiness, and also diminish it when they change, as all things do. This is not the same as feeling that nothing has any meaning. You must be the one who determines the meaning you give to each thing in your life. But at the same time give nothing so much importance that you let it define you. Many people fear change yet there are few mind-sets more powerful than knowing nothing stays the same. No experience, good or bad, can define you when you know it is going to change, and in this way you do not become attached to anything. Moreover, knowing your experience of reality is impermanent and subject to change in accordance with your self-directed mind, then you no longer fear anything because how can you fear something that is impermanent and that *will* change?

THE TEMPORNAUT

Tempornaut is a word that I use to mean time-traveller, just as astronaut means star-traveller, where *tempor* is the Latin word for time. This section of the book will revolutionise your idea of time and is intended to transform you into a mental time-traveller.

Some of the most revolutionary theories to have emerged from the field of physics are in regard to the nature of time. In the physical world, you experience the arrow of time in a forward linear direction. Time moves in a single direction from the past to the future and so you remember the past but not the future. However, this is just your *experience* of time and not the real nature of time. Studies in the field of physics have led to the conclusion that instead of time being fixed in *one* direction, *all* possible past, future, and present moments exist simultaneously *always*. Looking at time in this way means that there is only ever one single moment that is Now. This does not mean that only the present moment exists, while the past and future do not exist. What it means is that all past, *all* present and *all* future moments exist simultaneously such that they are one, single, ever-present Now moment. Indeed, the underlying nature of the Universe is timeless.

Timelessness in Physics

Here are a few thoughts from the most prominent scientific minds of modern times on the timeless nature of the Universe, as quoted in Gevin Giorbran's 2007 book Everything Forever. Albert Einstein said, "This distinction between past, present, and future is only an illusion." In The Grand Design (2010), Stephen Hawking wrote with reference to the quantum theory of alternative histories that "the universe does not have just a single existence or history, but rather every possible version of the universe exists simultaneously in what is called a quantum superposition." In The Elegant Universe (1999), Brian Greene wrote, "Just as we envision all of space as really being out there, as really existing, we should also envision all of time as really being out there, as really existing, too. The only thing that's real is the whole of spacetime." The theoretical physicist, David Bohm, who made significant contributions to quantum theory and to the philosophy of mind, said "Ultimately, all moments are really one, therefore *now* is an eternity."

Without having to understand the physics behind the timelessness of the Universe, it has profound implications for your view of reality in the context of conscious reality creation. We will now consider some implications of the timeless nature of the Universe, starting with a related idea that you are living in the past. This, however, is not an attempt to combine physics with metaphysics, but rather to show the parallels between the latest scientific discoveries and what was asserted by philosophers over two thousand years ago. For instance, the Greek philosopher Parmenides of Elea said, "Nothing was not once nor will it ever be, since being is *now altogether*."

Living in the Past

Since your experience of reality is a projection of your mind, it stands to reason that your present moment is but a reflection of your past, because it is *your* past mental contents that it is reflecting. This logic has its parallels in your physical world experience as well.

For instance, since it takes an estimated 8 minutes and 19 seconds for the sun's light to reach Earth, the sun you see when you look up at the sky, is as it was 8 minutes ago, and even near-by objects you see are time delayed albeit too negligibly for you to notice. Looking at a star in distant space is also tantamount to looking back in time. This is because a particular star may no longer exist in the Physical Plane present moment, but you can still see it because the light it emitted prior to being extinguished is still reaching the Earth. The same applies to sound-waves, making the sounds you hear also slightly time delayed. As you may already know, it is only because light travels faster than sound that you see the lightning bolt before you hear the crack of thunder.

In the context of your experience of reality, in the same way your present moment is a reflection of your *past* thoughts, what you most often think of, imagine and do in the *present* moment, is a preview of your 'future's coming attractions'. To the degree that you do not change your dominant thoughts, imaginings, and actions today, is the degree to which your future experiences will approximate to those of your past, with major deviations accounted for by the element of unpredictability that comes with living in collective consciousness.

Remembering the Future

Here is a revolutionary way to re-frame your concept of time. Just like you remember your past, you can remember your future and in turn, change your present moment. This is because there is no past or future as you are accustomed to thinking of them. Remembering the past is the same as remembering the future. In both cases you use your imagination, the only difference being that the past is based on memories that have already happened, whereas remembering the future is based on memories that have yet to happen.

Imagining what will happen in the future as if it were a memory creates a *present* moment experience based on your future imaginings rather than on those of the past. To change your present moment therefore, change the future by imagining it the way you intend.

In other words, concentrate on your intended future outcome as if it is taking place in the present moment, rather than remembering your past memories as if on some kind of repeat play-back. In this way, you mentally resonate with the frequency of the already existing *possibility* of what you imagine for yourself in potential form, and so increase the probability of experiencing it in physical form.

The Possible and the Probable

Just because something is possible does not necessarily make it probable. All futures are equally *possible* but they are not equally *probable*. The immediate probability of your future depends on your current mental frequency and what you are giving your attention to. If, however, you are not focusing on anything in particular, things are likely to remain little changed because it is your outer world that is providing the images you are sending to your sub-conscious mind. The Greek philosopher Aristotle expressed this most simply by saying, "the probable is what *usually* happens."

Since all possible futures already exist, which of those futures you experience is essentially up to you, and is a function of the rate of vibration of the mental images you hold and give your Life Force to. When you intensely focus on your desire, the possible future which resonates most with the frequency of your desire becomes more immediately probable than those that don't. If, however, you focus on your already existing circumstances, the possible future you move towards is the one that most matches the continuity of your current conditions, and hence is the one that is most probable for you. Having said this, if you are not directing and guarding your mind, then the sheer number of external parameters that can affect the mental and physical actions you take result in a huge number of possible outcomes that in turn makes your future more unpredictable and seemingly random. For this reason, endeavour to keep your positivity high, focus exclusively on your desired future as if it already exists, and find the resolve to guard your mind from unwanted or negative thoughts and mental images.

YOU DO NOT CREATE ANYTHING

Since all possible futures exist timelessly in potential form, it means you are not creating your reality by building it from scratch. Rather, conscious reality creation is about mentally focusing on the already-existing *potential* version of the reality you desire to experience. In other words, it is about directing Universal Mind to transform the *potential energy* of your desired future into *actualised form*. And your direction is always by way of what you think, imagine, feel, believe, and do, whether consciously or not.

If, however, you set out to try to change things already existing in the Physical Plane through mental manipulation or force, you cannot help but focus on your current conditions and so re-enforce them. It is therefore far more effective to focus on a version of reality as you desire it to be irrespective of your current conditions, than to focus on existing things and try to change them at their level. And bear in mind that the current version of your reality is itself just one of many potential realities, the only difference being, it was actualised into form while other better or worse versions were not. "The secret of change," as the Greek philosopher Socrates said, "is to focus all of your energy not on fighting the old, but on building the new."

Having said this, it is best to be wise in your imaginings and not fall into the trap of delusion. You must make sure that you *believe* what you imagine *is* possible. If you don't, neither will Universal Mind because remember, your mind *is* Universal Mind. This is not a suggestion, however, to limit your imaginings but rather, not to go to such extremes that they amount to little more than daydreaming. But even so, always remember by virtue of Universal Mind being infinite and limitless, It contains within its fabric *all* past, present, and future possibilities *always*. And so, it is only ever up to you to *believe* what is possible for you, and let no one else define it for you. As Thomas Edison advised us, "when you have exhausted all possibilities, remember this - you haven't."

Chapter 31

LIVING FROM THE I WITHIN

In this chapter we will consider the experience of your reality from the higher vantage point of the I within. Bear in mind once again that the Spiritual Plane of the Real You is not above the Physical Plane in distance, but only in degree of consciousness. It takes place in the same space and time as the Physical Plane, albeit unconstrained by both. And you *can be* the I within in any place and at any time.

THERE IS ONLY EVER ONE I

What follows is adapted from John McDonald's early 20th century book, The Message of a Master, and sets the scene for living from the vantage point of the I. Here is a summary of what he had to say about the Real You. I encourage you to give it your full attention.

"When you declare 'I am', 'I will', 'I did', you are making a most mighty and profound utterance. There are very few who realize the power released when the 'I' is expressed. The body you have is personal, but the 'I' you express is universal, for in all the Universe there is but one 'I'. When you work in the 'me' consciousness, you are working from the personal, limited standpoint. When you work in 'I' consciousness, you invoke and receive the help of the impersonal, unlimited resources of the Universe. If there is but one 'I' and you cannot express yourself without using it, it follows that as far as you individually are concerned, there must be but one 'you'.

Did you ever apply the pronoun 'I' to any other human being? Of course you did not. You could not. You might say 'he', 'she', 'they', 'you', 'we' but never 'I'. For there is but one 'I' and that is you. Yes, applied individually, there is [in fact] but one 'you'. Since the great and mighty 'I' is, when expressed individually, none other than yourself, you can see what power you have at your command. You can see what a wonderful being you are. You can see that you are now a master, not yet developed perhaps, but the qualities are there awaiting unfoldment and use. If you do not clearly understand what I have just given, pass it by for this time. You can later reason it out for yourself and see the truth of it."

KNOW YOURSELF

To know yourself is to know the I within. From the vantage point of your Real Self, you are above, independent of, and undisturbed by your ever-changing mental contents and impermanent physical world experiences. You know you are a spiritual being, created in the image of The Absolute, having a physical experience. You know you are immortal and eternal and you fear nothing. You know your will is a centre of Cosmic Will and yet one and the same with It. You know your mind is a creative centre of Universal Mind and yet one and the same with It, and Universal Mind mutually recognises your mind as being It.

You know you exist in an invisible world of limitless possibilities while your physical being exists as a projection of your consciousness in the world of actualised form. You are wholly objective to your physical world and everything within it, and it, is wholly subjective to you. You know your physical world experiences are impermanent and subject to change under your explicit direction. You know you have the complete freedom of choice to experience anything while every possible experience already exists eternally in potential form.

You are the Observer who is undisturbed by what you are observing in your physical world. You are attached to nothing. You fear nothing. You know you are already complete and nothing can be added to or subtracted from you. You take nothing personally for you know there is nothing outside your own consciousness to be personal in relation to. You know no-*thing* can define you.

From your perspective, which is the only perspective you can ever experience, you know your consciousness is everywhere at the same time, and you share in the Omnipotence and Omniscience of The Absolute. You know in the vast silence of infinite, timeless space, you are Every-Thing and you are No-Thing.

What a Difference Indifference Makes

Your Real Self is above the misguided belief that anything or anyone in the physical world can make a difference to you. Instead, your inner power is founded in indifference. But to be indifferent is not to be apathetic or not to care about anything or anyone. That can only ever be the indifference of the counterfeit ego.

The power of indifference is to know that no experience, whether wanted or unwanted, makes any difference to the You who is the Observer. It is to remain still and undisturbed by the ever-changing projections in your physical world experience, while also participating in them and knowing you have directive power over them.

Interestingly the word 'indifferent' has its origin in the Latin word *indifferentem*, meaning 'not differing or neither good nor evil' and it is a combination of the Latin words 'in' meaning 'not' and *differre* meaning to 'set apart'. From the perspective of the I therefore, to be indifferent means 'not to separate, or not to set apart, the opposites'.

In other words, indifference is to be above the opposites. It is only by rising above the opposites of good and bad that you can come to know your freedom of choice and its inherent power of detachment. Only then are you *personally* free to choose your desires, as you will discover in Chapter 34 on the Power of Desire.

EXERCISE FOR EXPERIENCING THE I

What follows is a very powerful exercise in discovering the I within adapted from The Arcane Teaching by William Walker Atkinson. For your information, how to enter a deep state of mental and physical relaxation is described in Chapter 37 on meditation, along with a most powerful guided meditation for experiencing the Real You called the 'I of the Ego'.

Calling Your Name

In a deep meditative state of relaxation, softly repeat your first name to yourself. This is the name you identify yourself with when you say 'My name is [e.g. John]'. It can also be a shortened version of your name, if that is what you most identify yourself with.

When mentally calling out your name, do so softly, earnestly, and with your full attention, as if you are trying to wake yourself up gently from a deep sleep. The more you mentally repeat your name, the more you will sense yourself being lifted higher and higher in degree of consciousness. As you call your name in this way, you awaken to your Real Self with a calm sense of inner power.

I encourage you to practice this exercise often, preferably before going to sleep and even to drift off to sleep in the 'centre' of your name. Few other exercises of such simplicity can afford you with the power inherent in calling out your name in this way.

BE YOURSELF

When you know yourself you can be yourself - your *Real* Self. To be yourself, however, is not to be true to your perceived strengths and weaknesses, or to any of the adopted beliefs of your personality. As your Real Self you have no limiting beliefs. No *personal* limiting belief, no matter how powerful or deeply ingrained it may seem, stands any chance in the face of Omnipotence.

As the Real You, you have no need to compare yourself, compete with, or depend on the opinion or approval of others as a measure of your worthiness. Any personal limitations become redundant when your self-worth and self-esteem have their foundation in knowing your true nature. Knowing who you really are - the eternal and immortal I -

is the only authentic source of inner strength you can ever discover. And when you look inwards, instead of outwards, for your strength, you will find that All-Power has been residing within you all along. And you say 'I AM *I*' and 'I *CAN* and I *WILL*'.

LOVE YOURSELF

The I within is your unshakeable foundation of real self-love. Only the counterfeit ego criticises you, makes you feel inadequate, or tells you, 'you are not good enough'. Its badgering criticism is the craftiest of mind tricks because, knowing it has no real power of its own, it rules you tyrannically in a desperate bid to stay in control.

Indeed, self-love has nothing to do with the assumed strengths and weaknesses of your personality. Self-love is to know that they are the fabrications of the counterfeit ego, and have nothing to do with the Real You. Nothing can add to or subtract from the I within. Any imperfection can only ever be a perception of the personal self. You are already *perfect*, always have been and always will be.

As your Real Self you love yourself Absolutely. There is never a question of how much you love yourself, or how deserving or non-deserving you think you are. Your love has its foundation in knowing your unique, immortal place in the Universe. It is to be in awe of the wonder of the infinite Universe and know that from your perspective you are at its very centre.

The self-love of the I within is pure bliss. But this is not an over-excited emotion that is subject to the swing of the pendulum. Pure bliss is a state of *being* that is free of all emotion and thinking. Pure bliss is to *be* and to *know* you *are* the eternal I within. And finally, once again, when you stop looking for 'the one' outside of you, you will realise that *You* are the one you have been looking for all along.

Chapter 32

THE POWER OF YOUR WILL

Your will is the single most directive power of your mind. This is because the full directive power of your will belongs to the Real You, and as you already know, higher degrees of positivity mean higher degrees of power to direct change. Remember also, that your will is a centre of Cosmic Will and is one and the same with It.

Your will is higher in degree of positivity than are your emotions and reasoning mind, which means it has directive power over them. When you give dominance to your will over your mind and all its activities, you become intensely positive to everything and everyone around you. Put another way, your power to direct change and influence your environment increases in proportion to an increase in the use of your will power. And the more you use your will power, the higher you raise your degree of positivity.

The superiority of your will power can be easily appreciated when you realise that while you have many desires, emotions, thoughts, and physical experiences, you only ever have one will. Therefore, while you can use your will power in many directions, it remains your one unchanged will. It is for this reason that your will power belongs to that part of you that is unchanging, which is the Real You, while all your ever-changing mental contents and outer world circumstances belong to your personal self.

AWAKENING YOUR WILL POWER

Your ability to use the directive power of your will increases in direct proportion to your identification with it. If, however, you do not allow the active participation of your will in directing your mind, then your will is left open to being manipulated by those whose will is more powerful than your own. Moreover, your thoughts, moods, emotions, and desires are determined largely by the impersonal operations of the Universal Laws and collective consciousness.

You may believe that you have little if any will power, but that is only because you have left it idle, not because you do not have it. The truth is you cannot acquire will power. Nor do you build up or strengthen your will power. Rather, you *awaken* your will and you train *yourself* to use its *already* existing power. The most effective way to train yourself to use the power of your will in any direction is through self-discipline. No one said it would be easy but the life-long rewards of disciplining yourself to use the incredible power of your will to direct your mind, instead of letting it wander idly and aimlessly, far outweigh any effort you may exert in this direction.

SELF-DISCIPLINE

Self-discipline is arguably the most important yet most overlooked ingredient of mind power. Many people struggle with the idea of self-discipline because they wrongly believe it to be a restriction on their sense of freedom. The truth is, however, that it is only through self-discipline that you can find your freedom.

Self-discipline gives you the freedom of choice to do what *you know must be done* in order to achieve your intended outcome, and to do it well and gladly. In the absence of self-discipline you are little more than the obedient servant of your mind's ever-changing whims, emotions, passions, desires, thoughts, fears, and beliefs. There is no freedom in having no *choice* over feeling how you feel, in not doing something simply because you do not feel like it, or in *having to* have what you want without also being willing *not* to have it.

It is you who must *decide*, it is you who must *choose*, and it is you who must *direct* your thoughts, emotions, moods, beliefs, desires, actions, and reactions. If you are not the one deciding, then you cannot be said to belong to yourself. Instead, you belong to whatever or whoever is deciding for you, be it your undirected mental contents or other people in your life.

Learn to Say No to Yourself

Self-denial is a key element of self-discipline. Self-denial is to deny yourself the misguided freedom of wallowing in your fears, of getting caught up in your emotions, and of having to have what you want and wanting it now, as if you were a child throwing a tantrum.

Moreover, self-denial is about respecting yourself enough to release those desires, limiting beliefs, and habits that you intuitively know do not serve you. Indeed, self-respect and self-dignity are born out of being able to say *no* to yourself. And only when you have the power to say no to yourself, do you truly have the power to say yes.

The Tantrum of the Untrained Mind

Be warned that when you first set out to restrict your mind to your will's direction, your counterfeit ego will kick and scream and, more often than not, remind you of every negative thought and image it can conjure up in an attempt to hold onto its unchecked freedom. Do not let this discourage you. Rather see it as a sign of just how little mastery you have over your mind, and imagine all those changes you can create in your life once you bring your mind under your direction. Let this encourage you to persist and do not let yourself off the hook. Tempering your mind under the direction of your will is not a quick-fix overnight process, but for the same reason it does not yield quick-fix temporary results. The reward of self-discipline and will power is higher degrees of positivity. And no other mental reward measures up to higher degrees of positivity, more so since it lasts a lifetime and becomes more rewarding day by day.

Think of your untrained mind as a 'spoilt' child who has been left to its own devices for far too many years, without any sense of self-discipline, structure, or direction. As is the case with all children, however, your mind wants boundaries and yearns for discipline and a structure within which it can thrive and in time be successful.

Rest assured that as you apply your will power and listen to your intuition (Ch. 33), your mind's child-like temper tantrums will lessen and become few and far between. As written in the Bhagavad Gita, "the mind is restless and difficult to restrain but it is subdued by practice." Remember always that if you do not discipline yourself to direct your own mind with the power of your will, you are effectively giving up your freedom of choice and your power to create your desired life. The more you identify with the true nature of your Real Self, the easier it becomes to use your will power with discipline.

The Student of the I

Let go of any negative connotation that you may associate with the term 'self-discipline' and instead, learn to see self-discipline as being synonymous with self-power. In fact, the true meaning of discipline has nothing to do with the modern idea of limitation, chastisement, or punishment for wrong-doing. Rather, the word 'discipline' has its origin in the Latin word *disciplina*, which means 'instruction, learning, or knowledge'. Moreover, discipline has the same root as the word 'disciple', meaning 'student or follower'.

A more appropriate definition for self-discipline therefore, is to bring your thoughts, desires, passions, emotions, and actions under the self-directed *instruction* of your will. It is to make the personal self with its many desires, thoughts, and emotions, the dedicated student of the Real You, until finally you no longer have any need for self-discipline, for the student will have, in time, become the teacher.

In other words, the personal self and the I will merge and act as one. But, since the I within is unchanging, it can never *lower* its degree of positivity to that of the personal self. It is up to you to raise your degree of positivity upwards to its level. In so doing, degree by degree, you find yourself *choosing* what you feel, think, say, and do with far greater ease, and will power no longer feels foreign to you but rather, it is your most natural mental faculty.

PERSISTENCE

Persistence is the mental child of will power and self-discipline. It is the willingness to press on, to get up if you fall, dust yourself off, and continue to pursue your goal. The following quote by Calvin Coolidge sums up the power of persistence: "Nothing in the world can take the place of persistence. Talent will not; nothing is more common than unsuccessful men with talent. Genius will not; unrewarded genius is almost a proverb. Education will not; the world is full of educated derelicts. Persistence and determination alone are Omnipotent. The slogan, Press On! has solved and always will solve the problems of the human race."

Persistence, however, is not about being obsessed with your desire or goal, and nor is it about letting its attainment define you. Rather, true persistence is to desire something *enough* to pursue it even if the odds appear to be against you. It is to use the power of your will to overcome the many obstacles you are likely to face on your path and to pay the price of attainment willingly and gladly, because your desire or goal is important enough to you. It is to enjoy every step of the way in the knowledge that every step forward, and even every obstacle, is one step closer to your ideal. And finally, persistence is to pursue your dreams with calm confidence, strength, and courage, while knowing that the whole Universe is on your side.

MENTAL CONCENTRATION

The power of mental concentration cannot be over-emphasised when it comes to directing your mind towards attaining your desires. The etymology of the word 'concentration' is 'the action of bringing something to its centre'. Concentration therefore, is the ability to focus your mind firmly on a definite purpose, subject, mental image or idea, and hold it there exclusively for a certain time, without letting your thoughts wander, your focus shift, or outside world things disturb or deter you.

If you have never attempted to concentrate in this way before, you may think it is easy, but true concentration is in fact very difficult for the restless mind whose thoughts are forever wandering. It is for this reason that to master concentration you must employ the power of your will. Moreover, the power of concentration includes the ability to *stop* concentrating on a particular mental image, idea, or subject at will, or in other words, to detach from it completely and focus on something else or on nothing at all.

Having said this, concentration is *not* about letting your mind focus involuntarily or aimlessly on something in your environment or on a thought or image that you keep playing over and over in your head. On the contrary, this is the surest sign of an undirected mind that has wholly escaped the direction of your will. You either concentrate consciously and with purpose, with the ability to stop concentrating and detach at will, or you don't. Anything less does not constitute true concentration. And as is the case with all your mental faculties, you either master concentration, or it masters you.

Exercises in Concentration

To use your mind effectively, you must learn to concentrate, and the route to concentration is through paying attention. The following exercise, adapted from the writings of William Walker Atkinson, is very powerful in learning how to pay attention. Take a simple object with which you are familiar and give it your full attention for a few minutes. Study the object and endeavour to see as many details as possible in it. Take a break and then come back to the object, and this time look for new details that you missed. Carry on repeating this process until you have discovered everything about the object. Do not fool yourself into thinking you have seen all the details at once. Rather, will yourself to discover more.

Do this exercise every day for one month, using simple objects at first and then more complex ones, until you can find all the details in the most complex of objects. This exercise strengthens your power of observation, heightens your ability to pay attention, and develops your ability to concentrate to such a degree that you scarcely need any conscious effort to do so. And when you master concentration in this way, you become a master of mental influence, for you will be able to focus all your Life Force and energy exclusively on anything you choose to, at will and with little effort.

Concentration for Conscious Creation

Learning to concentrate exclusively on a mental image of your desire or goal, impresses that image on your sub-conscious mind and hence also on Universal Mind. Concentration provides your mental image with the Life Force or energy necessary for it to manifest. In other words, by concentrating on something, you project your Life Force or energy directly onto it, rather than scattering your energy on many ever-changing idle or purposeless thoughts. In this way, whatever you have concentrated on receives the full power of your directed energy, and hence the sub-conscious process of creation is ignited faster. This is in fact the essence of conscious creation through visualisation, which is the subject of Chapter 40.

The Sun and the Magnifying Glass

The sun's light, concentrated through a magnifying glass, is a fitting analogy for the power of concentration, as was written in Charles F. Haanel's 1912 book The Master Key System. When a magnifying glass is randomly moved around in view of the sun's light then nothing appears to change. If, however, you hold the magnifying glass steady and allow for the sun's rays to be concentrated through it to a common point of focus, then the result is fire.

The same principle applies to your mind and anything you may want to concentrate on. In the context of pursuing your desires, your energy or Life Force is akin to the Sun, your mental focus is the magnifying glass, and the fire is the 'ignition' of the mental image of your desire. If you let your focus wander randomly on many and often conflicting things, then you scatter your energy and little or no change occurs. If, however, you mentally concentrate your energy on the single mental image of your desire, then the result is that you ignite the creative power of your subjective mind, and hence that of the entire Universe.

USING YOUR WILL POWER

It may be obvious to you by now that you cannot effectively apply the knowledge contained in this book in the absence of your will to do so. Whatever you want to do, whether it is to transmute your negative thoughts and emotions, to keep your emotions at optimal levels, to deny the full counter-swing of Rhythm's pendulum, to raise your mental frequency into an upward spiral, to guide your emotions with reason, to objectively protect your subjective mind, to discipline your mind, to persist, to mentally concentrate at will, or any of the upcoming practical techniques outlined in this book - the power of your will must come *first*. Without it you cannot hope to direct your mind or create the life you truly desire. But with it, doing so becomes child's play and life becomes your playground.

You innately know that you have tremendous will power and can probably think of a few times in your life when you used it with great success, because you had to. But the point is not to wait for pressure to bear down on you, and not to have to depend on your desire for something to be so all-consuming that *it* incites your will into action. The point is to be the master of your will, and not let it be swayed by all those things that are beneath it in degree of positivity. Here then are some exercises to awaken your will and train your mind in self-discipline.

Exercises to Awaken the Will

To awaken your will power you assert the I within by saying 'I CAN and I WILL' with a calm authoritative voice. In the words once again of William Walker Atkinson: "Let your prevailing thought be 'I Can and I Will'. Think 'I Can and I Will'. Dream 'I Can and I Will'. Say 'I Can and I Will'. And act 'I Can and I Will'. Live on the 'I Can and I and Will' plane, and before you are aware of it, you will feel the new vibrations manifesting themselves in action; will see them bring results; will be conscious of the new point of view; will realize that your own is coming to you. You will feel better, act better, see better, BE better in every way, after you join the 'I Can and I Will' brigade."

Exercise to Train Your Mind

As you know, you already possess and have access to your will power in its entirety. The only reason people do not use their will is not because they do not have any, but because they are mentally lazy and do not want it enough. Living unconsciously appears easier than living consciously because there is no mental effort involved in an undirected mind. But in life, you get what you pay for and by paying the higher price of training your mind and using your will, your life becomes a far more joyful experience in all ways.

Here is a simple exercise to use in training your mind. For one month, perform one task every day that you do not like doing or do not feel like doing. Every day, think of the one task that you would most want to avoid, pick that one to do, and do it cheerfully. Anyone can do something that pleases them, but it takes will power to do gladly something you do not enjoy doing. This is a very powerful exercise. Will yourself to do it for a month and do not let yourself off the hook, otherwise you are telling yourself you are content with an untrained mind and do not want to use your will power.

Exercise in Physical Actions

Will yourself to participate consciously in your physical actions. For instance, consciously will your hands to take specific actions of your choosing, and then observe the actions your hands take. Adopt this mental attitude once a day in the actions you take whether it is while taking a shower, getting dressed, or just washing the dishes. Take conscious, deliberate actions and think in terms of 'It is my will to do

[this]' rather than 'I must or have to', especially if it is something you do not particularly feel like doing.

Exercise in Verbal Actions

Will yourself to observe your voice. Really listen to your voice as you are speaking, just like you would listen to the voice of someone else that you were speaking with. Familiarise yourself with the details of the sound of your voice, its depth, its pitch, and its tone. Realise it is the voice that you use to express yourself verbally in the physical world. Moreover, become conscious of the words you speak and how you speak them. Deliberately direct and choose your tone of voice. Slow down your speech so that you are consciously ahead of the speed at which you are talking, and in so doing consciously choose your words both when speaking first and in responding to others.

Exercise in Mental Actions

Use your will to observe your thoughts, emotions, and desires as they arise. Neutrally observe and pay attention to your thoughts as they enter and exit your mind, as if you were watching them flash by on a movie screen. Notice how the part of you observing your thoughts is independent of and undisturbed by them. Practice stopping your thoughts in their tracks with your will power, and instantly replace them with another, or think of nothing.

Repeat this exercise with your emotions as they arise. Notice how by observing, rather than being caught up in their specifics, they have no independent power over you whatsoever. Practice using your will to stop both positive and negative emotions. Moreover, practice observing your desires. Sense how easily you can set your desires aside with the power of your will, and how any associated attachment or doubt has no bearing on that part of you that is observing them. Practice setting your desires aside as if you are deactivating them.

Exercise in Attention

Become aware of everything in your environment by paying attention to your surroundings. Really stretch your physical senses in this direction. Become aware of where you are looking and what you are seeing, of all the sounds you are hearing around you, whether it is the whirring noise of a fridge or the chirping of birds outside, of the variety of smells in the atmosphere both pleasant and unpleasant, and also of the slightest sensations of your body. You can also practice expanding your field of attention outwards, beyond your immediate physical surroundings, beyond even the city or country you are in. You can continue to expand your attention in ever widening circles using your imagination, until the entire Universe is captured within its field, and you will find that you can go on expanding your attention infinitely in space.

The aforementioned exercises raise your degree of self-awareness, grant you greater direction over your mental and physical actions, and hence also over the reactions and consequences that flow from them. At first it may feel strange as if you are mentally and physically slowing down, which in fact you are. In time, however, it will become easier and feel more natural as you adapt to being the Observer of your physical reality, while at the same time being its direct and conscious participant under the direction of your will as the *self-aware* personal self, not the automaton of the adopted script.

It must be said, however, that using your will power to direct your mind is not intended to transform you into a weak automaton or servant that takes commands, even if it may feel like it to your counterfeit ego. Never think of yourself as taking commands. Rather, be the one who is *giving* the commands by way of *your* direction. In other words, be the *Real Ego*, not its fake imposter.

THE EFFORTLESS INFLUENCE OF WILL POWER

When all is said and done, a person who has the power to influence everything and everyone in his environment without force is always a person who directs his own mind with the power of his will. As you already know, forcing someone or something to comply with your desires, physically or mentally, requires varying degrees of physical force and mental manipulation and the results are more often than not short-lived. In contrast, the physical world results that arise out of your self-directed mind, require no physical force and so your physical world influence appears to be effortless.

Having said this, when you use your will to direct your mind, your outer world influence will only *appear* to be effortless. This is because according to the Principle of Compensation, nothing is furnished for free and indeed, you will have exerted great mental and spiritual effort in the direction of rising above the Physical and Mental Planes of the personal self that you have identified with all your life. But the greater the effort you exert in this direction, the greater the reward you will gain by way of compensation for your effort.

Chapter 33
THE POWER OF INTUITION

The Real You shares in All-Knowledge beyond space and time and is not subject to the limitations of what is known in the Physical Plane. As a physical being you experience the *knowing* of the Real You as your intuition. This means that the intuitive messages you receive as a physical being are the *knowing* of the I within.

There is no logical thought process involved in *knowing*, nor is there any deductive or inductive reasoning. Knowing is not born out of intellect, intelligence, or an understanding of the subject at hand. Rather, knowing can best be described as a non-thinking state of deeply sensing something to be true, without it having to pass the test of reason. Intuition therefore, is not a brain process. You think in your *head*, you know in your *heart*.

INTUITION IS A FEMININE PRINCIPLE

Your intuition is above your reasoning mind in degree of positivity and it is also above the emotional mind of feelings. As you already know, your will power is the directive masculine principle of the Real You and the power of your intuition is the equally powerful but opposite feminine principle of the I.

Whereas your will *actively directs* your thinking and your actions, your intuition *calmly nurtures* your entire being. It provides you with all the answers you may need beyond reason, and seeks to keep you from harm's way just as a mother does her child.

In the same way that you cannot consciously think or act without your will to do so, you cannot *know* without your intuition. In other words, you consciously *think* and act through your will, and you consciously *know* through your intuition. This means that by not listening to your intuition, you limit your physical experience to a combination of logical and emotional thinking, but you do not *know*.

If you *think* you *know* everything, be very certain that you in fact know very little. In the words of the Buddha, "how can one ever *know* anything if they are too busy thinking."

Tuition from Within

In-tuition is tuition from within. It is your inner teacher. Learn to honour your intuition and its messages. When you are at peace with not having all the answers to the ever-changing questions of your personal self, they will come to you.

Slow down and heed the voice within, with its heart-felt whisper that tells you 'everything will be ok', 'let it go' or 'be careful'; or that *silently* advises you to take or not to take a certain action, to say or not to say something, to go to or avoid a certain area, or to trust or not to trust someone.

Among your intuition's many messages are solutions to problems that you could not solve logically, insightful answers to puzzling questions, a feeling that something is not quite right that stirs your attention, and an inner peace that tells you beyond any doubt that everything will be okay.

Your intuition is usually heard or sensed suddenly because it is beyond space and time and hence it is not limited by any of the constraints of the physical world. Moreover, the higher you raise your degree of positivity, the clearer you will hear your intuition's voice, because your positivity will be closer to its rate of vibration and so it will be more accessible to your senses, albeit not your physical senses.

THE POWER OF SILENCE

All knowledge resides in silence. To be silent literally means to *think* nothing. When you think *nothing*, you enter the infinite empty space of the *No*-Thing that is The Absolute within. And in the silent space of nothingness, everything becomes known to you. Indeed, this is the meaning of 'be still and know'. Having said this, 'everything becomes known to you' does not mean that you now have all the answers. On the contrary, in the silence of nothingness, there are no questions.

As human beings we naturally understand the power of silence by honouring someone who has left the Physical Plane with a moment of silence. Endeavour therefore, to honour yourself every day while here in the Physical Plane by cultivating inner silence. Set aside some time each day to silence your mind, even if only for a few moments. Empty your mind of thoughts, desires, worries, emotions, and silence the incessant chatter of the counterfeit ego. Let everything go. In this regard, a powerful exercise for experiencing mental silence is outlined in Chapter 37 under Expansive Meditation.

Moreover, through mental silence you become more comfortable with physical world silence and hence, you find yourself talking less and listening more. "Do not speak unless you can improve on the silence," as a Spanish proverb tells us.

Above all, however, when you silence your thoughts and empty your mind, your identification with the One Universal Mind increases, and hence It's identification with you also increases. And in the words of Lao Tzu, "to the mind that is still, the whole universe surrenders."

FAITH

True faith is born out of *knowing*. The most complete definition for faith is found in Hebrews 11:1 as follows: "Faith is the *substance* of things hoped for, the *evidence* of things not seen." Let us see what this means. The word 'substance' implies something tangible, so having faith makes your hopes tangible. And the word 'evidence' suggests that even if you cannot physically see what you desire with your eyes, it *already* exists if you look with your heart.

Some people when asked, will say they have faith, yet unbeknown to them they live in doubt. The only reason people live in doubt is because it is easier than to live in faith, albeit more painful. And the reason it is easier is because they are so accustomed to listening to the incessant mental chatter of the counterfeit ego, while also looking to their outer physical world for feedback about what is real. And whatever is declared real comes with a sense of permanency and hence an inability to see how things could change.

Kahlil Gibran, however, told us that "doubt is a pain too lonely to know that faith is his *twin brother*." This means that doubt is the equal but opposite pole of faith, which in turn means it can be transmuted. If you find yourself doubting whether something is possible for you, rest assured that in accordance with the Law of Polarity, somewhere inside you, you have faith that it *is* possible. To transmute doubt into faith, silence your mind. Let all your thoughts and worries go just for a moment and become one with the silence. In that moment you will *know* in your heart that all things are possible through The Absolute, as long as you believe.

Faith that is born in silence is built on an unshakeable foundation of *knowing*. And when you truly *know* something there is no room for doubt. Indeed, the kind of faith born out of knowing is not blind. It is the clearest you will ever see.

INTUITIVE LIVING

The intuition of the Real You is immeasurably higher in degree of positivity than your personal self's logic, thoughts, emotions, and desires. Just as you have one unchanging will but countless thoughts, so it is that you have one unchanging intuition.

Your intuition therefore, is intended to guide your mind alongside your will, with the difference being that your will incites action, whereas your intuition nurtures stillness. When you allow for your intuition to guide your mind, you *know* before you think, you *know* before you speak, and you *know* before you act.

Intuitive Reasoning

To reason *with* your intuition is what I call intuitive reasoning and is the highest expression of reason. Once again, it differs from using the power of your will to direct your thoughts because it does not incite action, but rather nurtures an inner sense of calm. Intuitive reasoning therefore, is to *know* in your heart *first*, and then *think* with your mind. For instance, when dealing with others slow down and let the calm feeling in your heart guide the *reason* behind what you think, say, or do, which in turn adds a certain warmth to your overall nature and relationships.

Intuitive reasoning can also be used when struggling to solve a problem logically. To do so, stop *thinking* about the problem and put it out of your mind. In so doing, you will find the solution will be *given* to you through your intuition. The solution may come to you in your sleep or while you are not focusing on anything in particular, and more often than not the solution will be far sounder and more empowering than anything you could have logically achieved.

Emotional Intelligence

By intuitively guiding your thoughts, you will find your emotions follow suit, as long as you allow them to be guided by your intuitive reason. In so doing, you will find that you are far kinder with your words, far more understanding of others, and hence far more patient in your overall life. You will also *know* when to be firmer with others and when it is best to walk away, rather than doing so in reaction to a bruised counterfeit ego.

Train yourself to slow down your emotional knee-jerk reactions, and take the time to *know first* and then react. In fact, most emotional reactions are habitual and are triggered by your sub-conscious beliefs. This means that emotional outbursts, whether positive or negative, are automatic and without your conscious input, even more so in the case of extreme lower emotions such as anger. Think about it this way - when was the last time you first quietened your mind for a moment, thought about a situation reasonably, and then decided to have an emotional outburst of anger? In the words of Lao Tzu, "The best fighter is never angry."

Moreover, endeavour to strike a balance between expressing your emotions spontaneously and being a person of intuitive calm reason. The more you use the power of your will and the more you listen to your intuition, then the more your spontaneity will match the optimal emotions of love, courage, confidence, and joy, and the less you will permit any extremes to overwhelm you. This is called emotional intelligence and empowers you to act and react intelligently, even in response to the unintelligent actions or words of others, which in turn affords you an inner calm and strength that cold logic and emotional overwhelm deny you.

Take the time every day to ask yourself how you are, just like you would a friend. Answer honestly, and get a sense of how you feel. If you feel sadness, anger, doubt, or even over-excitement, again quieten your mind and let your emotions dissolve in the silence. Your daily life can be likened to sailing a boat across a stormy sea as opposed to a sea that is calm with just enough wind. A mental storm of emotions tosses your mental boat about and where you land up is usually not where you intended to go. In contrast, when your boat sails gracefully across a calm mental sea, with the wind of positivity in your sails, you can *direct* and *know* where you are headed and so also increase the probability of arriving at your chosen destination.

THE UNION OF WILL AND INTUITION

Your will power and intuition are the masculine and feminine powers of the *Real* You and you have access to them in any place and at any time. The more you silence your mind and *know,* then the more you can use your will to *direct* your mind. And the more you use your will to direct your mind, the more you can enter the silence of intuition and know. The one enables and completes the other, and together they afford you with the balance of an inner drive and a calm mind.

The Two Doors of The I Within

Imagine two towering doors standing side by side. The one door opens outwards and the other door opens inwards. The door that opens outwards is the door of your Will. Upon opening the door, the power of your will pours forth and directs all those things of the personal self that are outside the Real You, including your thoughts, emotions, desires, and experiences. The door that opens inwards is the door of your Intuition. Upon opening the door, a vast stillness beckons you to enter, and when you do, you become one with it. And in the vast silence of nothingness you *know* everything.

The outward-opening door of your masculine Will is your door to Omnipotence. The inward-opening door of your feminine Intuition is your door to Omniscience. Within your mind you hold the key that unlocks the door of your Will, and within your heart you hold the key that unlocks the door of your Intuition. And when you unlock both doors, All-Power merges with All-Knowledge, and with the full authority of the Real You, you say 'I WILL' and 'I KNOW'.

Chapter 34

THE POWER OF DESIRE

To attain something you want, you must first desire it enough and then use your will to direct your mind and actions to attain it. In other words your desire must be *attractive* enough for you to be willing to direct your mind to achieve it. This may sound obvious but few people know what they desire, let alone how to use the power of their mind to attain it. Instead most people have many half-hearted desires, and even if they do have a *burning* desire, they become attached to it and equally doubt their power to achieve it.

Moreover, the very subject of 'desire' can be confusing as some esoteric teachings assert that one should have no desires. For instance, the Buddha said that "desire is the root of all suffering" and in fact there is great truth in this. One can say therefore, that desire is a double-sided coin, with one side being the desire to attain, and the other being to desire nothing. Together these two sides present a paradox. This chapter is intended to reconcile the two opposite sides of the coin of desire by striking a balance between the two.

THE I DESIRES NOTHING

As the I within, you desire *nothing* because you are already complete. In fact, nothing that belongs to the Physical Plane can ever define the Real You because your true domain is the Spiritual Plane, which is immeasurably above the Physical Plane in degree of positivity. This means that no desire can ever add to or subtract from the Real You, created in the image of The Absolute. Only your personal self has desires. Sometimes you succeed in attaining your desires while other times you do not, but in both instances the Real You remains equally undisturbed because you know that your ever-changing experience is a projection of your consciousness.

The One Unchanging Desire

There is only one desire that does not change and that is the desire for *nothing*. And being unchanging, it must belong to the unchanging I. By understanding that, as the Real You, you desire *nothing* for you are always complete and nothing is ever missing, you can rise above your desires of the Mental Plane. This does not suggest you do not have any *personal* desires but rather, it means that you are *above* them in degree of positivity and hence can direct them with the power of your will, while also being undisturbed by them.

Remember always that as the Real You, you know you are complete and desire *nothing*. And when you desire nothing, you are *personally* free to *choose* anything for the sake of the experience while letting nothing define you. There is a world of difference between *desiring* your desires and *choosing* them. Desiring keeps you focused on the fact that you do not have what you desire. In contrast, choosing your desire keeps you focused on the fact that it *already exists* in potential form and that you are simply *choosing* to experience it, which in turn, empowers you to believe that you *can* experience it.

THE COSMIC PRICE OF DESIRE

The cosmic price of desire is inner imbalance, which is a feeling that something is personally missing. This is not the same as the cosmic price you pay to *attain* your desire. But rather, it is the cosmic price you pay for the desire itself, irrespective of whether you attain it. As you already know from the Principle of Balance, a desire is born out of a *perceived* imbalance in your current circumstances, which itself is experienced as something missing or the need to change something.

In other words, to desire something you *first* perceive its *absence* in your life. This creates an outer world imbalance that in turn gives rise to an inner world imbalance, which you seek to balance by desiring the *opposite* of what you have. But if you did not perceive anything as missing in your life, you would personally desire nothing and would never feel the inner imbalance of desire. And the more desires you have, the greater the inner imbalances you permit. This is why some esoteric teachings assert that to be balanced you must have no desires because they cause suffering in the sense of inner imbalance.

Paying the Price of Imbalance

When you know that the cosmic price of desire is inner imbalance, you are free to choose whether or not to desire something. In other words, you decide if your desire is worth the price of imbalance that it creates within you. And if you decide it is worth it to you, then and only then, are you free to choose your desires and pay their price.

By knowing that every desire comes with its own price of inner imbalance, you are very careful about how many desires you choose to have. Moreover, the more passionate you are about your desire, the higher its price and so the greater the imbalance it creates within you. Interestingly, the word 'passion' has its origin in the Latin word *passionem*, which means 'suffering or enduring'. Likewise, the word 'pathos' is a Greek word that also means 'suffering' or more literally 'something that befalls you'. Indeed, this is why the suffering of Jesus Christ on the cross is referred as 'The Passion of Christ'.

Knowing this, you can also choose how much you are willing to *suffer* for your desire by deciding how *passionate* you are about it. Herein lies the paradox of desires. The more you want your desire the more you suffer for it. But the more you want it, the more you are willing to pay the price to *attain* it. On the other hand, the less you want it the less you suffer for it, and the less you are willing to go out and attain it. To reconcile this paradox you must be willing to suffer or *endure* the inner imbalance your desires create. And to do so *gladly*, your desire must mean *enough* to you.

THE POWER OF SINGLE DESIRES

Since desires cause inner imbalances it makes sense that it is best to choose one desire at a time. In other words, by choosing one desire at a time you minimise the inner imbalance created within you, and this also requires that you think very carefully about what you choose rather than randomly having many desires. It is up to you of course to *choose* which desire means the most to you at any given time.

Moreover, by choosing one desire at a time you can focus your energy on balancing a single imbalance. In contrast, by having to endure the many imbalances that come with many desires, you do not know where to begin or what to focus your energy on, and hence you scatter it aimlessly. And more often than not you lack the mental clarity to even begin because of just how imbalanced you feel.

It may sound obvious but to choose a single desire, you must first know exactly *what* you desire and *why* you desire it. In this way you become a person who knows what they want, why they want it, and what it is worth to them, which in turn enables you to pay the right price for your desire and to set it aside if you decide it is no longer worth its price. So the question is what do you want?

What Do You Want?

You will probably find from your own experience that many of your desires are often focused on things you think you cannot have or on something you previously had but 'lost'. In the same way that chocolate can become the dieter's single most alluring desire, so it is that what you *think* you cannot have, or what you believe is being denied you, often becomes your single desire with little thought for if you really want it. So ask yourself this: if you knew you could have what you *think* you cannot have, would you *still want it*? And would you still want it, if you knew you could have something even *better*? In answering these questions honestly, you may find many of the desires you cling to are just your counterfeit ego wanting to have its way.

Here is another question to ask yourself: if you really knew you could have *anything*, what would you want? The personal self may come up with a long list of desires like a child let loose in a toy store, but remember that the Real You only ever has one answer, which is 'nothing'. There is great power to be found in the mental equilibrium of desiring *nothing*, while being ready to direct the power of your will towards attaining *anything*.

The Power of Desiring Out of Nothing

Knowing that as the Real You, you desire nothing, the next question to ask yourself is this: what *one* thing do I *personally* desire to *experience* most right now? Think very carefully before you answer and *know* in your heart that what you choose is what you *truly* do desire. Personal desires that have their foundation in the 'nothingness' of the I are accompanied with such mental clarity, strength, and motivation, that you feel as if the whole Universe desires it with you and will conspire to help you in the attainment of your desire.

If your answer to this last question is still nothing, do not fight it. Enjoy the inner balance and freedom that comes with *personally* desiring nothing. The chances are that, by virtue of being a human being living in the Physical Plane, you will sooner or later desire something, only this time you will know *why* you do beyond a shadow of a doubt. And again, your desire will have been born out of the I's 'nothing' and hence, your inner strength and drive to attain it will be incomparable to just desiring something arbitrarily.

By choosing your desires in this way, you transmute your desires into choices. Instead of just *desiring* what you desire, you *choose* what you desire. And instead of saying 'I wish I could have this or that', you say 'It is my *will* to *experience* what I *choose* to experience'.

Choose with Your Heart not Your Head

When you choose your desire, choose it with your heart, not your head. Desires that originate in your head tend to reflect the desires of your counterfeit ego's need to control, and its child-like demands to satisfy itself. In contrast, desires that are felt in your heart are more pure in nature and are born out of *knowing* what you truly want.

The more you specify all the 'must-have details' in your desire, the more likely it is that the counterfeit ego is the one doing the desiring. In contrast, the more open or flexible you are about your desire's outcome being whatever is best for you, the more likely it is that it is your heart's desire. For instance in your head, you may desire to be in a relationship with a *specific* person and are not willing to entertain the idea of being in a relationship with anyone else. If, however, you ask your *heart* what you truly want, you will *know* that it is not so much a specific person you desire, but a loving relationship with a partner that is ideal for you. Having to have someone *specific*, or anything else specific, is usually a sign that your counterfeit ego is holding your true desire captive and is adding its usual limitations to it. What you truly want has more to do with how attaining your desire would make you *feel* than who or what is making you feel it.

Put simply, know *exactly* what you want and how you want to feel, but be open to the outer world specifics, which means do not limit the outcome. Another way of saying this is that your heart's desires are limitless, whereas your head's desires are limited. Whether you desire with your heart or your head is up to you, but do remember that desires are referred to as your heart's desires and *not* your head's desires, for a reason.

Whenever you desire something, whether it is specific or not, always be willing to say 'this or something better'. This means that even if you desire something specific you are at least willing to desire something better than what you specified. Your willingness therefore, to say 'this or something better' and really mean it, is your personal litmus test for detachment. If, however, you cannot say 'this or something better' and mean it, you can be very certain it is just your counterfeit ego insisting on having its way.

Know Your Desire Intimately

Know everything about your desire. For instance, if it is your dream home you desire, mentally walk through it, imagine every room, and familiarise yourself with every corner. Mentally entertain your friends and see your loved ones enjoying it with you. Smell the food that is cooking in your kitchen. Lie on your comfortable bed in your ideal bedroom. Walk in your garden, smell the flowers and sit under one of its trees, or enjoy the view from your balcony.

Know everything about your desire, and know it well. Knowing your desire, however, is again not about being specific in the way discussed previously. The difference is that you imagine your home exactly as you desire it to be but you avoid for instance, *attaching* an already existing home to your desire while refusing to entertain anything else. In the same way you imagine, for instance, your ideal relationship with your ideal partner exactly the way you want it to be and know exactly how you feel in it, but you avoid *attaching* a specific person that you may desire to that relationship, unless already in a relationship with that person. In this way you do not limit your desire to already existing conditions and hence, you do not become *attached* to what you are *attaching* to your mental image. Rather you trust, that if an already existing home or the specific person you desire are the ones that can best fulfil your desire, then they will certainly be the ones that are brought into your life, and if not, then something or someone better for you will fulfil your desire.

THE PURPOSE OF YOUR DESIRE

It is one thing to know exactly what you want, but it is quite another to thing to know *why* you want it. Knowing why you want something ensures you have the necessary motivation to pursue your desire through to its attainment, and also empowers you to add the necessary emotion to your desire when concentrating on it. The easiest way to know why you desire something is to discover what it symbolises for you. And what it symbolises for you is its *purpose* or in other words, why it is personally *necessary* in your life.

As the saying goes 'necessity is the mother of invention', so there must be a reason or purpose for your desire in order to invent it or in your case, set out to attain it. Most people, however, stop at a mental image of their desire without knowing what the image means to them, and hence never find the motivation to pursue their desire.

If you choose, for instance, to desire more money, a mental image of money is just an image of money but what it symbolises for you may be financial freedom, your own business, travelling, buying your dream home, the ability to enjoy a fuller life, or even to help others in need. A mental image of a house is just a house but what it symbolises may be a combination of comfort, family, shelter, sharing your home with your loved ones, or providing a safe place for your family. And an image of a relationship is just a relationship but what it symbolises may be sharing your love, intimacy, deep friendship, companionship, or starting a family of your own.

Put simply, what the mental image of your desire symbolises is *why* you want it and knowing why you want something gives you *reason* enough to pursue it. In turn, the reason you want it determines how necessary it is for you, and in the words of the Roman emperor Julius Caesar, "nature must obey necessity."

Once again, ask your heart not your head *why* you desire what you desire. By knowing why you want something and how necessary it is to you personally, you can then more easily choose the *single* desire to pursue at any one time. And the one you choose to pursue is the one that is most important to you by nature of its purpose in your life.

Everyone has his or her own reason for desiring something and the reason behind your desire is personal to you. There is no need to tell anyone what you desire or why you desire it, and in fact it is important that you keep it to yourself, as will be discussed in Chapter 44. If, however, you do not have a convincing enough reason for desiring something, the chances are you either do not really want it or it is just your counterfeit ego comparing itself to others and wanting something it thinks it cannot have.

Once you know what you want and why you want it then there are only two ways you can really prevent its attainment. Attachment and doubt is one way, and desiring it too much or too little is the other. With this in mind, we will now consider how to rise above attachment and doubt, to reach a mental state of detachment, before turning our attention to what it means to desire something *enough*.

THE POWER OF DETACHMENT

To detach from something you desire does not mean not thinking about it. After all it is natural that you do think of your desire *enough* to keep you moving in its direction. Rather, detachment comes down to *how* you think about it, and to be detached means not permitting *doubt* in your mind and not being *attached* to the outcome, or in other words not being obsessed with having to have it.

The first step to detachment is to let go of any misguided notion that your desires can complete you. How many times have you attained what you thought would make you happy only to realise that nothing much changed or that the sense of fulfilment wore off soon after its attainment? Despite this, most people keep on looking to their desires for their happiness and completion and if one desire does not do the 'trick' they quickly move onto the next one. What they do not know is that what they are in fact looking for is the *desireless* I within.

Let Nothing Define You

As the mighty I within, nothing in the Physical Plane can define you. And when your desires do not define you, you are free to choose any desire for the experience inherent within it, rather than misguidedly believing that if you do not attain it, you are somehow incomplete.

The instant you let a desire define you, it has power over you and you usually lack the power to pursue it and so, it remains little more than a desire you *desire*, but never *choose* to attain. In contrast, when you are the one who defines your desires you gain the power inherent in them. Remember always, your desires *belong* to your personal self but your personal self must *never* belong to your desires. Whatever you let define you limits your directive and creative power to the same extent. Moreover, since your mental contents and outer world circumstances are always changing, for all intents and purposes they are unreal. How then can you define yourself by something that is not real? Never permit any desire, or anything else for that matter, define who you are. Remember you are the *unchanging* and *undisturbed* I within and nothing can add to or subtract from you.

How to Rise Above Attachment and Doubt

To rise above attachment and doubt stop labeling what you desire as good and its opposite as bad. In nature you do not judge the opposite poles of the same thing as being good or bad. You do not say the north pole of a magnet is good and the south pole is bad, any more than you declare the anode of a battery to be good compared to the bad cathode. In other words, you *naturally* reconcile the opposites into a balanced whole. And the reason you do so, is because you have no vested personal interest in the difference between the two poles.

When it comes to your personal desires, however, you judge what you desire as good and its opposite, which is usually some version of your current conditions, as bad. This causes you to become attached to your desire and resist your current conditions. Your attachment to your desire creates an imbalance that is counter-balanced by swinging you to the opposite side of resisting your current conditions, which is experienced as doubt in your ability to attain your desire. What you fail to realise, however, is that the only reason you are attached to your desire is because you took a one-sided position by judging it as good in the first place and its opposite as bad. And the more you label what you desire as good, then the more attached you become, and your attachment feeds your doubt, which in turn feeds your attachment, all courtesy of the pendulum's counter-balancing swing.

In so doing, you fail to focus on your desire exclusively, as your doubt and resistance cause you to also focus on your unwanted existing conditions. And hence, the two opposing mental images cancel each other out and nothing or little changes.

What you also fail to realise while mentally swinging between attachment and doubt, is that your existing conditions give rise to and hence are necessary to your desire, and that the two are the same thing only different in rate of vibration. This means that you are inadvertently declaring the same thing to be both good *and* bad at the same time. This can be likened to wanting to generate electricity out of a battery by allowing only the anode side to work and denying the cathode's role.

Judge Nothing as Good or Bad

As you already know, as the Real You, you are above the duality of good and bad and hence, do not distinguish between the two or engage in the futility of judging the same thing as good *and* bad. By adopting this higher vantage point as your personal self, you once again choose any *personal* desire for the *experience* and not because it is good and its opposite pole is bad. In so doing, you do not permit the one-sided extreme of attachment, which in turn creates no reason for the pendulum to swing to the opposite end of doubt.

Moreover, the instant you judge something as good, you give it the power to make you feel bad if you do not attain it, or even if you do attain it and it changes in some way. In other words, when you judge something to be good, you are telling yourself that this thing makes you happy, and whatever makes you happy is what one day can make you sad when it changes, as all things do. It cannot be stressed enough that the key to mental freedom is to let nothing define you and to rise above the judgement call of good and bad.

In Winning Through Enlightenment (1980), Ron Smothermon wrote that "in order to have something, you must be willing not to have it." This is a profound statement in the context of rising above the duality of good and bad in your desires. What it comes down to is the only real freedom you have, which is your freedom of choice.

FREEDOM OF CHOICE

You can only exercise your freedom of choice from a place of non-attachment to your desire and non-resistance to its opposite. If you *must have* what you want, then you are attached to it, and so the only way to detach from it is to be also willing *not* to have it. Think about it this way - if you *have to have* your desire, you are not *free* to choose it because the freedom to choose something must include the freedom to choose not to have it.

You probably know from your own experience, that you attract to yourself with ease those things or experiences you are not attached to. This is because, whether you realise it or not, you have already acknowledged their other 'bad' opposite side and are not bothered about it. In other words, when you desire something but are not attached to the outcome, which means you are equally content with not having it because it does not define your happiness, then it more often than not comes to you effortlessly and you do not even realise you created it. Put simply, choose what you desire, pursue it with all your heart, pay whatever the price for its attainment, and be confident. But let go of the idea of having to have it and remember it is just an experience. In so doing, you gain the power *it* would otherwise have over you and guard yourself from spiralling downwards in positivity in a state of panic, fuelled by doubt and attachment.

By telling yourself you have to have something, you give yourself no choice in the matter. Unbeknown to you, this creates a mental prison from which you cannot escape because you have deluded yourself into believing you are already free. Therefore, give yourself the *real* freedom of choice, it is the only real freedom you have.

Freedom of Choice is Free Will

Freedom of choice exercised under the direction of your will is known as free will. Anything less than using the power of your will to choose your desires free from the attachment that comes with having to have them, amounts to being their servant and by no means their master. To exercise your free will, you must once again rise above the perceived duality of good and bad. Otherwise you are *forced* to choose good over bad. But there is no real freedom in having to choose one side, even if you have deluded yourself into believing you are free.

Endeavour therefore, to loosen the grip on your desire, let go of the idea of having to have it and grant yourself the freedom of choice of being *alright* with not having it. Then and only then are you truly free to pursue it with all your heart and without being burdened with fear and panic. In other words, when you are willing not to have something, there is never a question of 'what if it doesn't happen'.

DESIRE IT ENOUGH

People usually fall into one of two extreme categories. They either do not desire something enough or they desire it too much, with no consideration for the point of balance between the two which is to desire it *enough*. On the one hand if you do not desire something enough, you never quite find the energy to pursue it. And on the other hand, if you desire something too much you cannot help but be attached to having it because you are constantly reminding yourself that you do not have it, which in turn leaves you spinning your wheels on the same spot with little progress.

Stop Short-Circuiting Your Desires

In the Physical Plane, when a device is overcharged with energy in the form of an electrical current without any insulation, then the excess energy causes overheating. Overheating results in an electrical short-circuit and the device usually explodes or becomes faulty. In the same way, by giving something in your life too much importance, be it a desire, person, or experience, you send too much energy through its 'circuit' and it metaphorically blows up in your face while you are left wondering what went wrong. To insulate yourself from such 'explosions', do not overcharge anything with too much energy, which means do not give anything so much importance that it has the power to define you and how you feel.

Give Nothing Excess Importance

It is of course natural to be more interested in certain things and to give those people, things, and goals that are personal to you greater importance than to those that are not. For instance, the importance you give to your children, your partner, or your family, is naturally greater than what you give to strangers. Similarly, the importance you give to one desire is greater than what you may give to another.

Giving nothing too much importance therefore, does not suggest having no personal interests, goals, or hobbies, nor is it about treating all people neutrally. Rather it is about letting nothing define you, and hence avoiding obsession, which is attachment taken to an extreme. And where extreme emotions cloud your objectivity and mental clarity, obsession blinds them completely. The key therefore in pursuing any desire is for it to be important enough to you. But enough means *enough*, and anything more is too much.

Lessons from a Steam-Engine

The optimal energy or importance to give your desires can be likened to the optimal temperature of the fire that powers a steam engine. If the temperature of the fire is too low, not enough steam is generated to move the steam engine.

If, however, the temperature is too high, the fusible plugs of the engine are likely to melt because there is no way for the excess heat to be used for powering the steam engine, which in turn causes the engine's boiler to explode, dumping water on the fire, putting it out and effectively bringing the steam engine's trip to an end.

How important something is to you can be likened to the fire which powers the steam engine, where the steam engine is your pursuit of your desire. Too little importance does not yield enough energy for you to pursue your desire. In contrast, too much importance stops you dead in your tracks because it gives rise to attachment and doubt. And finally, optimal importance maximises the probability of attaining your desire quickly and efficiently.

How much importance is enough, depends on you. You can only know if you are giving something too much importance by paying attention to how you feel about it. If the thought of your desire weighs you down, or makes you feel upset that you do not have it, then you are more than likely giving it too much importance. On the other hand, if thinking about your desire leaves you unmotivated, it is unlikely to be important enough for you to pursue it. And finally, if the thought of your desire makes you feel light on your feet, strong, confident, and motivated to pursue it without the mental heaviness of obsession, then you are at optimal importance.

Burning Desires Burn Out Twice as Fast

Having a burning desire for something may go a long way in enabling you to put the necessary effort into its attainment but it comes with its own risks. On the one hand, maintaining the same constant sense of *burning* for your desire is unlikely because, as Lao Tzu said "the flame that burns twice as bright burns half as long." On the other hand, the excess 'fire' inherent in your burning desire, could cause you to *burn out* mentally and physically before it does.

Depending on desiring something excessively in order to go out and get it is usually evidence of a general lack of self-discipline and a weak will. In contrast, by employing your will power, you exert the necessary mental and physical effort without having to endure the inner turmoil and extreme imbalance of burning desires, which arise when operating at a level of emotions and passions alone. In other words, to incite your will into action you have to desire something enough, or in other words it must attract you enough. But without your will's participation, your desire floats aimlessly in the Mental Plane, just as your idle daydreams do.

Arguably you could focus on your desire obsessively and use the sheer power of your will to overcome your doubt. However, this is the difficult and unlikely route to attainment because you are working against the force of nature as you must constantly fight the swing of the pendulum to stay on the extreme side you want.

If, however, you maintain an inner sense of calm optimism and mental strength, you limit the pendulum's counter-swing because you create no extreme for it to counter-balance, and even if it does swing, the degree is so negligible that you can quickly and easily correct it. So instead of being beset with doubt and obsession, you are free to pursue your desire joyfully and also to enjoy the experience.

In Joyful Pursuit of Desire

To pursue your desire joyfully is to know in your heart that what you *truly* desire desires you too in the same measure, and is waiting for your mental instruction to be created. If you want your desire enough, you train your mind to comply with your will's direction, you do not scatter your thought power on idle daydreaming, you do not permit doubt to cloud your mind, you pursue your desire with calm confidence and courage, and you are willing to pay the price of its attainment, whatever it is, as long as your desire is worth it to you.

But in all this, you know it is just an experience and has no bearing on the Real You, which in turn frees you from the obsessive feeling of having to have it. And so you enjoy the pursuit of your desire with all your heart for the experience itself, but without doubt and without attachment to the outcome.

Confident Expectation

Confidently expect to attain your desire with faith in the immutable Law of Mentalism that mind is creative through thought. The word 'confidence' has its origin in the Latin word *confidere*, meaning 'with full trust and reliance'. Confident expectation therefore, means to expect the fulfilment of your desire with trust in, and reliance on, the creative power of your mind *through* the One Universal Mind. This kind of confidence leaves no room for doubt and likewise leaves no room for arrogance.

Confident expectation, however, does not mean expecting your desire every moment, wondering where it is, why it has not happened yet, or thinking that the Universe has 'forgotten you'. This is anything *but* confidently expecting something, and is in fact a sign that you do not expect it at all. In life you usually get what you expect to get and not what you want. This is because you are not attached to what you *expect* to receive and take it for granted. In contrast, what you *want* to receive is something you wish for but are not quite sure you can receive. For instance, if you expect to be paid by month end, you do not wonder about it as you have an underlying unspoken expectation that you will receive your pay-check. In other words, you take it for granted that you will be paid and do not wonder about it.

Remain Calm with a Strong Resolve

Do not get excited at the first signs of your desire's manifestations. Mentally acknowledge every sign and keep going. Over-excitement discharges your energy or Life Force that you would otherwise use to keep on moving towards your desire's attainment.

Moreover, do not allow yourself to become arrogant in your pursuit, or to take your eye off the ball. Guard yourself from falling into the trap of believing that nothing and no one can stand in your way, because as you already know this attitude by its own force, more often than not, triggers the return swing of the pendulum to the other extreme of reversing all your efforts.

Do not try to physically force anything or anyone in order to hurry your desire along, and do not partake in mental manipulation of others in the misguided belief that it is the only way to attain your desire. Remain calm and patient with a strong resolve. Moreover, knowing that there may still be a long way to go before you attain your desire is a reminder to use your energy reserves wisely. Above all, identify your mind with the One Universal Mind and it too will identify Itself with your mind. In so doing, you can then trust Life implicitly to take you to your desired destination.

OPTIMAL EMOTION FOR DESIRE

It is a misconception that you must work yourself into an extreme positive or frenzied state of emotional excitement when you focus on your desire, for instance during visualisation (Ch. 40). Always keep your emotions positive because emotions add energy to your desires, as water adds nourishment to a seed. Your *e*-motions incite *energy* into *motion* and hence positive emotions create positive energy. But do not permit extreme emotions. Just like you do not drown a seed with excess water, you do not permit your desire to be 'drowned' by emotional overwhelm.

To temper your emotions, you incite your masculine reason with the guidance of your intuition. Use your intuitive reason and rational mind to keep your emotions at optimal levels that inspire and motivate you, but at the same time allow for an inner sense of calm confidence. If your emotions overwhelm you and cause you to lose objectivity, immediately rein them in and centre yourself, knowing that extreme emotions lead to extreme actions, which in the absence of objectivity are often miscalculated.

TAKE WHAT YOU WANT FOR GRANTED

Metaphysical teachings assert that you must visualise your desire in the present moment as if it *already exists* and is already part of your life. In other words, you must believe that you already have it. Now, if you already had what you desire, then you would hardly be emotionally excited about it in your physical reality, or at least not for long. In the same way that you are not excited about and even take for granted, all those things you already have in your life, so you should avoid emotional extremes in your desires. And by avoiding extreme emotions, you avoid the counter-swing of the pendulum. As is the case for all experiences in your life, it is far more effective to maintain a positive mental state of calm strength and inner courage that does not depend on your desires or anything else, but rather depends only on knowing your true nature as the I within.

What You Desire Already Exists

Take for granted that what you want *already* exists in your life and stay calm about it. This is not fanciful thinking because remember you live in two worlds, and in the world that is invisible to your eyes, what you want *does* already exist. Interestingly, the etymology of the word 'granted' can be traced back to the Latin word *credentem* meaning 'to believe' or 'to trust'.

Taking what you want for granted therefore, is to believe that it has already been granted or given to you and it has been received. And when you already have something, you do not sit around wondering where it is. But you still pursue it with the same motivation, knowing it is up to you to bring it from the invisible world into the physical world in which you have your experience through your mental and physical actions.

Be Grateful for What you Take for Granted

You can most definitely take things for granted *and* be grateful for them at the same time. In fact, taking things for granted has *nothing* to do with gratitude or a lack thereof. For instance, you can be grateful for the opportunity to enjoy the magnificence of a sunrise but you take it for granted that the sun will rise.

Therefore, believe that you have already received, take what you have and what you desire for granted with a sense of gratitude, and avoid arrogance. And always remember that the greatest gift ever granted to you as a human being with a physical experience, is your God-given power to create the reality of your *choice* under the direction of your will and the guidance of your intuition. Take it, use it wisely, and be eternally grateful for it.

BE PATIENT

You must be willing to be patient when you set out to attain any desire. Patience is of paramount importance in the Physical Plane because of the time lag between the mental causes you set in motion and their physical world manifestations or effects. Without patience, you let doubt cloud your mind and so you are unlikely to find enough resolve to overcome any obstacles you may encounter. To be patient, however, does not mean to sit back and do nothing. On the contrary, it means to be willing to do whatever it takes to attain your desire, no matter *how long* it takes. Interestingly, the words 'patience' and 'passion' have the same root which is 'to suffer'. To suffer however must not be confused with any sort of punishment or retribution for your desires. Instead, to suffer in this context simply means to *patiently endure* the inner imbalance that is created by your desires until such time that you attain them.

SUCCESS IS A DEMANDING WOMAN

Taking what you desire for granted, however, does not mean that success is a done deal. Rather, to take what you want for granted is founded on knowing the underlying nature of the Universe, but bear in mind that paying the cosmic price for success is also part of the nature of the Universe. To succeed in attaining your desire therefore, you must gladly exert all the necessary mental and physical effort with self-discipline and persistence.

Success can be likened to a demanding woman with the highest self-regard, and indeed metaphysical teachings refer to success as being feminine in nature. Success never pursues you. You must pursue her. Half-hearted flirting leaves her cold. She demands your earnest desire. She does not tolerate you even glancing at another woman with desire. You must have eyes only for her. She demands that you court her earnestly and pursue her persistently. Then and only then will you perhaps win her hand. But having attained success, she will still expect you to appreciate and protect her otherwise she will leave your side with little warning. If, however, you give her no reason to leave, she will stay by your side and gladly reward you for all your efforts for many years to come.

CONSCIOUS CREATION THROUGH DESIRE

To wrap up this chapter on desire we will now look at desire in the context of conscious reality creation. As you already know from the Law of Gender, your desires are a feminine principle of mind and your will power is a masculine principle. When you desire something enough you direct it by concentrating on a mental image of your desire with the power of your will. And you affirm to yourself over and over again 'I WILL and I CAN'.

You use the creative power of your imagination, which is the subject of the next chapter, to create the ideal mental image of your desire. And you keep the mental image of your ideal at the forefront of your objective mind. The more you hold the mental image of your ideal in mind, the more it is impressed on your subjective subconscious mind where all creation takes place.

You concentrate on the mental image of your ideal with optimal emotion and laser-like precision. You direct your energy or Life Force towards it, which you know is necessary for its creation. The more you focus on your desire, the more you keep a mental image of it in mind with the power of your will, and the more you keep your emotions at optimal levels, then the easier it will be for you to gladly pay the cosmic price of attainment, whatever it is.

Once your creative subjective mind takes over, use your objective mind to protect it from doubt and conflicting images or thoughts. It is then just a matter of time before your desire is projected in your outer physical world, provided you keep on taking the necessary physical actions towards attaining it and intelligently deal with resistance, which is the subject of Chapter 36.

Universal Mind Takes Over

When the mental image of your desire is firmly impressed on your creative subjective mind, it means it is also firmly impressed on the subjective Universal Mind, because the two are the same mind. And the degree to which you identify your mind as being one and the same with Universal Mind is the degree to which It will identify Its unity with your mind, in mutual recognition of each other. And when you truly know that your mind *is* Universal Mind in its entirety, then your desire becomes wholly a *desire* of Universal Mind and so, It takes over the creative process.

And as Paulo Coelho said in his book The Alchemist, "when you want something, all the Universe conspires in *helping* you to achieve it." But you must truly want it *enough*, and be willing to pay the price for it because a half-hearted desire of your own, in which you have no real conviction, is at best a half-hearted desire of the Universe in which it has no conviction. And to have *conviction*, is to be in a state of being convinced *without* doubt, whereas to have no conviction means to be *convinced of* your doubt.

Finally, when you know all possibilities already exist in potential form and that no desire is too big, too complicated, or too difficult for something that has the inherent potential of All Power, then you also have Omnipotence on your side. And when you truly know you have All Power on your side then nothing is impossible for you through The Absolute.

Chapter 35

THE POWER OF IMAGINATION

Imagination is the creative faculty of your mind. It is not constrained by space or time, it knows no boundaries, it is not limited by physical world circumstances, it does not measure the impossible against the yardstick of the possible, and it does not care for mathematical equations, philosophical debates, logical proofs, or even knowledge.

Imagination even has the power to sway your will. Although you must will yourself to do something, if you imagine that you cannot do it then usually you don't. A person of strong will power uses their imagination wisely to awaken their will, whereas a weak-willed person is left subject to his imaginings. Few people, however, know of the incredible power inherent in their imagination, believing it to be a fanciful pleasure reserved for children. But nothing could be further from the truth.

YOUR MENTAL WORKSHOP

The truth is your imagination is the mental workshop in which you can create anything you desire. It is the mental workshop of the inventor in which all the inventions throughout history were first fashioned. It is the secret workshop of the sculptor in which he first gives life to his statues. And it is the single most powerful workshop of the reality creator in which he moulds his reality just as he desires to experience it. By cultivating a strong imagination, you will find that creating and holding mental images of your desire becomes child's play rather than hard work.

Some of the greatest minds of our times have left us clues as to the immense power of the imagination. Albert Einstein said that "imagination is more important than knowledge; logic will get you from A to B [but] imagination will take you everywhere; and that imagination is the preview of life's coming attractions."

Moreover Nikolas Tesla, who is arguably the greatest inventor of all time, had this to say about imagination: "My method is different. I do not rush into actual work. When I get a new idea, I start at once building it up in my imagination, and make improvements and operate the device in my mind. When I have gone so far as to embody everything in my invention, every possible improvement I can think of, and when I see no fault anywhere, I put into concrete form the final product of my brain."

THE IDEA AND THE MENTAL IMAGE

Anything you desire to experience in your life starts off as an idea that you imagine. The idea of a thing can be likened to the seed of its creation. The word 'idea' has its origin in the Platonic philosophy of archetypes and in the same Greek word meaning 'ideal prototype'. In a literal sense therefore, an idea is the original *ideal* mental pattern from which something is brought forth or copied. In other words, it is the original mental image of a thing in its ideal state, as opposed to its actual physical counterpart which may or may not match the ideal.

The imagined mental image of an idea determines what is to be created. It is the mental blueprint or representation of the idea and is what is presented to your sub-conscious mind. Remember that your mind works in mental images but this does not only mean you think in images, but that images held in your mind are created or brought forth into the physical world.

The 'mental image' of an oak tree held in Universal Mind, is how the oak tree grows from an acorn that can in no way contain the physical oak tree itself. And there must be some Divine Intelligence through which the mental image of an oak tree unfolds into a physical oak tree that in no way resembles the acorn.

The Power of Mental Images

Consider the following words from John McDonald's book Message of a Master. "Mind, no matter what form it is contained in, holds images. And any image firmly held in any mind in any form, is bound to come forth. This is the great, unchanging Universal Law which, when we cooperate with it intelligently, makes us absolute masters of conditions and environment."

The ability to consciously choose, construct, and hold any image in mind is the privilege of human beings in the physical world, and is what sets us apart from the other kingdoms. Just like the mind spark in an acorn brings forth an oak tree without judgment, so your sub-conscious mind brings forth those images impressed on it with no consideration as to whether the image is wanted or unwanted - just the image. Knowing this is reason enough to stay focused on the mental images of all that you desire to experience in life and to clear contradictory images from your mind.

The Mental Image is 'Real'

Bear in mind that both your ever-changing mental images and outside conditions are unreal because they are impermanent. But if you were to label either of them as being real, it would have to be the mental image. This is because it is the cause while your outside conditions are the effect or in other words, a physical world projection of your mental image. This concept is best understood in the context of constrained and unconstrained causes as was discussed in Chapter 26. To become the *Causer*, you must consciously impress a mental image of your desire on your subjective mind and hence on Universal Mind, irrespective of your outer world conditions.

Remember that the Universe of solid things is not real. It is but a reflection of the image of those things held in Universal Mind. Think about it this way - the movie you see on a movie screen is not real. It is just a projection of the images held in the film-reel, and what you see on the screen changes in accordance with a change of the image in the reel. In the same way, your ever-changing circumstances in the physical world are not real. They are but projections of the mental images you hold in your mind and the projection changes in accordance with a change in the mental image.

MENTAL ARCHITECTURE

Without a clear mental image of what you want to create, an idea remains a seed that is never quite planted. For this reason, you must construct a mental image of your desire in your imagination. The first step in this direction is to identify with the power of your imagination and then employ its power constructively for the purpose of creating a mental image of what you want to experience.

Get out of the habit of using your imagination for purposeless daydreaming or wishful thinking, for that is in fact reserved for children. Instead, use your imagination to construct, invent, design, and plan the ideal of what you want to create in physical form. Instead of imagining how things could go wrong or get worse in your life, discipline yourself to imagine only how things are already going right and can get even better. There is nothing fanciful about using your imagination in this way. In fact, you could hardly do anything more constructive, mentally or physically.

While the term mental image suggests something that is visual this is not quite accurate. A mental image in fact involves and invokes all five senses, and seeing is just one of them. Indeed, you can bring a mental image of a rose to mind far easier if you first physically smell a rose, or an image of a lemon if you first taste its sourness. A mental image of your ideal outcome is more tangible and more believable when you mentally see it, and even more so when you add sound, touch, taste, and smell, as well as colour, movement, and feeling.

Having said this, you can still create your desire even if your mental image is unclear, but the outcome becomes more certain and the process more enjoyable, if you actively involve all your senses. The more real something feels in your imagination, the more real it becomes for you. Here are some exercises that can aid you in the direction of employing and creating mental imagery of this kind.

Exercise in Mental Construction

No matter what your experience has been to date, as long as you have had at least one vivid dream, then you can also use your imagination in the same way to see your desire. To help you do so you can first create a mental image by constructing it from scratch, as if you were a mental architect.

Start by contemplating the idea of the image in your mind and next see the outline or framework of the image as if it were an architect's blueprint. Once you have the mental blueprint or outline in mind, you can begin to fill in the outline with colour. Think back to the last time you coloured an outlined image in a children's colouring book and you will find this far easier to do.

Having added colour to your mental image, next see it in three-dimensional form, as if the two-dimensional image on a piece of paper was lifted off the paper to create a three-dimension form that includes depth. Draw on your memories of those things in your mental image to add sound, smell, taste, and other sensations where appropriate. Your memory bank of sensations and experiences is the richest source of materials to use in constructing your ideal mental image. In other words you can use ideal images of things already in your memory, whether you have personally experienced those images or seen them in say a magazine or movie. Since memories are stored in the sub-conscious mind, it is far easier to draw on them when in a relaxed meditative state (Ch. 37).

Finally, bring your image to life by adding movement as if you were watching a movie. Again draw on your experience of movie watching to assist you in this. Bear in mind, however, that while it is beneficial to learn to visualise vividly in this way, simply imagining as best you can is sufficient. You may find that you *feel* in your imagination more than you *see*, and this is just as effective.

Exercise in Dreaming

Another way to trigger your mind's visualising capacity is to pretend that you are dreaming. Put simply, when creating the mental image of what you want to experience, pretend that you are seeing a dream. In this way your mind shifts into a dream-like state, which makes seeing moving mental images with sound and other sensations far easier because that is what you do when you are dreaming.

Exercise in Mental Imagery

You can become masterful at mental imagery by practicing with everyday things. Here are some helpful guidelines. Start with small objects and then work yourself up to larger objects. For instance, take a small pebble. Hold it in front of your eyes and study it intently. Study its shape, its colour, its size and how it feels. While keeping it in place in front of your eyes, close your eyes and imagine the pebble in your hand, exactly as you experienced it. Attempt to see its exact colour and size and sense how its surface felt to your touch.

Next, open your eyes and study the pebble again as you did previously. Now put the pebble behind your back, and attempt to see the pebble in front of you with your eyes open as if it were there hovering in mid-air. Repeat these exercises with different objects already in your memory bank, such as your house keys, your favourite mug, or something as simple as a pencil.

Once you have mastered seeing small objects, move onto bigger ones such as a house, or something even bigger like the view from your balcony, patio, or window. When you have had enough practice bringing to mind and even 'seeing' with your eyes open, both small and large objects, you can begin to apply this method to visualising the ideal mental image of your own personal desires with ease.

IMPRESSING YOUR SUBJECTIVE MIND

Recall that whatever image you want to impress on your subjective mind must first pass through your objective conscious mind. For this reason you must use your imagination to focus on a mental image of what you want with your objective conscious mind, until your sub-conscious mind takes over.

You will know that a mental image has been impressed on your sub-conscious mind when the image comes to mind naturally without having to engage your focus consciously. In other words, you will find that bringing a mental image of your desire or intention to mind will feel less and less like a conscious process and more like an involuntary or automatic process. Moreover, the mental image will begin to feel part of *you*, rather than something *outside* of you.

How quickly a mental image passes down to your sub-conscious mind depends on your mental focus and on any conflicting images you entertain. The more attached you are to *having to* have what you want, the more the conflicting images that are likely to come to mind. In contrast, the less extreme you are in your desire, the less you will entertain conflicting mental images because there will be little for the pendulum to counter-balance.

Lessons from Children's Play Putty

A mental image is created in the Mental Plane when it has been *impressed* on your sub-conscious mind, and hence on Universal Mind. Not every thought or mental image, however, is impressed on your subjective mind. To do it effectively, you must think the same thought, or imagine the same mental image, often enough.

To understand this, it is helpful to think of your sub-conscious mind as children's mouldable play putty, and every thought you have or image you imagine, can be likened to pressing the putty lightly with your finger. Thinking of the same thought or mental image over and over again means you press the putty in the same place over and over again. And the more you do so, the deeper the impression it makes on the putty. However, if you doubt your mental image or have conflicting thoughts, it is like wiping out the last impression that was made by your intended thought. And so, the more conflicting your thoughts are, the more you remove the impression of your intended outcome on the putty that is your sub-conscious mind.

Put simply, to impress your sub-conscious mind with your desire, you must think the same thought, or imagine the same mental image, over and over again, while limiting conflicting thoughts or mental images. Once your ideal is impressed on your subjective mind, it no longer takes conscious effort to think about or imagine it.

Finally, as you already know, impressing a mental image on your subjective mind directly impresses that mental image on Universal Mind. Thereafter, what is left for you to do is persist in maintaining an overall positive mental attitude while taking the necessary physical action towards your desire's attainment and intelligently dealing with any obstacles or resistance that you are likely to face. This then brings us to the subject of taking action and dealing with reaction which is the topic of the next chapter.

Chapter 36
TAKING ACTION, DEALING WITH REACTION

Taking action is about actively participating in the creation of your desire in the physical world. So far, we have considered mental action while this chapter focuses on its equal but opposite physical action. Physical action is the cosmic price you must be willing to pay in order to attain your desire in your outer world.

TAKING ACTION
When you choose a goal or objective, set out to attain it with courage and self-confidence, trusting in your own ability that you can and will attain it, provided that you exert the necessary effort in its direction. It is up to you to make every physical effort to attain your intended outcome when physical action is called for, provided it is important enough to you. You cannot just sit back and urge your desire to be attained by thinking about it all day. As an aside, however, there are some desires that may not require physical action. For instance, in the case of distant healing or in desiring a more spiritual experience free of the attainment of physical world things. Nevertheless, it is physical world desires as opposed to purely mental desires that more often than not do require physical action.

Lessons from Driving
Think of your mind as the engine that drives the 'car' of physical action. The better the condition of the engine, the better the driving experience, but the engine is of little use to your car, if you do not drive it. Put another way, you do not expect your car to drive itself somewhere, no matter how clearly you hold the mental image of your destination in mind. It is you that must do the driving. With the same logic, you have to take physical action to move in your desired direction in the physical world.

Inspired Action
Bear in mind that taking action does not suggest that you must run around in a frenzied state doing anything and everything that pops into your head in an attempt to try force the outcome you intend as quickly as possible. The key is to take inspired action. Put simply, inspired action is born out of *knowing* your next step by listening to your intuition and engaging your reasoning mind. At the same time it means taking *no* action when you find yourself emotionally overwhelmed, for instance, at times of over-excitement or anger.

Emotional extremes can be very motivating, but remember that they deny you objectivity. And in the absence of objectivity, you significantly increase the chances of taking miscalculated actions that do not serve you or your goal, and that you will later regret.

Finally, inspired action also includes taking a break to rest, unwind, and replenish your reserves. Remember that taking action is just as important as relaxing, but ensure that your action determines or directs your relaxation and not the other way around. If you sit around doing nothing waiting for the inspiration to do something, it seldom, if ever, comes.

THE REACTION TO YOUR ACTION

Recall that the Law of Rhythm and the Principle of Balance state that any action gives rise to an opposite reaction, as is also affirmed by Isaac Newton's Third Law of Motion. This means that the physical actions you take *will* give rise to opposite reactions in the physical world. And reactions are usually experienced as outer world obstacles or resistance. This is not the Universe's way of sabotaging you or testing your resolve. You must understand that it is *your activity* that creates the opposite reaction that presents itself as resistance.

In fact, resistance in reaction to any action taken is how nature works. For instance, without air resistance an airplane could not stay airborne and birds could not fly. This means that resistance is *necessary* in order for the actions you take to yield the results you desire. Learning to see obstacles or resistance as nature's way of actually *getting* you where you want to go rather than *stopping* you, enables you to work with the obstacles you will face on your path, rather than fight them.

Lessons from Aerodynamics

The mechanics of aerodynamics are a perfect analogy for the actions you take, and the resistance to your actions in the physical world, as was explained by John McDonald in The Message of a Master.

In aerodynamics, the term 'thrust' is analogous to action and the term 'drag' is analogous to reaction. Thrust is generated by the propeller of an airplane. The thrust *opposes* the drag that is caused by air *resistance* to the front part of the airplane. In drawing an analogy with your goals or desires, the airplane can be likened to your goal, the thrust is the action you take, and the drag is the resistance you must overcome in your outer physical world.

In aerodynamics, the thrust of the propeller must *overcome* the resistance of the drag during takeoff in order for the airplane to become airborne. In the same way, your actions must overcome the resistance you face in the outer world for your goal to be attained. In level flight when constant speed is achieved, thrust *exactly equals* drag and the airplane remains airborne without having to exert excess thrust. In the same way, once you attain your goal, your actions then naturally equal the resistance you face so that you no longer have to overcome excess resistance, which means you will have overcome your obstacles. This is what is meant by the saying 'to be in the flow', where everything just seems effortless.

Incidentally, if you want to land a plane then thrust (action) is reduced below the level of drag (resistance). In the same way, you can send your goals into a crash landing if you let the resistance you face overpower the actions you take. This is why persistence is such an important determining factor in your success. To persist is to keep on taking *extra* action until resistance is overcome and your goal is attained. Thereafter, you continue to take mental and physical actions but your actions serve to sustain what you have achieved rather than to overcome resistance.

Do Not Resist Resistance

If you label the physical actions you take as good and the resistance you face as bad, you resign yourself to not overcoming the obstacles and hence not attaining your goal. The question is not whether or not you will face resistance or obstacles. You *will*. And the bigger your goal, the *greater* the resistance you are likely to face, in the same way a Boeing 747 needs to overcome more drag than a light aircraft. It is *what* you do when faced with obstacles that matters and the simplest answer is not to resist them because 'what you resist persists'.

Resisting obstacles is akin to *adding* to the drag your plane faces while also *reducing* the thrust and still expecting to take flight. When dealing with obstacles work with, through, and around them, but do not resist them or wonder why the Universe is thwarting your plans. Working *with* an obstacle is to be willing to adjust your plans accordingly if called for, working *through* an obstacle is to persist in the actions you take, and working *around* an obstacle is to look for a solution to help you move past it.

When you know that resistance in reaction to your actions is the way nature works, and is in fact *necessary* to your success, then you treat obstacles with the same respect that you do your actions. In so doing, you perceive resistance as proof that your intended outcome is on its way, rather than evidence that your efforts are just not working.

Remember always that things are seldom what they seem, and obstacles are in fact sign posts on your way to success.

Do not confuse the process with the outcome. This means that during the *process* of attaining any goal, you will encounter problems, resistance, and even some disappointments, all of which may confuse you and cause you to doubt your ability, yet are necessary to get you to your intended outcome. If you confuse the *process* with the *outcome* and give in to the obstacles, you are effectively switching off the lights of the lampposts that are guiding your way. Persist, be patient, and allow for things to clear up. As Lao Tzu said, "Do you have the patience to wait until your mud settles and the water is clear?"

THE GREAT ADVENTURE OF LIFE

Life is a wonderful adventure. In any adventure, you set out with a sense of purpose and do your best to direct your course while not always knowing what to expect. You do, however, know full well that there will be obstacles along the way to overcome. The thought of the obstacles, however, do not frighten you but rather they entice you. Indeed, if adventures were plain-sailing without a single obstacle, there would be no sense of achievement. In the same way, wherever possible endeavour to let the obstacles you face in life add to your enjoyment and not take away from it.

Treat your experience of reality as the Great Adventure of Life, and heed the words of the Little Prince, from Antoine de Saint-Exupéry's book of the same name, that "what makes the desert beautiful is that somewhere it hides a well." Instead of labelling the obstacles on your path as 'problems', see them as intriguing puzzles that are waiting to be solved, knowing that all puzzles must have a solution. Sometimes the solution comes to you in a moment of doing nothing and other times in a moment of doing something. As long as you believe there is a solution, the solution will be made apparent to you, but at the same time be content with not having all the answers.

Problems are indeed life's puzzles. Hidden within every problem therefore, is its own solution because in order for something to be a problem it must have the seed of its opposite within it, which is its solution. Just like every mathematical problem has its solution, so life's problems have theirs. This means you must look *within* your problems to find their solutions, rather than looking outside of them.

The Art of Making Mistakes

Become skilled at the art of making mistakes and at the art of correcting them. In life, there is no such thing as failure. There is only feedback. When you stop beating yourself up about the mistakes of the past, you will realise that they have brought you closer to where you want to be, even if only by letting you know what you should not do in order to get there. In contrast, the more you focus on your mistakes or perceived failures with guilt or self-recrimination, the more likely you are to repeat them in time. Accept your mistakes, learn from them, correct them wherever possible, and let them go. In so doing, you will find your mistakes transforming from a jailer that keeps you captive, into the friend who gives you the prison door key.

Incidentally, the word 'error' has its origin in the Latin word *errorem* meaning 'to wander or to stray'. To make an error therefore can be likened to wandering off your path. By keeping your path in mind, however, and recalling the steps you took, you can and do find your way again. But bear in mind that sometimes wandering off a certain path opens you up to a whole new world of opportunity to explore. Trust life, flow with change and travel lightly by letting things go. If you fall, pick yourself up, dust yourself off, take a break whenever necessary, and then carry on.

If what you are looking for is a problem-free and mistake-free life, all you have to do is get rid of all of your goals and all of your desires. This affords you with a more permanent sense of inner balance and if this is what you desire then by all means do so.

Having said this, it is human nature to set goals and have desires, and the higher the nature of your aspirations, the higher you raise yourself upwards in degree of positivity. Indeed, it is an inner Spiritual desire that urges the self-conscious man to raise himself to elevated heights of positivity. Heed these words from a poem by an unknown author, "As I sail through change, my resolve remains the same. What I *choose* are magic moments. Ships are safe in the harbour but that is not what ships are made for."

REALITY CREATION MANAGEMENT

Making and adhering to a plan of action is the key to completing any project. Having said this, most people fail to make a plan for the single most important project of all, which is their own life. In the same way that a skilled project manager creates a project plan for the project at hand, you must become the manager of your life. The most effective way to do so is to make and adhere to a plan for whatever it is you intend to create and experience in your life.

Think about it this way - when you set out to attain any goal, any action you take moves you either *towards* its attainment or *away* from it. And the easiest way to determine if you are heading in the right direction, and to keep on doing so, is to create a *plan* of action *before* taking action. A plan can be likened to a map that enables you to navigate unchartered territory. Without one you are unlikely to get very far, whereas with one you know where you are heading and also if you are on or off track. Planning also enables you to predict some of the possible obstacles that you may encounter, and in this way you can prepare for them ahead of time or even prevent them.

Put simply, a plan of action includes specific steps that take you towards your ideal outcome, specific time frames for each step, how to implement each step, an evaluation of external factors that you could reasonably encounter, and regular evaluation of your progress. Having no definite plan or vision for your life usually leaves you aimlessly wandering about. Having said this, as is the case in all things, strike a balance between planning your life while also allowing it to flow effortlessly. To make a plan is not about being in control of everything, but rather it affords you with a sense of direction of where you want to go. And as the saying goes, 'if you do not know where you are heading, you will land up where you are headed'.

APPLICATION UNLOCKS THE POWER OF KNOWLEDGE

In closing this chapter on taking action and dealing with reaction, it must be said that you *must* apply the knowledge you gain in this book in order to gain its rewards. Carefully read this excerpt from The Kybalion: "The possession of Knowledge, unless accompanied by a manifestation and expression in Action, is like the hoarding of precious metals - a vain and foolish thing. Knowledge, like Wealth, is intended for Use. The Law of Use is Universal, and he who violates it suffers by reason of his conflict with natural forces."

One Step at a Time

Most people, when first introduced to the idea of conscious reality creation, want to 'change it all' and they want to 'change it now'. As is the case however with any new tool you use, you must first learn to use this knowledge wisely and take it one step at a time. The most effective way to learn something is to start at the beginning and, as Lao Tzu told us, "the journey of a thousand miles begins with a single step." Do not be in a hurry to change your life overnight. If you are too eager to run before you walk, then you are likely to stumble. And it is not the getting up that is the problem, as much as it is the probability that you will begin to question this knowledge and your power to direct your mind. Do not let this happen.

Be wise and guard yourself against unreasonable haste. Indeed, 'great haste makes for great waste' and paradoxically, the slower you take things, the faster you will find your life changing in the ways you desire it to. The Greek philosopher Plato said that "the penalty of *too much haste* is *too little speed*."

Having said this, taking it slow or not rushing, does not mean putting it off, not taking it seriously, or applying the knowledge half-heartedly. It simply means being patient, taking it one step at a time, and learning to direct your mind *first*. Be very certain that if you want to *create* your life *before* you make the effort to *direct* your mind, your circumstances will remain very little changed.

Warning: Danger Zone

When you first set out to apply this knowledge, the chances are you will still be operating more at the level of the counterfeit ego than the Real Ego. For this reason, be wary of your counterfeit ego grabbing this knowledge as just another one of its many futile tricks to stay in control. To guard you from this, here are some tell-tale signs that you are operating from the counterfeit ego and not the Real Ego.

You try to control everything in your life, including other people, and wonder why your world is not yielding to your command. You blame yourself for what does or does not show up in your life, and even in the life of others, and tell yourself that it is your fault. One moment you are feeling empowered and nothing can stand in your way, and the next you are feeling powerless and tell yourself 'you will never get this right' or 'none of this works'. You over-think and over-analyse every thought, emotion, and experience. And finally, you live in your mental world so much that you stop truly *living* life, which really amounts to living in a fantasy world with no real intention of directing your mind or creating your life.

If you recognise yourself in any of these descriptions, there is no need to be discouraged. Simply take a break from it all, let it go, re-group, and come back to it later. It is far better to live in ignorance of this knowledge than to mentally torment yourself in this way. Your intention is to direct your mind and consciously create your life, while also allowing life to *flow*, and trusting it to take you where you are supposed to go. Endeavour therefore, to strike a balance between becoming the master of your mind and joyfully participating in your life *as it is*. Remember, being happy is not so much about changing everything as it is about changing how you *perceive* everything, while knowing that nothing is permanent. As Wayne Dyer said, "change the way you look at things and the things you look at change."

PART VI
PRACTICAL CONSCIOUS CREATION

Chapter 37
THE POWER OF MEDITATION

Meditation is the single most powerful technique that you can use to raise your degree of consciousness and self-awareness. Put simply, it is the involvement of your mind for a specific purpose, while in a calm and relaxed mental and physical state. The recorded use of meditation dates back thousands of years, and interestingly the words 'meditation' and 'medication' are very closely related in their etymologies. Indeed, meditation is the most self-healing medication available to mankind, and its results range from the ordinary to the miraculous, depending on what you use it for and how you apply it.

DISPELLING MEDITATION MYTHS
Most people wrongly associate meditation with being a difficult and boring practice with little practical benefit, reserved mainly for monks and other deeply spiritual human beings. The truth, however, is that meditation is a natural practice and for the most part quite simple. It has a number of scientifically proven physical and mental benefits, and is available to every human being as the single most fulfilling mental method for raising one's degree of positivity.

Benefits of Meditation
Some medically documented health benefits of meditation include significant stress reduction, marked improvements in the quality of sleep, a more positive mental disposition, a significant decrease in the aging process, an increase in physical and mental energy levels, and immune system enhancement. Although not as well documented, but still most definitely worth noting, other meditation benefits include healing yourself and others, self-protection, and conscious creation through visualisation, as you will learn in the chapters that follow.

RELAXATION FOR MEDITATION
The first step in meditating for any purpose is mental and physical relaxation. Bear in mind that the relaxation exercise described here

explains how to enter the 'relaxed meditative state' referred to in the various practical techniques described in this book.

Body Position

You can relax for meditation while sitting on a chair, sitting on the floor, or lying down. If you choose to sit in a chair, sit upright and adjust your body into a comfortable position, with your feet flat on the floor, your back supported by the chair, and your hands resting lightly on your lap. If you prefer to sit on the floor it is preferable that you sit on a soft carpet or mat. Sit with your back upright but not tense, legs crossed and your hands resting gently on your thighs.

Alternatively, lie down flat on your back with your arms resting to your side. Be aware that if you lie down, you may find that you drift off to sleep, which is fine if your intention is simply to relax ahead of sleeping. But if not, it is best to sit upright for meditation.

Breathing

Deep *rhythmic* breathing is the most effective way to relax, especially since it creates a connection between your self-conscious and sub-conscious mind. To breathe rhythmically, start by inhaling slowly and deeply through your nose to a mental count of four. As you do so, feel your lungs and diaphragm gently expand. To assist you in deep breathing, it is best to feel you are inhaling from your diaphragm and not from the back of your throat. Hold your breath for a moment and then slowly exhale through your mouth, again to a mental count of four. As you do, feel your lungs emptying and your diaphragm returning to its normal position. Continue to breathe rhythmically in this way, by mentally counting to four as you inhale and again to four as you exhale, while keeping an even tempo or rhythm.

Counting Backwards

When you have reached an even tempo of inhaling and exhaling, each to the count of four, begin to count backwards slowly from 40 to 1. With every descending number, feel yourself relaxing further. With practice, as you become more accustomed to relaxing, you can reduce the number you count down from to 20 or 10. With enough practice you will be able to enter a relaxed meditative state at will, any place and any time you choose, without any countdown.

Relax Your Body

As you count backwards, relax each part of your body in turn. Start with the top of your head, forehead, eyes, and face. Next work downwards to your shoulders, chest area, arms, hands, and fingers, then your stomach, pelvis, thighs, knees, and calves, and finally your ankles, feet, and toes. Do not *think* about relaxing your body as this causes mental tension. Simply release any tension that is being held in each part of your body and relax your muscles. Feel soft waves of relaxation washing over your entire body from head to toe until such time that your body feels so relaxed that it would take conscious effort for you to move any part of it.

Relax Your Mind

To relax your mind, simply place your attention on your breathing without strain. Observe your breathing. Thoughts or worries may race through your mind but do not fight or resist them. Simply let them float away without giving them your attention and you will find that in time such uncontrolled thoughts will become fewer and fewer.

Remember to focus on your breathing but again do not *think* about doing it. Endeavour to get out of your *thinking* head area, and enter the stillness found in your heart area. If you find your mind wandering or focusing on your thoughts, then gently bring your focus back to your breathing. When both your body and mind are relaxed you can then begin the meditation technique of your choice, whether it is visualisation, self-healing, or something else.

Practice Makes Perfect

I recommend you first practice this relaxation technique alone a number of times, until you can enter a relaxed meditative state with relative ease. This will make it much easier for you to combine it with techniques such as visualisation, rather than having to *try* so hard to relax that you never quite get around to doing the technique itself. You may already have your own preferred relaxation technique and by all means use the one that works best for you.

THE TWO DIRECTIONS OF MEDITATION

There are two main directions in which you can use meditation. The first is *contractive* or inwards, and the second is *expansive* or outwards. Both are equally important to each other and offer balance to your meditation sessions, which brings your efforts into greater alignment with the balance the Universe seeks. I coined the terms Contractive and Expansive Meditation because I believe that they most accurately describe the meditation process for conscious creation. They were inspired by Walter Russell's 1950 Home Study Course. I will briefly describe them here but their application and relevance will become much clearer to you in Chapter 40 on visualisation.

Contractive Meditation

Contractive Meditation is to focus *inwards*. It means to concentrate on a single point or idea. In the context of visualisation for conscious creation, it is about *exclusively* concentrating on the mental image of your desire. You *contract* your mental focus inwards as if the power of the entire Universe were concentrated in your single mental image.

Remember the word 'concentrate' literally means 'the action of bringing something to its centre'. Another way therefore of looking at Contractive Meditation in the context of visualisation, is the action of concentrating on the mental image of your desire as if it were at the very centre of the Universe, which from your perspective, it is. Think about it this way - since from your perspective you are at the *centre* of the infinite Universal Mind, and your mental image is your *only* focus at the time, then the mental image itself is at the centre of Universal Mind because all your awareness is concentrated within it.

Expansive Meditation

Expansive Meditation is the opposite of Contractive Meditation. It is to expand your consciousness outwards *without* concentrating on *anything*. The following description provides you with a visual idea of what Expansive Meditation is.

First become aware of your body, wherever you are physically. Without focusing on anything specific, expand your consciousness outwards to *include* the room or area you are in. Expand it further to include the house or building you are in. Continue to expand your consciousness further beyond the walls, trees, mountains, oceans, and the atmosphere until the entire planet and Solar System is captured within your consciousness.

Sense your consciousness continuing to expand further until you can no longer see anything but the emptiness of space. Notice also how you can continue to indefinitely expand your consciousness without ever meeting a point beyond which you cannot extend it further. And the more you do so, without focusing on anything, the more you enter the *nothingness* of infinite empty space and *silence*.

You will notice that your awareness is at the very centre of this infinite expansion of your consciousness. And when you *remove* your awareness from the 'you' in the centre, you then merge *with* the nothingness and silence, and your consciousness *becomes* infinite Universal Consciousness. This description gives you a clear idea of Expansive Meditation. Visualising what has been written here in a relaxed meditative state is very powerful for experiencing mental silence when accessing your intuition (Ch. 33). The main point of

Expansive Meditation is to *not* focus on anything and ultimately to let your awareness merge with silence and nothingness. In the context of visualisation for conscious creation, Expansive Meditation is about *releasing* the mental image of your desire from your concentration, into the infinite Universal Mind, as you will learn in Chapter 40.

Lessons from a Wind-Up Toy

To gain a better understanding of these two directions of meditation, it is helpful to think of your mind as the spring inside a wind-up toy. Contractive Meditation feels like winding your mind inwards to a single point and holding it there, as you would do when winding up a toy. In contrast, Expansive Meditation feels like unwinding your mind back outwards, which can be likened to *releasing* the turn-key of the wind-up toy from your hand.

When playing with a wind-up toy, you exert physical *effort* to wind it up, but *none* to unwind it. In the context of imagining your ideal, you exert mental effort to concentrate or wind your mind inwards to a single point of focus, which is the mental image of your ideal.

When you are done concentrating, you unwind your mind by *releasing* all mental effort, which is simply a case of letting your mental image go and is akin to sending it outwards to Universal Mind in order for it to be created. Put simply, you first concentrate on a mental image of your desire and then you release it. This will be discussed in more detail in Chapter 40 on visualisation.

INSTRUCTIONS FOR MEDITATION

Select a quiet place for your meditation time where you will not be interrupted. When you first learn to meditate, it is helpful to use the same seat, place, or bed, to allow your brain to associate it with relaxation and meditation, and hence make it easier for you to enter into the desired mental state. It is also preferable whenever possible, to silence your phone and switch off any equipment that may disturb you. Moreover, ask any people that may be present in your home not to disturb you, unless of course it is an emergency.

Before You Go to Sleep

It is best to meditate before you go to sleep, even if just to relax, unwind, and still your mind after your day's activities. In this way you enhance the effectiveness of your meditation on your subjective subconscious mind, as it will have the ability to absorb the message or feeling of the meditation all through the night while your objective mind is asleep. For the same reason, however, be mindful of the thoughts you think, what you read, what you watch on television, or what you listen to before going to sleep, because that too will be your sub-conscious mind's focus for the next few hours while you are asleep, without any way for you to consciously intercept its focus.

A SHORT LESSON IN BRAINWAVES

An interesting subject to consider in the context of meditation is how it relates to the activity of your brain. As is the case with everything in the Universe, every part of your body, including your brain, vibrates to its own rhythm. Your brain has its own unique set of brainwaves and each set corresponds to a specific rate of vibration or frequency range that is measured in cycles per second (Hz) by EEG recorders. EEG stands for electroencephalography, which literally means a recording of the electric activity of the head or brain.

In neuroscience, the human brain's brainwave ranges are referred to as Gamma, Beta, Alpha, Theta, and Delta Levels, in order of *highest* to *lowest* frequency. Moreover, each brainwave range has its own set of characteristics that represents a specific level of brain activity and hence a unique state of consciousness or level of mind.

Gamma Level (25 - 100Hz)

The Gamma Level of mind has only recently been measured with the introduction of digital EEG recorders. Gamma brainwaves have the highest frequencies and are in the range of 25-100Hz, with 40Hz being the average measured in human beings.

Research shows that higher Gamma frequencies are associated with bursts of profound insight, high-level information processing, peak mental and physical performance, as well as with higher degrees of will power, self-discipline, and overall mental positivity. Higher levels of Gamma frequencies can therefore be said to be associated with higher degrees of positivity.

Beta Level (12 - 25Hz)

The Beta brainwave frequency range is 12-25Hz and is associated with normal waking consciousness, including alertness, objectivity, and critical reasoning. Ordinary daily activities are performed at the Beta Level of mind. It is also linked to heightened levels of stress and anxiety. The Beta brainwave range is associated with the objective self-conscious level of mind.

Alpha Level (7.5 - 12Hz)

The Alpha brainwave frequency range is between 7.5 and 12Hz and occurs during periods of relaxation with one's eyes usually closed or while daydreaming. A light meditative sate of relaxation, in which a person is relaxed but still aware of his surroundings, is characteristic of the Alpha Level. It is associated with heightened imagination and mental imagery, as well as memory recall.

The Alpha Level is the brainwave frequency range between the self-conscious and sub-conscious mind, and so is said to be the gateway between the two. For this reason, lower Alpha frequencies are optimal for visualisation. The more relaxed you feel mentally and physically, while still being able to consciously direct your thoughts, the greater your capacity to directly engage with and impress your creative sub-conscious mind at will.

Bear in mind that watching television induces the Alpha Level, which explains why people are easily conditioned in accordance with what they watch on television. This is why you should not have a television in your bedroom and nor should you fall asleep while watching it, more so if you are watching the news or a disturbing movie. Television sets the tone for your sub-conscious mind's operations while you are watching it and even more so if you fall asleep. For this reason either watch television with your full attention or limit your viewing to a bare minimum, or none at all.

Theta Level (4 - 7.5Hz)
The Theta brainwave frequency range is between 4 and 7.5Hz and is present during deep meditation and light sleep, which includes the REM (rapid eye movement) dream state. Theta Level is associated with the sub-conscious mind and is also known as the twilight state because it is normally measured when one drifts off to sleep from the Alpha Level or arises from an even deeper dreamless sleep, which is the Delta Level.

Mental silence and physical stillness is experienced at higher Theta frequencies, as well as more vivid visualisations or so-called visions, provided one is able to remain self-aware at this level. The deeper you relax, while remaining consciously aware, the more you approach the Theta Level, but too much relaxation could cause you to fall asleep.

Delta Level (0.5 - 4Hz)
The Delta frequency of brainwaves is the slowest at between 0.5 and 4Hz. It is present in deep dreamless sleep where one is completely detached from any sense of self-awareness. The Delta Level is said to be the *unconscious* mind and it is also associated with deep healing and regeneration, which underpins the importance of deep sleep for any healing process.

THE I OF THE EGO MEDITATION

'The I of the Ego' is a very powerful meditation that will perhaps for the first time allow you to establish a direct, positive realisation that you are not your body or your personality, but that your Real Self is superior to and master of both. Repeat this meditation at least once a week or more often if preferred. Each time you repeat it you will find your identification with the I within becoming stronger. It is arguably the most important of all the exercises in this book as it enables you to *feel* what it means to *be* the I within.

Guided Description

In a relaxed meditative state, mentally scan your body up and down, slowly and with your full attention. As you do so, sense how there is a distinct someone that is doing the scanning. This someone doing the thinking is your Real Self - the I within.

Mentally send your attention to your feet. Sense how, although they are your feet and are necessary to your physical experience, if they were not attached to your body, the someone within who is doing the thinking, would be unaffected. You can repeat this exercise with other parts of your body, as well as with your vital organs.

Next, imagine yourself exiting your physical body and studying it from the outside. Realise how essential your body is to your physical existence but also how it is distinctly separate from the you that is looking at it from the outside.

Next, ask yourself 'Who am I?' The first thing that may come to mind is your name, age and certain personality traits. Imagine having another name or another age, and again notice how that someone within who is doing the thinking remains unaffected by any name or any age you may choose.

Think of your strengths and weaknesses. Mentally set them aside one by one and notice how the thinker within is undisturbed. Get a real sense of how your strengths and weaknesses do not belong to you in any real way. Repeat this exercise for your likes and dislikes, and other personality traits, as well as for your desires and fears.

You will notice that the more you set aside your personality traits, likes and dislikes, and desires, the more the someone within, who is doing the thinking, persists in full force and even feels stronger.

Next, imagine yourself acting out a specific role, for instance that of an actor in your favourite movie or of someone you admire in life, irrespective of whether they are male and you are female, or vice versa. Notice how you can play any role just as well as you play your own role in life, and that again the someone within who is doing the thinking is unchanged and unaffected.

Next, mentally say the words 'I AM' with a calm authoritative voice. Mentally repeat 'I AM' three times, slowly and deliberately. Notice how saying 'I AM' strengthens the I.

To end the meditation, be still in the silence and let yourself mentally float in the awareness of being defined by nothing. Feel the sense of inner peace and strength of being the I - the Observer. Sense how you have complete directive power over your mind, personality, thoughts, desires, and emotions, and at the same time, how none of them can define you.

Whenever you feel ready to do so, gently bring yourself out of the meditative state by counting upwards from 1 to 5, feeling wide awake, alert and better than before with every ascending number.

MEDITATION IN PRACTICE

Having looked at the basics of meditation, as well as the very powerful 'I of the Ego' exercise, the next few chapters teach you how to practically apply meditation for a specific purpose. You will learn how to increase your Life Force, self-protection, visualisation, auto-suggestions for impressing your subjective mind, and mental healing.

You may be tempted to dive straight into these techniques but you will save yourself many hours of frustration by *first* training your mind to follow your will's direction. To do so, use the exercises outlined earlier in the book and spend 30-40 days mastering concentration, self-discipline, awakening your will, and training your imagination through mental imagery, as well as the relaxation technique described in this chapter.

THE 40-DAY RULE

A common question that arises in conscious reality creation, is how long does it take? Since your experience of reality is a projection of your consciousness, a more accurate question is, how long does it take to create a lasting change in your consciousness? Although there is no definite answer, a time frame referred to in some metaphysical texts is 40 days. This means the *minimum time* required for conscious creation in the Physical Plane is 40 days.

Interestingly, 40 days for major transformation is a theme found in religious and sacred texts and in cultural traditions. It is considered to be the number of *completion*. For instance, the 40 days of Moses on Mount Sinai, the 40 days of Jesus in the desert, the 40 days of the Buddha's meditation under the bodhi tree, 40 days of fasting, 40 days of mourning, and in some cultures, 40 days must pass before a newborn baby leaves its home for the first time.

The 40-Day Conscious Creation Plan
Make 40 days a rule when it comes to conscious creation. This means once you have chosen your single desire, create a 40 day plan, which includes *both* visualising and using auto-suggestions aimed at your desire for 40 days. Visualise and use auto-suggestions every day for 40 days *continuously*. Do not skip one day, and if you do, start again. Keep a brief journal to keep track of your progress but make sure you keep it, and your mental efforts, private.

Bear in mind that the 40 days, in this context, aim for a shift in your *consciousness* and therefore need not include taking physical action if there is no action to take at the time. If after 40 days there is no change in your conditions, then continue until there is, provided it is still important enough to you, and also take all necessary physical action where appropriate.

Chapter 38

INCREASING YOUR LIFE FORCE

Life Force is the force behind the creation of all things and is what sustains the Universe. In other words, Life Force or energy is the *limitless* living force of Universal Mind through which undifferentiated potential *energy* is differentiated into actualised form. Since everything is consciousness, then your energy is also part of this Universal Life Force, and how you use it depends on your degree of positivity.

PERSONAL LIFE FORCE

Optimal levels of personal Life Force are necessary to keep you mentally and physically healthy in the Physical Plane. Any physical or mental action you take uses up your personal reserves of Life Force, which explains why it is essential that you get adequate amounts of sleep to replenish your energy. At the same time, however, it is never advisable to overload your system with Life Force as it is very much a *force* in the same way that electricity is.

Having said this, most people are faced with the problem of too *little* Life Force, not too much. If you spend most of your day feeling mentally and physically lethargic, your personal energy reserves are running low. The most common reasons behind low energy levels are worry, stress, over-work, idle thinking, emotional overwhelm, and ordinary daily activities. Moreover, there is little or no consideration for *intentionally* replenishing your energy reserves other than through sleep, which itself is usually restless and not sound enough to provide you with adequate Life Force reserves.

Learn to Access Universal Life Force

The key is to learn how to *directly* access Universal Life Force in order to supplement, replenish, and increase your personal reserves, which you can then use for any purpose you choose. The Universal supply of Life Force is limitless. It is the *only* source of your own energy reserves and you have direct access to it. With this in mind, you guard yourself from arrogantly believing your power originates in you personally, and instead have reverence for The Absolute as the Single Source of all Universal Life Force.

By learning how to receive Universal Life Force *intentionally*, you are able to replenish and raise your energy levels at will, and also let it flow through you to everything and everyone around you. You must also train yourself not to dissipate or waste your stores of energy on negative thinking, stress, and fears. Instead, you can use it wisely, for instance by directing it to the mental images of your desires through concentration, which is the basis of visualisation (Ch. 40).

We will now consider four very powerful exercises for increasing your Life Force, but bear in mind that no method, no matter how powerful, is intended to replace adequate amounts of sound sleep on a daily basis. Sleep is not only important to your Life Force reserves, but is fundamental to deep cellular regeneration and healing.

1. MINDFUL EATING

Although it is obvious that food gives us energy that we use to carry out physical and mental tasks, very few people maximise their ability to increase their Life Force through eating. What the 'right foods' are, is beyond the scope of this book, but it is obvious that food in as natural and raw a form as possible can provide you with far greater energy than those foods that have had their energy literally cooked.

By following the simple set of instructions for mindful eating outlined below, you will experience a significant increase in your daily energy levels. You will also find that you make naturally healthier food choices by choosing more nutritional food over food that has been made to taste artificially good and addictive, yet offers you little or no nutritional value.

Instructions for Mindful Eating

Say grace or in other words, give thanks for the food that you are about to eat. In so doing, you bless both the food that is giving you its energy, and yourself that is receiving it. There is no need to say grace aloud and it can be as simple as mentally saying, 'thank you for the food that I am about to eat'.

Importantly, do not eat in an emotionally charged state because otherwise you will charge your meal with your emotions and hence amplify them within you. If you feel stress, go for a walk or do something to release that stress before you sit down to your meal.

Moreover, eat consciously by paying attention to how and what you are eating. Endeavour to distinguish the taste of the variety of foods you eat, and also how the food makes your body feel after you have eaten it. Eat slowly and deliberately, put your utensils down between each mouthful or your sandwich down between each bite, and chew your food very thoroughly. Get out of the fast food habit of eating on the run. Instead, get into the habit of seeing your meal time as a sacred time during which you nourish your body that houses your Spirit.

2. THE STAR EXERCISE

The second technique for increasing your Life Force reserves is a physical technique called the Star Exercise. It is wholly based on the technique of the same name from Eugene Fersen's 1927 book, The Science of Being - Twenty Seven Lessons. The following instructions have been paraphrased from this seminal work on consciousness.

This exercise is an easy, physical method for directly accessing Universal Life Force. It works automatically by virtue of the Law of Attraction without any need on your part to believe that it works. The more you do it, the more you will benefit, as it helps restore both your physical and mental balance. Rest assured that the Life Force goes precisely where it is needed naturally and without any need for your conscious input. Although not necessary, it is preferable to do the Star Exercise outside or near a window to benefit from fresh air, and to wear comfortable clothing with no shoes. Moreover, it is best to do it on an empty or near empty stomach. The exercise is done standing up, but if for whatever reason you cannot stand upright, you can equally benefit from the exercise by doing it lying down or sitting on a chair, and assuming the same position as will now be described.

Instructions for the Star Exercise

Stand upright with legs shoulder-width apart, your arms outstretched to the sides at shoulder level, with your *left* palm facing *upwards* and your *right* palm facing *downwards*, and your head facing forwards. This is the Star Position and it opens you up to effortlessly receiving and transmitting Universal Life Force.

Incidentally, the reason the left palm faces upwards and the right palm downwards is because the left palm *receives* energy, which then flows throughout your body, and the right palm *gives* out surplus energy once the body has received all that it needs. In fact, this is why religious figures depicted in an image or statue usually have their left palm facing upwards and right palm downwards, which is the gesture of blessing someone or something.

While in the Star Position, relax your body and release any tension you may feel. Breathe deeply by inhaling through your nose and exhaling through your mouth. If your arms feel tired or heavy do not strain to keep them up. You can slowly lower them while maintaining the direction of your palms to maintain the energy flow. Slowly raise your arms again to their original position once rested. Although not necessary to *physically* receiving Life Force, you can add a *mental* element to this exercise by attuning your senses to feeling the energy flowing through your body and mentally saying to yourself, 'I am one with Universal Life Energy, it is flowing through me now. I feel it'.

For the first month, Eugene Fersen instructed that one is to perform the Star Exercise twice a day and for no more than three to five minutes each time. The recommended times are upon getting up in the morning, and just before going to sleep. As you become accustomed to the inflow of Universal Life Force you can increase both the duration and number of times you perform it. By making the Star Exercise part of your daily routine, you will enjoy immeasurable mental and physical benefits and in so doing, increase your degree of positivity.

3. POWER WORDS

This technique is based on John McDonald's book The Message of a Master and involves a set of so-called Power Words. By focusing on the following words, you transfer the power each word holds to your subjective mind, which serves to raise your Life Force and positivity.

Selection of Power Words
PEACE - POISE - JOY - LOVE - HARMONY - KINDNESS - JUSTICE
WISDOM - GRATITUDE - SILENCE - FLOW - FAITH - BALANCE
INSPIRATION - PERSISTENCE - ACHIEVEMENT - CONFIDENCE
ATTAINMENT - ATTENTION - ALERTNESS - CONCENTRATION
UNDERSTANDING - INTELLIGENCE - KNOWLEDGE - MEMORY
LAW AND ORDER - PURPOSE - SUCCESS - STRENGTH - LIFE
ACTIVITY - SPIRIT - ENERGY - HEALTH - VITALITY - YOUTH
OPTIMISM - WILL - SELF-DISCIPLINE - DOMINION - POWER
GUIDANCE - MASTERY - CHOICE - DIRECTION - PROTECTION
CREATE - EFFICIENCY - HAPPINESS - POSITIVITY - FREEDOM

Instructions for Power Words
Set half an hour to one hour aside every evening for this technique or whenever you feel your energy levels are low. Choose a quiet place where you will not be disturbed. The right attitude for this exercise is to be mentally calm without focusing on your body, thoughts, or worries. Focus on each word separately or choose those words you feel meet your needs at the time. Sense the meaning of each word. Visualise what it symbolises for you rather than its general definition, and endeavour to *feel* its effect on your mental state. Each word acts as nourishment to your mind, just as food does to your body. And the inherent power of each world will continue to yield positive effects at

all levels even after the exercise has been completed. If your mind wanders, as it is likely to do at first, gently bring your attention back to the exercise and continue with it. There is no need to strain to do this or any other exercise.

Do not, however, use these words as affirmations because they are likely to raise mental resistance. For instance, do not say 'I am Love' unless you are feeling positive at the time and have full conviction in what you are saying. It is best that you focus on the word Love alone, and to visualise and feel what it means to you. Finally, if English is not your mother tongue, translate the words into your language of preference, and feel free to add other words which resonate with you.

4. PSYCHIC ENERGY MEDITATION

The final method for increasing your Life Force reserves is a meditation based entirely on Joseph J. Weed's 1970 book, Psychic Energy. Bear in mind that the term 'Psychic Energy' is an alternative for Universal Life Force. You can do the meditation described here every day upon waking up, before going to sleep, or whenever it intuitively feels right for you to do so. It is very powerful and its benefits are immediate, long lasting, and cumulative.

Instructions for Increasing Psychic Energy

The first step is to enter into a relaxed, meditative state while sitting on a chair, on the floor, or lying down, as described in Chapter 37. It is recommended that you breathe normally for this exercise *without* giving attention to your breathing.

When mentally and physically relaxed, turn your attention to your heart area. Mentally visualise your heart emanating a pink light, similar to the light of a pink-tinted light bulb, only brighter and more brilliant - hold this image for a mental count of 9. Next, transfer your attention from your heart to the top of your head carrying with you the pink light emanating from your heart and see it as a sphere of pink light resting immediately above your head like a cloud - hold this image for a mental count of 15. Then visualise this pink coloured cloud growing in size, larger and larger as it gradually envelops your whole body, just as if you were sitting in a radiating, egg-shaped pink cloud - hold this image for a mental count of 12.

Now, shift your focus to the vicinity of your throat and visualise a brilliant blue light emanating from your throat centre, and hold this image for a mental count of 9. Next, transfer your attention to the top of your head taking this blue radiant light with you and see it as a brilliant blue sphere hovering immediately over your head - hold this image for a mental count of 15. Then mentally see the ball of blue light begin to expand until you are completely bathed in a shining blue light - hold this image for a mental count of 12.

Now, visualise a brilliant white light radiating outwards from your forehead from a point between your eyebrows - hold this image for a mental count of 9. Next, transfer your attention to the top of your head taking this white light with you and seeing it rest as a sphere above your head - hold this image for a mental count of 15. Next, mentally see this ball of white light expanding until it envelops you entirely - hold this image for a mental count of 12.

To complete this meditation, with your eyes closed, sit quietly for a few moments in the knowledge that you have started great forces in motion. Consciously feel the Universal Life Force as it flows through your body and let your awareness merge with it. Finally, slowly bring yourself out of a meditative state by counting upwards from 1 to 5, feeling more alert and wide-awake with every ascending number, and feeling fully refreshed and alert upon opening your eyes.

All the exercises described in this chapter are effective in raising your reserves of Life Force. I recommend that you start using the Star Exercise immediately as it takes no *mental* effort or concentration and is very easy yet immeasurably powerful. All it takes is the discipline to do it, and the same applies to eating more mindfully.

Moreover, I recommend that you focus your efforts on first training your mind as previously mentioned for 30-40 days before using the Power Words and Psychic Energy Meditation exercises. As the meditation is somewhat complicated, you may find it helpful to record it in your own voice, pausing appropriately for the required counts, and then use the recording to guide you through it.

Finally, since all four exercises raise your Life Force reserves there is no need to apply them all every day. It is more effective to choose the one that you are drawn to most and master that first.

Chapter 39

MENTAL SELF-PROTECTION

Having learnt how to increase your Life Force reserves, you will now learn how to protect your reserves and energy field from negative energy. In this context, the word 'negative' *does* carry the connotation of something that is harmful, or in other words energy that can harm you mentally and physically. As is the case with all opposites, positive and negative energy exist side-by-side in the Mental Plane, and even the most positive and well-intended person can be affected by negative mental energy.

USING LIFE FORCE

Since Universal Mind is impersonal, Its Life Force can be used to serve both good and evil purposes. It can be no other way because otherwise Universal Mind would not be impersonal and nor could it receive instructions from its individual mind centres, including your own. Remember that whatever one of Universal Mind's life centres thinks, It *thinks*, so if a person's thoughts are good or evil is owing to them, not Universal Mind.

As You Sow So Shall You Reap

Any person using Universal Life Force for evil or unworthy purposes will in time, by Law, fall victim to his own mental trappings, dealings, and intentions. And ignorance of this does not serve as any form of protection. Recall that in accordance with the Law of Attraction 'as you sow so shall you reap' and 'like attracts like'. This serves as a warning not to attempt to use your mind for any unworthy or evil purpose that by definition is the intention to cause harm to anyone or anything. You are *free* to choose to use your mind in whatever way you wish, but you are not free from the *consequences* of your choices.

Forewarned is Forearmed

Being well-intentioned does not serve as adequate protection from negative energy. This does not suggest, however, that you must fear negative energy because it is far lower in degree of positivity relative to positive energy. Moreover, remember that positive thought-waves are amplified by other positive thought-waves and are *only* neutralised or diminished by negative thought-waves.

Keeping your mental nature positive by entertaining higher thoughts and permitting only higher emotions, is itself the first step in self-protection. Having said this, it does not benefit you to 'stick your head in the sand' and ignore the existence of negative energy. Forewarned is forearmed.

The self-protection techniques outlined here serve to protect you from the negative thoughts or ill intentions that others' may have towards you. They also guard your mind from mental manipulation, protect your energy field from negative energy and thought-waves in your environment, even if not targeted towards you, and help clear existing negative energy from your energy field.

In other words, these techniques raise your degree of positivity further and *keep* it raised, so as not to leave you exposed to having your positivity diminished by negative energy you are unaware of. Put simply, they immunise you against negative influences, and the more you put them into practice, the greater your immunity. The exercises outlined here are largely attributable to the various writings of William Walker Atkinson.

ASSERT THE I WITHIN

There is no greater self-protection than asserting the I within, and it requires no special meditation technique to do so. Whenever you are in the presence of someone you sense is trying to manipulate you with their words or actions, *silently* tell yourself with strength and conviction 'I AM I', and back this up by *mentally* saying the following statement to the other person: 'Leave me alone. My inner power rejects your influence'. You will immediately notice a marked change in your inner strength, whereas the person trying to manipulate you will instantly back off and appear confused, and the next time you meet them they will treat you with respect.

You do not, however, have to wait to be in the direct presence of a manipulative person to assert these statements. It is just as effective to repeat them mentally to yourself as often as you will. A non-specific variation of the second statement is, 'My inner power casts off all adverse influence and manipulation - I am protected by All-Power'. By mentally asserting this statement, you protect yourself from negative manipulation and adverse mental influences that you may be unaware of, whether specifically targeted at you or not.

You also diminish the possibility of meeting anyone who would attempt to negatively manipulate you or try to cause you harm since your degree of positivity will be far higher in comparison to that of most people you meet. In your presence, others will sub-consciously sense they have no directive influence over you, and so will not even attempt to manipulate you.

Moreover, asserting the inner power of your will in this way, you become increasingly immune to negative energy or thought-waves in the atmosphere wherever you are. You will find yourself able to remain mentally calm, strong and centred, even if those around you are not, and so you will be able to calm them as well.

I Deny Your Positivity Over Me

When you are in the presence of someone you feel has a *higher* degree of positivity relative to your own, you can again assert the I within because their will is *positive* to yours and hence can sway it. Instead of doing so with every person you meet, do so when you feel mentally weak and vulnerable in someone's presence, or in awe of them and ready to yield to their command whether verbal or mental.

Remember that a higher degree of positivity does not mean to have positive thoughts or to be 'good'. It is always a matter of degree of directive will power and hence influence over all those things of a lesser positivity in comparison. Even if the person in question could *positively* sway your will, you are still *not* the one directing your will and for all intents and purposes, have submitted your will to theirs.

Therefore, when faced with a person of higher positivity, *mentally* assert the following statement: 'I deny your positivity over me' and immediately tell yourself 'My Will is a centre of Cosmic Will'. In this way, you immediately raise your degree of positivity to match their own, which ensures you have direction over your own will and hence can interact without being swayed, or alternatively, you raise your degree of positivity above theirs.

Bear in mind that this does not mean you should not want people of higher positivity to influence you positively. The point is for you to be the one who *chooses* how to *use* someone else's words or advice. In all cases, however, affirming the I within is most appropriate when you are in the presence of someone about whom you feel something is not quite right. Instead of becoming suspicious of everyone you meet, learn to listen to your intuition and you won't go wrong.

POSITIVE WILL ATMOSPHERE

Another very powerful technique for mental self-protection involves mental imagery, and is aimed at creating a protective shield around you, referred to in Arcane teachings, as a Positive Will Atmosphere. This serves to strengthen your aura and shield you from adverse outside influences, while also making you highly *positive to* those people you come into contact with. To create this protective shield around you, all you have to do is imagine it and use the power of your will. You can do so in a relaxed meditative state or when wide awake. Get a very strong sense of your own will. Then imagine the power of your will extending outwards from your body until you are surrounded by an oval-shaped energy field of positively charged will to a distance of three feet or around one metre.

Moreover, imagine this protective energy field as a pulsating or vibrating *force field* of clear *white* light, off of which all outside harmful influence immediately rebounds and is dispersed. Metaphysical texts assert that pure clear white light is the colour of Spirit and 'Spirit is the master of all things'. Surround yourself therefore by the shield of white light, any time you feel in danger mentally or physically, and again listen to your intuition for its guidance.

Repeat this Positive Will Atmosphere exercise every morning at first. Doing so in a wide awake state should not take more than a minute and in time you will begin to sense the permanency of the protective shield around you. Thereafter, you can repeat the exercise less often.

OMNIPOTENCE

In closing this chapter on self-protection, do not be misled into thinking that the aforementioned statements or the protective force field are just fanciful and offer no *real* mental protection. In fact, they offer more protection than you realise. And in the same way you take every precaution to protect yourself from harm's way in the Physical Plane, so should you do the same in the Mental Plane, and even more so as it is invisible to your physical senses.

Having said this, there is *nothing* to fear. Protecting yourself in this way is not aimed at making you fearful of the Mental Plane. In the same way that you take care to cross a road without being fearful, so you should also take care to protect your mind without fear. Also bear in mind that nature has its own in-built protection in the Mental Plane, just as your physical body does in the Physical Plane.

The main aim of mental self-protection therefore, is to keep your positivity higher and lessen the risk of it being lowered by negative thought-waves in the atmosphere that in turn serves to deplete your Life Force or energy reserves. Finally, by mentally protecting yourself in this way, you surround yourself with the power of Omnipotence in both the Mental and Physical Planes, so truly there is nothing to fear, yet there is much to be gained.

Chapter 40
VISUALISATION

Visualisation is a technique that combines meditation and the power of your imagination to focus and concentrate on the ideal of your desire, definite purpose, or objective. While older metaphysical texts refer to visualisation as mental imagery, modern texts on the subject use the term creative visualisation.

VISUALISATION ESSENTIALS

As you already know, conscious reality creation is a result of the interaction between the masculine and feminine principles of your mind in *opposing* directions, aimed at creation. Put simply therefore, visualisation involves using your *masculine objective* mind to impress an ideal mental image of your desire on your *feminine subjective* mind, and hence on the subjective Universal Mind. You use your masculine *will* to concentrate on a mental image of your feminine *desire* and mentally keep it in place.

Essentially, you mentally form and concentrate on a mental image of things and conditions as you desire or intend them to be, as if in the *present* moment. It is best to adopt a child-like imagination under the conscious direction of an adult's will power. Instead of *thinking* of an image, engage your heart in the process. In other words, let the mental image you imagine come from your heart rather than trying to *think* about it. This ensures that your mental images are founded in a deep sense of knowing and feeling of the heart, whereas trying to think about the image could bring up conflicting thoughts and keep your mind active rather than relaxed. Keep your visualisation sessions simple. Be calm and maintain a positive mental state.

The step-by-step visualisation instructions that follow assume that you know what you desire and its purpose, largely free of attachment and doubt, and that you have practiced both the concentration and imagination exercises described earlier.

Think With Your Pencil First

When you first start to use visualisation, you will probably find that your mind wanders and that it is somewhat difficult to imagine just what you want. To maximise the effectiveness of your visualisations from the outset it is helpful to write down a description of your desire. This is not the same as over-analysing, limiting, or attaching specifics to your desire. But rather, this exercise is aimed at giving your untrained imagination a ready platform from which to work off, rather than you having to *think* of the details while visualising. Bear in mind that trying to *think* while visualising, inhibits mental relaxation because it induces Beta Level or wide-awake brainwave activity. In contrast, by writing about your ideal beforehand, you can allow your visualisation to flow from your heart effortlessly and hence, remain in the ideal relaxed mental state of Alpha Level.

You only need to write down a description of your desire before that desire's *first* visualisation. But you can adjust your written ideal by adding or subtracting details. Write down what you want, why you want it, and exactly how you want it, and also how you imagine yourself feeling when experiencing your desire. Use the *present* tense *not* the future tense. For instance in the example of your ideal home, you would write 'my house *is*', not 'my house *will be*'. Familiarise yourself with every aspect of the ideal version of your desire. There is no need to write an elaborate descriptive essay. Short bullet points suffice if you prefer, as long as you get it all down. Keep your written desire in a safe place and keep it private. Do not show it to anyone *whatsoever*, the reason for which is explained in Chapter 44.

Read what you have written calmly before visualising, as this prepares your brain for the visualisation. Having said this, *do not* try to *remember* what you have written *during* your visualisation. Do not even think about it. And certainly do not worry about it. You may find you imagine different or even better mental images than what you have written down, and of course that is fine. We will now look at the three essential steps of visualisation.

STEP 1: RELAX

Select a time and place for your visualisation during which you will not be disturbed. If you are new to visualising or meditation, it is best that you sit upright in a chair to avoid drifting off to sleep, which is likely to happen at first if you lie down.

Having said this, lying down naturally promotes deeper relaxation, and is perfectly fine if you cannot sit upright. When in position, enter a relaxed meditative state as described in Chapter 37. This *slows* your brain's activity and creates a direct, open link between your objective and subjective mind. It is best that you first learn to relax before doing so for visualisation. Nevertheless, take as long as you need to relax ahead of your visualisation but not so much time that you are wasting your time *trying* to relax. As you become more skilled at relaxing with practice, entering a relaxed meditative state need not take longer than 1-3 minutes.

Cultivating Inner Calm and Strength
Here are some powerful techniques to strengthen and calm your mind ahead of visualisation. They can be done while you are relaxing but they are not *essential* to visualisation. As you *inhale*, imagine your consciousness contracting *inwards* and as you exhale, imagine it expanding back *outwards* into infinite space. Simply feel your mind winding inwards and outwards rhythmically as you inhale and exhale. Since your mind *is* Universal Mind, you can imagine that it is Universal Mind in its *entirety* contracting inwards and expanding outwards as *you* breathe. Calmly remind yourself that whatever you desire already exists in the invisible world of all possibilities. Identify with the Real You by feeling your awareness rising upwards and mentally call out your first name calmly a few times, as was explained in Chapter 31.

The Gentle Smile
Another powerful suggestion is to smile gently as you relax and to maintain the smile throughout the visualisation session. This does not mean a big tense grin on your face. Rather, simply turn the edges of your lips *ever so slightly* upwards without any tension. *Gently* smiling in this way has a physiological effect of triggering a sense of positivity and optimism without your conscious input. Try it out for yourself now and you will feel the proof of this. It is far easier to imagine your ideal outcome when smiling gently, and also far more difficult to bring an unwanted or contradictory image to mind. There is no need, however, to think about it or try to remember to smile during visualisation. Instead, let it come and go naturally.

Setting Your Intention
Once you are relaxed, mentally say in a calm, confident voice, 'It is my will to use all of my abilities to create [whatever it is you want to create] in my physical reality'. This not only sets your intention from the outset, but it also commands your mind to use *all the power* available to you, whether you are consciously aware of that power or not. Finally you can also mentally say a short prayer or mantra that resonates with you. You are now ready to visualise.

STEP 2: VISUALISE
Having relaxed and stated your intention, the next step is to clearly imagine yourself, others, and your physical world conditions exactly as you desire or intend them to be, as if in the *present* moment. Visualise your mental image for at least 3-5 minutes. This may sound like a short period of time, but to the untrained mind it is not. As your skills

of concentration improve you can increase the time you spend mentally imagining your ideal, although 5 minutes is optimal.

In the Present Moment

It is fundamental that you visualise your desire as if it already exists in the present moment. The reason is because Universal Mind, being infinite, is not subject to space or time as you experience it. This means that the future has no validity as a time-frame for Universal Mind. If you visualise in the future, you keep your intention in the future, which never comes. And this is because, as you already know, there is only one *present* moment and it includes *all* past, present and future possibilities in the *present* moment. Moreover, by visualising in the future, you inadvertently acknowledge, and hence focus on, your current conditions in which you do not have your desire.

Imagining Your Ideal

Visualise the mental image of your desire in the mental space in front of your mind's eye, which is the space mentally in front of your eyes when you close them. An alternative method is to see your mental image on a mental white screen that fills your mental vision. Do not *think* about, strain, or force the image to come to mind because again this induces the wide-awake Beta Level of brain activity, which makes it more difficult to impress it on your subjective mind. Rather, it is very effective to let the images come from your heart, not your head.

Imagine your ideal with as much clarity as possible. While *seeing* the image visually is not essential to manifestation, it strengthens your creative power. Moreover, it makes it easier to believe what you are seeing with optimal emotion and generates motivation. The more you *see* it in your mind, the more you *believe* it, and the more you believe it, the greater the probability that you will see it in your physical world.

Concentrate on the mental image by using the power of your will to keep it in place. If you find your mind wandering, which it is likely to do at first, gently bring your attention back to the mental image of your ideal without feeling frustration.

To sharpen your skills of concentration make sure to practice the concentration exercise in Chapter 32, and also review the imagination techniques from Chapter 35. Do not become frustrated if you cannot imagine the image with clarity. Take your time, be patient, and remember not to force anything. Your mental images will become clearer and sharper with practice, and even if they do not, you can still create your experience with success. After all, a person who remains focused on their ideal without mentally seeing it is far more likely to attain it than is a person who can visualise vividly but whose focus is scattered. Keep the *idea* of your ideal in mind and the mental image will come.

Add Emotion

An effective way to add emotion to your visualisation is to remember the purpose behind your desire and let the feeling of what your desire symbolises wash over you (Ch. 34). When adding emotion to your mental image, however, be careful not to switch into obsession mode by adding too much emotion.

Keep it light and as long as you are feeling light and not weighed down, you are in optimal emotion drive. It is more effective to maintain an overall mental state of positivity than have too much emotion about any one desire. In other words, if you are generally positive, then you are positive about all things, including that which you desire to experience. In this way, the desire itself can in no way define or affect your overall positivity.

STEP 3: RELEASE

The final step in visualisation is to release the mental image of your desire after you have concentrated on it. Most texts on the subject overlook the importance of this step, yet it is fundamental to the process. This final step takes anywhere between 1-3 minutes.

To release your mental image in the way described here, is in alignment with the Universal search for balance, as was explained in Contractive and Expansive Meditation in Chapter 37. A good analogy for understanding the importance of releasing your mental image is breathing. Concentrating your Life Force on your mental image can be likened to *inhaling* it (contractive) in the same way you inhale through your nose and hold the air concentrated in your lungs.

In contrast, releasing your mental image is akin to *exhaling* it (expansive) back into the infinite space of Universal Mind where all creation takes place. This can be likened to exhaling the air from your lungs back into the atmosphere, so that you can take the next breath, which is your next visualisation session. Put another way, this final step releases your mental image from the involvement of your directive objective mind and hands it over entirely to your creative subjective mind, which is one with the subjective Universal Mind.

The simplest way to release the mental image of your desire that you have been concentrating on, is simply to let it go, and let it leave from the view of your mind's eye, which serves to release it from your objective thinking mind. Having said this, what follows is a very powerful releasing technique that you can use if it appeals to you.

The Vortex of Creation

When you have a clear mental image of your ideal in mind, imagine a radiant ball of vibrating energy hovering in front of you, and then place the mental image of your desire inside the ball. Next, mentally look outwards into empty space and see a whirling vortex open up in the distance. Imagine this whirling energy flowing in a clockwise direction with an entrance or portal in its centre, which you know leads to another dimension.

With your mental image in the energy ball, release the ball by seeing it fly off into space towards the whirling vortex, and then see it entering the portal. Once it enters, see the portal closing, and sense how in that very moment you have planted a seed of creation in the invisible world of limitless possibilities. Being unconstrained by space and time, sense how your mental image has already manifested in the here and now, even if it is not yet accessible to your physical senses.

And So It Is, Thank You

To complete releasing your mental image, mentally say 'and so it is, thank you' with a tone of gratitude and with a sense of lightness. This short affirmation solidifies your belief that what you have mentally concentrated on has *now* been created, and also acknowledges The Absolute for your directive and creative power to create your ideal.

This brings you to the end of the visualisation session. Upon completing it, gently bring yourself out of the meditative state by counting upwards from 1 to 5, feeling more alert at each ascending number, and feeling wide awake and better than before with your eyes open on the count of 5. You can increase the count to 10 if you feel you need more time to return to full alertness. Finally, when in a wide-awake state, immediately put the visualisation out of your objective mind.

This marks the end of the visualisation process itself. As you become more familiar with visualising through practice, the entire three-step process should not take more than 10 minutes. Although this is not set in stone, it is best to keep your visualisations short and powerful. This ensures maximum concentration, whereas trying to keep mentally *focused* in a meditative state for longer periods of time is far more difficult, and not necessary for effective visualisation.

DO NOT THINK ABOUT IT

There are two reasons to put the visualisation out of your mind and not think about it. The first is that mentally recalling the visualisation drains it of the Life Force you have directed towards it because you have to use *its* Life Force to view it mentally. In so doing, you take energy away from its creation. The second reason is that by thinking about it, you do not release it from your masculine objective mind to your feminine subjective mind. This really amounts to holding a seed in your hand and never planting it in the soil, yet expecting it to grow.

You can think about your desire itself during the day and send it more positive mental energy, which in fact strengthens it, as long as you are not obsessing over it. But do not think about the details of any visualisation, no matter how powerful it made you feel. Finally, for reasons you will learn about shortly, talk to no one about your visualisation.

INS AND OUTS OF VISUALISATION

Here are a few additional suggestions about visualisation. If you find yourself struggling to relax, or spiral into any sense of doubt during your visualisation, simply come back to it another time. Having said this, be determined to use the power of your will and do not let yourself off the hook easily.

Do Not Think

Bear in mind that at the level of consciousness for visualisation your awareness is beyond time and space. Do not think about how much time has elapsed or if it is enough. If you want an idea of how long each session lasts, simply jot down the time before you start and again once you finish. In this way you can keep a log of your times. Do not think about all the instructions set out in this chapter or wonder if you are doing it right. It is most important that you relax and let your visualisation flow more from your heart than from your head.

How Many Times?

Visualise your intended outcome at least once a day and at best three times a day. The optimal time of day is in the morning upon waking up, and in the evening before going to sleep. The third time is preferably around midday. You can set one session aside for a longer visualisation and keep the other two shorter. If, however, three times a day is not practical, keep it to once a day. It is best that you do *not* skip a day until your desire has manifested, or to continue to visualise it for at least *40 days*. Alternatively, feel free to stop at any time if your desire is no longer important enough to you.

Replenish Your Life Force

Remember that any mental or physical activity diminishes your Life Force reserves. When you visualise, you project and direct energy towards your mental image, which uses up your energy reserves. It is important, therefore, to replenish your Life Force reserves (Ch. 38) if you are to continue visualising effectively, otherwise you will find yourself running out of energy, which in turn makes it far more difficult to concentrate on your mental image. It is best to set some time aside for replenishing your Life Force reserves every day, irrespective of whether you visualise or not.

A Word of Warning

While visualisation is the single most powerful tool for consciously creating your reality, be careful not to become a 'visualisation addict'. Do not feel like you have to first visualise every little thing you want. Choose one desire at a time and stick to it. If you fall into the trap of having to visualise everything, you run the risk of 'living' solely in your mental world and so stop participating in your outer world.

Finally, just because you have successfully visualised the mental image of your desire for a few minutes does not mean that you can then go about the rest of your day worrying about it or being in an overall negative mental state because you do not have it. If you fall into this trap, you undo *all* your efforts. In fact, it is preferable to think of your desire during the day randomly without visualisation, than to visualise it three times a day and then doubt it for the rest of the day. Get on with your day, trust Life, and place Omnipotence behind and in front of your words, thoughts, and actions.

THE MAGIC LANTERN

To close this chapter, we will look at an analogy for visualisation called The Magic Lantern, as described in William Walker Atkinson's 1909 book, The Arcane Formulas. The Magic Lantern is akin to a modern-day projector which works by passing an image held in a slide in front of a concentrated light, so that it is projected onto an outer surface in front of it. The image in the Magic Lantern's slide is your mental image, the concentrated light in front of which it is passed is your focused will, and the surface onto which the image is projected is your outer world. In other words, the mental image is the feminine creative principle and your will is the masculine directive principle, used to *focus* on the image and *project* it outwards.

The reflection of the image in the slide is reproduced on a *larger scale* on the surface onto which it is projected. Just like the 'image' of the oak tree in the acorn is projected as a larger physical version of the oak tree in the outer world, so your concentrated mental images are projected in your outer world in full-scale physical form.

Moreover, the accuracy of the projection on the outer surface depends on the strength and focus of the light in the lantern. In the same way, the accuracy of the projection of your mental image in physical form depends on the power and focus of your will. If your will is weak, then the projection of your mental image in your outer world is also weak. If the rays of the Magic Lantern's light are not properly focused then the projection on the surface will be out of focus. And in the same way, if your will is not focused on holding your mental image in place, then your outer world experience of it will be weak or less definite.

Finally, if the slide containing the image is faint or faulty, then its projection on the outer surface will be the same, and the projection of any fault on the slide will be magnified. Likewise, if the mental image you focus on is not clear, or if it is riddled with doubt and unwanted factors, then that too will be your outer world experience of its projection. Endeavour therefore, to have a clear, correct, and accurate mental image of your desire, and mentally hold it in place with a strong and focused will until it is projected or manifested in form in the physical world, as it must be by Universal Law.

Chapter 41
AUTO-SUGGESTION

Auto-suggestion is a very powerful method used to impress a positive suggestion directly onto your subjective mind. It literally means 'to put forth an idea to one's own sub-conscious mind by oneself'. Put simply, an auto-suggestion is a statement *suggested* to your subjective mind *persistently* until such time that it is adopted as its own and hence acted upon automatically without your conscious input.

SECOND-PERSON AUTO-SUGGESTION

The well-known technique of reciting positive statements to oneself is commonly referred to as 'affirmations'. However, auto-suggestions differ from affirmations in one very important way. Affirmations are stated in the *first*-person. In contrast, auto-suggestions are stated in the *second*-person and you address yourself using your name as if you are addressing someone else. For instance, say your name is John Smith and you want to impress on your subjective mind that you are a strong person. Using affirmations you would usually say something like '*I am* a strong person', whereas using an auto-suggestion you would say 'John Smith, you are a person of great strength'.

The reason behind using second-person auto-suggestions to impress your subjective mind, and *not* first-person affirmations, is simple and fundamentally sound. It is William Walker Atkinson who first taught this alternative method of auto-suggestion, most notably in his 1915 book Suggestion and Auto-Suggestion.

The Suggestor and Suggestee

The reason for using second-person auto-suggestions and not first-person affirmations when impressing your sub-conscious mind is because, being subjective, it *receives* suggestions and is also *subject* to direction. By saying 'I am' there is no suggestion being given to your sub-conscious mind, or in other words, there is no one directing it.

Remember always that your objective mind *gives* the direction and is the 'suggestor', and your subjective mind *receives* the suggestion as the 'suggestee'. This is in line with the directive masculine and receptive feminine principles of the Law of Gender. Using first-person affirmations to direct your sub-conscious mind is tantamount to trying to direct it without giving it direction, and this explains why most people who use first-person 'I am' affirmations usually gain little from them. Say you feel weak, if you tell yourself 'I am strong' then you are unlikely to believe it if you *feel* weak, but if you address yourself as if speaking to someone else and say with encouragement '[your name] you are a strong person', then you sit up and listen. Stop reading now and try it out for yourself by using a first-person affirmation and a second-person suggestion for something you want to change within yourself. The difference will become very obvious.

'I AM' AFFIRMATIONS

Only use first-person 'I am' affirmations to affirm the I within. Think about it this way - since complete objectivity belongs to the I within, then it is *self*-directing and not *subjective* to anything. Since you *are* the I within, you can never direct a suggestion to it because you *are* it. And since, from your perspective, there is only ever one I, there is nothing outside of it to direct it.

Moreover, by reserving 'I am' affirmations only for the I, you never inadvertently define your unchanging Real Self with anything that belongs to the personality. Remember always that nothing can define the I, and as the Real You, you are already complete. Having said this, if you already use 'I am' personal affirmations that you feel work for you, continue to use them but I strongly suggest you also try second-person auto-suggestions to see the difference for yourself.

We will now consider a few powerful affirmations to assert the I within, and how to tailor-make auto-suggestions for the personal self, before looking at how to apply them practically in your daily life.

Powerful Affirmations

As mentioned earlier, only use 'I am' affirmations when asserting the I within. Here are a few very powerful affirmations that you can use to identify with the Real You.

I AM Affirmations

I AM
I AM I
I CAN and I WILL
I KNOW and I WILL
I THINK therefore I AM therefore I WILL
I AM asserting the mastery of my Real Self

Since this book is based on the idea of living life from the vantage point of the I within, which is Top-Down-Living, I suggest that you use these affirmations *first* for 40 days before moving on to second-person auto-suggestions. Use a calm and authoritative voice, feel the inner strength that arises from the affirmation, and feel what it is like to have no personal emotions, desires, fears, and thoughts, yet always ready to direct your mind with your will.

Choose one affirmation that appeals most to you, or combine a few into one. A combined affirmation could read as follows: 'I AM I. And I CAN and I KNOW and I WILL'.

PERSONAL AUTO-SUGGESTIONS

No one knows the best auto-suggestions for you better than you. It is hence most effective to create tailor-made suggestions for yourself. It is helpful to think with your *heart* of what you most need to hear from others. In this way you can create suggestions based on what you *know* you want to believe about yourself. And in fact you will find that what you most need to hear from others is what you most need to tell yourself.

Tailor-Made Auto-Suggestions

Remember always to include your name, for example 'John Smith' or simply 'John', in front of each of your tailor-made statements. The effectiveness of this cannot be over-stated. Now let us look at just what a tailor-made auto-suggestion is.

Address yourself as if you are trying to encourage your closest friend in whom you have full belief. Motivate yourself in the same way you would motivate anyone else, and be firm in what you are saying. Tell yourself, as if speaking to someone else, exactly what you want yourself to do and become, and how you expect yourself to act.

If, for instance, you feel weak and fearful in your actions and decisions with little conviction in yourself to achieve your desires, a tailor-made auto-suggestion would read like this:

'[Your name] you are courageous and fearless. You fear nothing. [Your first name] do you hear me? *Nothing*. Pull yourself together. Make a decision right now to go out and create what you want. You can and will do it. You are the most fearless and courageous person I know. You are positive this very minute. Are you listening to me? You are positive, fearless, and confident, right now. There is nothing you cannot achieve and I know that you already know this. Now go out and do what you know must be done to achieve your desire. Do it now. You can and I know you will. Go for it'.

Powerful Auto-Suggestions

Here are a few broad suggestions that you can include in your tailor-made auto-suggestions.

[Your name] all things possible are possible for you

...you trust Life and are open to change
...you are free to choose your experiences
...you naturally focus only on what you want to experience
...you direct your own mind and conquer all fear and doubt
...your intuition always guides you in the right direction - listen to it
...you create your experience of reality in the way you desire it to be
...what you desire in your heart is already yours
...you enjoy success in every area of your life
...abundance flows to you in great measure
...you are wealthy and prosperous in every way
...you have the power to transform your personality
...you have the confidence and courage to achieve all that you desire
...you honour and care for your body
...every cell in your body is Divinely Intelligent and self-healing
...you always pay attention intelligently and consciously
...love and joy is your natural state of being
...you act with love towards everyone and everything
...I love you more than anyone else in the world
...I love you just the way you are
...I will always love you - there is nothing to fear in love
...every day, in every way, you are getting better and better

Every Day in Every Way
The last auto-suggestion in the aforementioned list is an affirmation
that is adapted from Emile Coue's 1922 book Self-Mastery Through
Conscious Autosuggestion, and originally read, 'every day, in every
respect, *I am* getting better and better'.

It is very powerful and complete as both an affirmation and
second-person auto-suggestion because the words 'every day' suggest
an on ongoing daily process, and 'in every way' covers every aspect of
your life, while 'getting better and better' guards against any resistance
as it is not extreme and just suggests you are *better* today compared to
yesterday. You can adjust this auto-suggestion for something specific.
For instance, 'every day in every way you are getting healthier and
healthier' or 'every day in every way you are more and more positive',
and remember to address *yourself* by saying your name at the
beginning of the suggestion.

AUTO-SUGGESTION IN PRACTICE
It is best to choose one single tailor-made auto-suggestion at a time. In
this way you give your subjective mind a single idea to focus on, rather
than overwhelm it, and hence the suggestion is impressed on your

mind with greater ease. As is the case with all subjective mind work, do not *think* about or analyse the suggestion. Bear in mind that it is your non-reasoning sub-conscious mind you intend to impress and hence, the less you *think* about it the better.

Say It

When *saying* auto-suggestions you must speak with encouragement. Use a firm strong voice that conveys full belief in the person you are addressing, which of course is yourself. Do not let your voice convey any sense of pity. Remember always to speak to yourself as if you are motivating someone else that you truly desire to succeed and have full conviction that they can and they will.

See It

See or visualise yourself already possessing and displaying all those qualities you wish to develop in yourself. As you say the auto-suggestion to yourself, *see* yourself as what is being suggested to you, and really *feel* what it feels like to embody those qualities. The clearer your mental image of yourself, as you want to be right now, the deeper and clearer the impression that is made on your subjective mind by the accompanying auto-suggestion.

Act It

Finally, act on the auto-suggestion in your outer physical world. Act as if you embody those qualities you wish to embody. Do so as if you are acting in a play, which as you already know, you are. Remember from Chapter 7, that your personality is an actor in a play and its role is its assumed or adopted role. Acting 'as if', is very powerful because just like thought tends to take form in action, so action tends to act upon thought and so impresses your subjective mind further.

WHAT TIME AND HOW OFTEN?

Using the 40-Day Rule explained in Chapter 37, the optimal number of times to say an 'I am' affirmation or personal auto-suggestion is 40 times a day for 40 days. You can use a string of beads to keep count. If your tailor-made auto-suggestions, however, are very long then you can reduce the number of times to 20 or 10 times a day but stick to the 40-Day Rule. You can also split it into 2 daily sessions, once upon waking up and again before going to sleep, or you can say them any time during the day.

It is also effective to say the affirmations and auto-suggestions in a more relaxed mental state. Learn them by rote without the need to read them, and then mentally say and visualise them in a relaxed meditative state. It is also very helpful to record a tailor-made auto-suggestion in your own voice, and let it play on repeat while you are asleep or again, in a relaxed meditative state.

ALWAYS SPEAK WELL TO YOURSELF

Always speak well to yourself. Most people, however, are their own worst critic and criticise themselves with words they would never dare tell another, and for no valid reason. Never speak badly to yourself because you are inadvertently giving your subjective mind an auto-suggestion, which in time it will accept and adopt as its own. If you catch yourself speaking badly to yourself, immediately and earnestly apologise to yourself just as you would to another person, and replace your self-criticism with a positive auto-suggestion.

Moreover, only speak well of yourself to others. This does not mean boasting but rather, it means not putting yourself down when speaking to others. If someone compliments you, do not contradict them by telling them why their compliment does not count and do not play yourself down. Instead, graciously accept compliments and say thank you, while not depending on them for your own self-worth.

To close this chapter, it cannot be stressed enough how powerful a tool second-person auto-suggestion is in creating change in your life. You will be surprised at just how *obedient* your subjective mind will become to your objective demands of it.

Chapter 42

MENTAL HEALING

While the creative and directive power of the mind can be used in the direction of any desire or pursuit, there is perhaps no pursuit more worthy than healing yourself and others. This is because health is the foundation of your physical existence. Indeed, the wealthy man that has every material possession he could ever want and then some, has little use for any of them in the absence of his health. It is every human being's right to be perfectly healthy to the day we leave the Physical Plane naturally, having lived a long and healthy life.

Healing is no different to what has been discussed so far about consciousness. Since everything is energy vibrating at different rates, it stands to reason that any disease, whether deemed incurable or not, is also energy that has its own frequency. Moreover, since energy can be transmuted along the lines of its own kind, then it also stands to reason that any disease can be transmuted into its opposite, that of mental and physical health, which is our natural and intended state.

A discussion of the theory and techniques of mental healing could fill a book of its own, but this chapter on healing will focus on the fundamentals that suffice for you to apply mental healing in your life, for effectively healing yourself and others. The most notable sources of inspiration for this chapter are William Walker Atkinson's 1907 book The Secret of Mental Magic, and Jose Silva's 1989 book, You the Healer, which was written with Robert B. Stone, as well as my own experience and applied knowledge on the subject.

THE PREMISE OF HEALING

The basic premise of healing is that all is mind. This means that every cell in your body has a mind of its own, or rather *is* mind. To distinguish this from what you are accustomed to calling your *thinking* mind, in this chapter I refer to your thinking mind as your *central* mind, and the mind of your cells as your *cellular* mind. The difference is that your cellular mind works along unconscious or sub-conscious lines, whereas your central mind has the capacity to work along conscious lines through thought. Herein lies the secret to healing.

Being sub-conscious means that your cellular mind is subjective in nature and hence is subject to direction. In other words, your cellular mind is the subjective feminine principle, while your central mind is the objective masculine principle. The higher your positivity as regards self-awareness, the greater is your directive power over your subjective mind and hence the greater your ability to create the changes you desire in your body in the way of healing.

Cells are the Body's Building Blocks

To understand the mental nature of your body, you must first come to understand that everything in your body, including your blood, every organ, tissue, nerve, and bone, is a complex combination of a community of *individual cells*, which you refer to for instance as 'my liver', 'my blood' or 'my heart', and that work together to perform certain functions. Put simply, the building blocks of every part of your body are varieties of human cells, and every cell has a mind, hence the term cellular mind.

The Objective Director - The Subjective Healer

In ignorance of the subjective mental nature of our cells, human beings live in fear of disease. Moreover, in the presence of disease, this fear is compounded and overpowers the objective mind, whereas it is the objective mind that should be directing the subjective mind of the body. It is somewhat surprising that people can fully believe that they have the power to influence others and their environment and attract anything they desire to themselves, yet be plagued with doubt when it comes to directing change in the one thing that is closest to them mentally, which is their own body.

Nevertheless, the truth is that you have the capacity to heal your own body under the direction of your objective mind. If you are ever faced with disease, from anything as simple as the common flu or a stress headache, to an illness that is medically vastly more serious, endeavour to think of your central mind as the director of the healing and your subjective cellular mind as the healer.

In other words, your directive objective mind *directs* the healing and your creative subjective mind *carries out* the healing instructions it *receives*. Indeed, it is the innate intelligence within each of your cells that does the healing, while your central mind directs what is to be healed. Mental healing therefore is not only a case of 'mind over *cell* matter', but also, it is objective mind over subjective mind. Your objective central mind is *positive* to your subjective cellular mind, given its *directive* nature and the cellular mind's *receptive* nature.

Forget what you have been told is incurable and adhere to your new understanding of consciousness. Know that nothing is incurable, even more so when you know that the source of your power to heal your body is the Omnipotence of The Absolute. In fact, there is nothing miraculous about healing. It is only our ignorance that makes it appear miraculous. But do not let this mislead you into believing it is easy. Simple, yes, but not easy, as it requires mental concentration and belief, both of which are difficult for the untrained mind. Again, this emphasises the importance of awakening your will and training your mind through self-discipline using the exercises in this book.

The Prerequisites for Mental Healing

The basic prerequisites for mental healing are the same as those for any conscious creation, but are arguably more necessary for the purpose of healing. The first is positivity in the sense of self-aware consciousness. The next prerequisite is faith. Faith here is not so much to have faith in a Divine sense, but rather it is about not having doubt or fear in your central mind. This is because your doubt or fear will be impressed onto the subjective mind of your body and its cells, which given their receptive subjective nature will act on those states, and so little will change as far as your health is concerned. The mental attitude for healing therefore, as is the case with anything you intend to see manifest, is earnest desire, positive expectation, and belief. The three together are the foundation of faith.

Moreover, the optimal level of emotion with which to apply the techniques that follow is a mental state of confidence, strength, and courage, free from their relative extreme counterparts. Whether you are healing yourself or someone else, endeavour to maintain this mental state and release any sense of fear. Think about it this way - if a disease is *already* present, you have nothing to lose by applying these techniques and potentially everything to gain, so there is nothing to fear and everything to hope for.

MENTAL HEALING TECHNIQUES

The following mental healing techniques lead directly from the previous two chapters on visualisation and auto-suggestion. The method is the same, the only difference being the specific purpose that it is used for. As you read and apply these techniques, bear in mind the following basic premise of mental healing: the subjective cellular mind of your body is receptive and follows the direction of your objective central mind through concentrated thought. Put simply, the intelligent application of the central mind over the cellular mind is the Alpha and Omega of mental healing.

1. Visualisation for Healing

Visualisation for the purposes of healing is fundamentally the same as that for any purpose, as outlined in Chapter 40. The first step is to relax in a meditative state, the second is to visualise the ideal outcome you intend, and the third is to release it. As is the case for all visualisation, the optimal number of times to visualise for healing, is two to three times per day, once in the morning, and once before going to sleep when your subjective cellular mind is most open to direction, and preferably a third time at midday.

Three Screen Method

An alternative method of visualisation for the purposes of healing involves how and what you visualise in the second visualisation step. This is outlined in Jose Silva's You the Healer, which I highly recommend as a practical book on healing.

Instead of simply visualising the outcome you intend as if existing in the present moment, you visualise it in three stages. The first stage is to imagine the health *problem* as it is, the second stage is to imagine the health problem being *corrected*, and the third stage is to visualise yourself in *perfect health*. Each stage can be visualised either in your mind's eye or on a separate white screen in direct view of your mind's eye. If the health problem is inside your body, then visualise the actual organ or whatever part of the body may have the problem, by mentally looking inside your physical body.

More specifically, in using the white screen method, on the first screen imagine the health problem as is, for no more than 1 minute, then move the screen to the left of your mind's eye so that you can no longer see it.

Next, bring another white screen to your mind's eye and this time visualise the problem being corrected. There is no need to be medically correct or biologically exact in what you are seeing or mentally doing. For example you can visualise your white blood cells sprinkling healing energy over diseased cells, which cause the diseased cells to return to perfect health or simply disappear from the body. Visualise this correction stage for about 3-5 minutes, and again move the screen to your left as before.

Finally, on a third mental screen, visualise your organ or body in perfect health, and see yourself enjoying your health in the present moment. Imagine your body surrounded by a pure white light that acts as a protective sphere of perfect health, and then release the image as you would any other mental image. Visualise this for about 1-3 minutes. Remember to adjust your visualisations thereafter to include any physical world improvements when visualising the health problem as is. Keep your visualisations brief and remember that since you are using your own Life Force in the direction of healing, you must replenish your reserves of Life Force daily (Ch. 38).

2. Auto-Suggestion for Healing

Auto-suggestion for healing is little different from what has already been written on the subject in Chapter 41. It is recommended to combine visualisation with auto-suggestion for healing. For instance, as you give the instruction to the cellular mind of the specific part or organ of your body, then visualise that part of your body acting on the instruction and being perfectly healed.

In the same way you would make a positive suggestion to your subjective mind in the second-person, make a positive suggestion to your subjective cellular mind. Identify the cells, organ, or part of your body you intend to heal and directly *tell* them exactly what to do, as if you were giving an instruction to another person. It may be as simple as instructing them to recall their previous state of health and to re-produce it. While you do not have to be medically or biologically exact in your instructions, it may be helpful to research a disease that you are looking to correct, to add authority to your words. State your auto-suggestion in the second-person as a *positive* statement of what you *want* your cells to do, not a *negative* statement of what they must *not* do. As you mentally part with your subjective cellular mind, do so with some strong words of encouragement, in the same way that a caring doctor would do for his or her patient.

It may feel strange at first to speak to your cells in this way, but there is nothing fanciful about it. Just as you will your arm in order to raise it, so you can and must will your cells in the direction of health that you want them to take by way of suggestion. In the same way that your hand, which itself is made up of a countless number of cells, yields to your command without necessarily 'hearing' it, so the cells in any part of your body will yield to your mental command and will follow the instruction inherent in it.

DISTANT HEALING

The method for healing others at a distance, also known as remote healing, is the same as the aforementioned visualisation and auto-suggestion healing techniques. In each case, you simply replace your cellular mind and your own body, with that of the person you intend to send healing thought-waves to. Use your objective mind to instruct the subjective cellular mind and overall sub-conscious mind of the other person, both of which are *subjective* to your *objective* mind.

Recall from Chapter 22 that thought-waves are not constrained by space or time and you can effect change in someone's subjective sub-conscious mind by way of mental induction. In other words, since the other person's sub-conscious mind is impersonal and subjective in nature, as is the case throughout nature, it is able to receive and act on instructions from any source, including your own objective mind.

While it is your objective mind that is sending or *giving* the healing instructions to the subjective mind of the person you intend to be healed, it is *their* mind that does the actual healing, not yours. Your objective mind is the *messenger* not the healer. This means that you cannot take responsibility for the result of another person's healing, because while you can convey the message, it is up to their own subjective mind to accept and act on it consistently. Having said this, the greater your own belief and conviction in the instructions that you are giving, the more readily they will be accepted by the other person's subjective mind.

Bear in mind that while this chapter is focused on the healing of human beings, the same principles apply to the healing of any other living creature, including animals and plants. Distant healing is very effective in animals and plants because their mental operations are largely along sub-conscious lines and hence far easier to direct.

Asking Permission

Since mental healing directly *influences* the mind of another person, it is best always to ask permission of that person first, for several reasons. The first reason is out of respect for that person's mind and individuality. The second reason is so that the person can work *with you* rather than unravel all your mental work with his or her own fear and negativity. And finally, you do not want to inadvertently interfere in the other person's life path without their permission. You can explain the process in a brief and logical way as has been written here so as to dispel any limiting beliefs the other person may have about the idea of healing. Having said this, it is best to keep the details of the visualisations and auto-suggestions that you give the other person to yourself, so as not to scatter your concentrated mental energy.

Bear in mind that most people doubt their own capacity for self-healing and may associate distant healing as some form of magic. It is, however, only out of ignorance of the objective-subjective mental process involved that makes healing appear magical. Knowledge, as is the case in all things, is the key.

Do not be surprised if the other person shows some resistance to your suggestion for distant healing. It is my belief, however, that given the innate 'will to live' inherent in every living creature, when faced with a life-threatening illness no one would deny your request to offer mental healing, even if they do not necessarily believe in it. If they accept your offer, you can boost their belief by directing an auto-suggestion to them that they are open to and believe in their own innate healing power.

The exception for receiving the express permission from another person to send healing thought-waves to their subjective mind is in the case of that person being unable to communicate with you owing to their particular condition. If the person in question is a young child, ask permission of his or her parents. Alternatively, you can let your intuition guide you if time is of the essence.

It is my opinion that there is no more noble purpose in using the innate power of your mind than the purpose of healing yourself and others. Even so, someone may still refuse your offer for mental healing because of a misguided belief that their illness or disease is somehow God-sent, even if they are willing to consult a medical doctor and take medication for the very same illness. Nevertheless, whenever you ask another person for their permission to perform distant healing, always accept and honour their decision.

Establishing a Mental Connection

Establishing a mental connection with the person you intend to send healing thought-waves to, although not necessary, increases the effectiveness of your work. A technique described in metaphysical teachings is called the Astral Tube. This involves imagining a so-called 'vortex ring' that is similar to a smoke ring produced by a steam engine, with a diameter of 6-12 inches or 15-30 centimetres.

Using your will and imagination, see the ring lengthen or extend outwards from your mind in the shape of a tube that travels quickly towards the other person's mind. You do not have to visualise the entire distance that it travels and it suffices that you get an *intuitive* sense of the connection. Once established, you send the healing auto-suggestions as thought-waves through the Astral Tube, and imagine them travelling quickly towards the intended person, and being received by them.

An alternative method for establishing a mental connection is to imagine the person in your direct presence as if they were sitting in the same room with you and preferably on a chair opposite you, but with no concern for where they may physically be. You then speak directly to the person as if they were with you at the time. This method is equally effective, and which one you use is up to you.

Distant Healing in Practice

Once again the only difference between healing yourself and others is that in distant healing, the body and cellular mind you visualise and give suggestions to, is that of the other person. If you imagine the person sitting in front of you, you can speak to them and give them direct suggestions using their name.

For distant healing, it is recommended that you visualise once every three days if an illness is not life-threatening, and once a day if it is. Moreover, it is most effective to perform the visualisations when the other person is asleep, which ensures their objective mind does not interfere with your healing messages, which it could do if it was engaged in an outer world activity.

Working with Time Zones

If the person lives in the same time-zone as you, then before going to sleep, program your mind to wake up at the most appropriate time during the night when the other person's subjective mind is most open to programming. In a relaxed meditative state while lying in your bed, simply instruct yourself to awaken at the best time, feeling refreshed and alert and able to concentrate on any subject. Do not think about what the best time is and rest assured you will wake up.

Having said this, when you wake up you may find it difficult to be mentally alert enough for visualisation and to remain focused on the healing at hand. If you find yourself falling back to sleep or unable to maintain your focus, you can get out of bed and do your mental work seated. Alternatively, find out when the other person is most likely to be asleep, intuitively choose the best time to perform the mental healing, and once you have done so, go to sleep yourself. If the person is in a different time-zone to your own, ask them what hours they are asleep, calculate the corresponding time in your own time-zone, and perform the distant healing during that time.

Life Force and Self-Protection

When you are involved in distant healing, it is best that you increase your Life Force reserves on a daily basis, as you are sending your reserves *away* from you. Moreover, before you start your distant healing session, I recommend you do the self-protection Positive Will Atmosphere exercise in Chapter 39. Whenever you are operating in the Mental Plane *outside* your own mind, it is always helpful to take precautions, although distant healing itself is not dangerous in any way when applied properly and intelligently as described here.

DIVINE ASSISTANCE

Whether you are healing yourself or someone else, it is very powerful to ask for Divine assistance in the matter. This simply involves asking The Absolute or any other Divine Being, which includes your Higher Self, to assist you in the healing by working through your mind. Divine assistance essentially turns your mind into a *conduit* or channel for Divine healing energy, which you mentally direct to your body or someone else's body through visualisation and auto-suggestion.

Once again, this need only involve your imagination, a sincere desire to be healed or to help heal another person, and a belief in what you are doing based on your understanding of consciousness. Asking for Divine assistance helps to relieve you of any doubt you may have in your mind's healing powers, especially if the illness is life threatening. It also helps preserve your own Life Force because you are no longer directing your own personal energy towards healing but rather Divine Energy, which when flowing through you will equally benefit you.

THE ROLE OF DOCTORS AND MEDICINE

Under *no circumstances* is mental healing intended to replace medical advice. Always consult a professional doctor. Not only do doctors have a profoundly important purpose on this planet to which they have committed many years of study, but it is also a deeply ingrained belief in the collective consciousness of society, that doctors and medicine are fundamental to healing. Use this belief, therefore, to your advantage by always consulting a doctor you trust and respect.

There is also no denying that throughout history and even more so today, we have seen hugely significant discoveries in the field of medicine that have helped humanity cure diseases once deemed incurable. Modern medicine has vastly improved the overall state of our health and longevity. This is reason enough not to deny yourself access to centuries' worth of medical wisdom that is the foundation of today's medical profession. Always remember, mental healing of yourself and others is intended to supplement and support your medical therapy, and not to replace it outright.

Chapter 43
THE POWER OF PRAYER

The power of prayer is the single greatest power behind miracles. Even if you feel that you have exhausted all possibilities, or that something seems impossible for you given your current conditions and you cannot muster up one shred of evidence that things may change, prayer makes it possible. Having said this, prayer is often overlooked in teachings about conscious creation yet it is little different to visualisation. The key difference is that visualisation is an *intention* towards which you direct your own Life Force, whereas prayer is a *request* that you leave wholly in the hands of Omnipotence because it is directed to The Absolute or to a Higher Power.

Prayer is a most powerful meditation and should be approached in the same way you meditate, by physically and mentally relaxing first. But even if your mind is frantic and you feel that you cannot mentally calm yourself, by all means still pray. Prayer alone can grant you an incomparable sense of inner calm and peace.

HOW TO PRAY

Few people actually know how to pray. Jesus Christ taught us the most effective method of prayer as written in Mark 11:24. Here is the only instruction you will ever need on how to pray. "All things which you are *praying* for and *asking* for, *believe* you have *received*, and it *shall* happen for you." This version of Mark 11:24 is a direct translation from the *original* New Testament Bible written in Greek. Let us now look at each part of this instruction for prayer in turn.

"All things ..."

This means that through prayer you can ask for *anything whatsoever*. There is no request too big or too small, and there is no question about what is possible or not. Remember that God is above the relative opposites of big and small or difficult and easy.

The Absolute is unconstrained by space and time and is not limited by your own perception of what is possible or not, other than to the extent that you believe It is. You must come to *know* in your heart that all things are equally effortless to create, heal, and transform for the One that is All-Powerful.

"...which you are *praying* for and *asking* for"

This tells you that prayer is a *request*. It is *not* a desire. It is worth noting that the original Greek version of Mark 11:24 uses the word «αιτεῖσθε» *(pronounced: etisthe)*, and means 'to ask for'. But this has been *wrongly* translated in some modern versions to mean 'to desire'. There is, however, a world of difference between asking and desiring. *Asking* comes with an *expectation* that you will receive, otherwise you would not ask. In contrast, to desire something is really to *wish* for it, and is usually *not* accompanied by any expectation to receive.

"...believe you have received"

The most important part of this instruction for prayer is to *believe* you have *received*. Put simply, to receive what you pray for, you must *first* believe that you have already received it in that moment, without concern about the when or the how.

In other words, it is not to believe that you *will* receive, but rather to believe you have *already received*. To believe therefore, is to have the kind of faith described in Hebrews 11:1, as "the substance of things hoped for and the evidence of things not seen." Ultimately, to believe is not about believing in your *personal* power to change something but rather in the *Omnipotence* of The Absolute to change everything.

Believing that you have already received in prayer is similar to visualising in the present moment. To pray for something in the future is to fail to understand the true nature of space and time in the Spiritual Plane. Moreover, by praying for something in the future, you cannot help but acknowledge that you currently do not have it in the present moment. In so doing, you get caught up in the 'how' and question if it is possible. This is more often than not followed by the debilitating fear of 'what if it's not', which is again born out of not understanding the true meaning of Omnipotence.

When you pray therefore, believe that you have *already* received *without* any doubt. For instance, instead of praying for sunshine tomorrow, *feel* the sun's rays warming your skin while you pray. Instead of praying for a problem to be solved, see the problem as already perfectly solved while you pray. And instead of praying to be healed of an ailment or disease, feel the joy of being in perfect health while you pray. In each case be truly grateful while you pray for that which has already been *granted* to you.

"...and it *shall* happen for you."

The last part of the instruction for prayer tells you in no uncertain terms that as long as you *ask* and *believe*, then what you are praying for *will* happen for you. In other words, you will receive. It does not say you *could* maybe receive, or that The Absolute will think about it depending on the circumstances. In contrast, it is *definite* that you *shall* receive, with the only contingency being to ask for it and to believe you have received it. Put simply, asking and believing are the prerequisites for receiving.

Bear in mind that the word 'shall' implies the future, but based on your understanding of the nature of time, this *includes* the present moment or any other moment thereafter experienced as time in the Physical Plane. Even if you do not see an instant manifestation of your request through prayer, believe that it is only a matter of time in the Physical Plane, without any concern about how long it will take, because it has already manifested in the Spiritual Plane.

This then is the correct method for prayer - ask, believe, receive - in that specific order. If you ask but do not believe, you cannot receive. And if you believe but never ask, then likewise you cannot receive. If however you ask and *truly* believe that you have received, then you already have. Few people truly ask and even fewer come close to truly believing. Endeavour therefore, always to Ask - Believe - Receive.

WHEN TO PRAY

When you believe that something is possible within your own God-given creative power, it is preferable that you *will* it for yourself through visualisation. In contrast, when you feel it is improbable or even impossible, especially if you are attached to the outcome, then request it in the way described here through prayer. Having said this, whether you *request* in prayer or *intend* through visualisation, remember that the *source* of power is the same and unchanging. All power originates in the Omnipotence of The Absolute.

Bear in mind that visualisation and prayer is one and the same process because in both instances you are accessing the power of Omnipotence. Once again, the only difference is that visualisation is an *intention* towards which you direct your own Life Force, whereas prayer is a *request* that you leave wholly in the hands of Omnipotence.

Of course you could pray for everything but there is great reward to be had by directly participating in the creation of your own life, as it is intended for you to do. In so doing, you acknowledge yourself as a co-creator of your life, rather than never acknowledging your God-given power to do so.

The Greek philosopher Epicurus put it this way: "It is a folly for a man to pray to the gods for that which he has the power to obtain by himself." Endeavour therefore to make both visualisation and prayer part of your life and know always that in both cases you are accessing the Omnipotence of The Absolute.

THE POWER OF GIVING UP

Contrary to mainstream advice focused on *never* giving up, to give up is a powerful step in conscious creation, if you know *how* to do it. But most people deem giving up cowardly or an abandonment of their dreams. This, however, is in ignorance of the fact that to 'try, try, and try again' may be the less courageous and less effective thing to do. You have probably at some point, been faced with a dilemma of whether or not to give up on something you deeply desired. The usual advice is to 'keep trying' but never giving up can be the most tiring, time-wasting, and energy-draining thing you can do. If, however, you know how and when to give up, it is one of the most powerful steps you can take.

Give Upwards

Giving up is giving *up*-wards. This means to *give* whatever it is you are giving up on, *up* to a Higher Power. Send it upwards to The Absolute or even to your Higher Self who shares in All-Knowledge and All-Power, to sort it out for you. When you have tried everything else, to give up in this way is really the most powerful action you can take. A saying attributed to Albert Einstein is that "Insanity is doing the same thing over and over again while expecting different results." Use this as your guide to giving up. When you have tried everything, usually a number of times and in different ways, but are still getting the same unwanted results or see that nothing is changing, then give it upwards in its entirety to The Absolute.

You are the only one who can be the judge of whether *not* giving up on something is harming you and holding you back from living a happy life. The inner voice of your intuition will tell you to persist or it will advise you to stop and hand it over. Listen to it and honour its advice. When you are just too tired to try yet another way, give it upwards. Incidentally, the etymology of the term 'give up' correlates with the old French word *surrendre*, meaning to 'deliver over'. So giving up is to *deliver* your intention over to The Absolute.

A Powerful Decision

Never say 'I give up' with a sense of resignation. Rather let it be a powerful decision. Always imagine your intention being sent upwards and really ask and believe that it will be created for you. Then let it go in its entirety and know it is in the hands of Omnipotence. Refusing to give up on something is sometimes the very thing that prevents you from receiving what you desire because it is a sign of attachment and keeps you swinging between obsession and doubt.

It is better to give up than to live in *hope* in the *absence* of faith because hope *without* faith is just *doubt* by another name. Know that handing it over to a Higher Power opens you up to the realm of miracles. Indeed, adhering to the advice to 'let go and let God' is at times the only way of receiving that which you desire in your heart.

THE ESSENTIAL PRAYER

Whether you intend for yourself to experience something through visualisation, ask for it through prayer, or give your desire upwards, always make prayer part of your daily life to simply say thank you with gratitude for your life.

When you take the time each day to truly thank The Absolute for everything you already have in your life, from the mundane to the more important, then you cannot help but adopt an attitude of joy and gratitude. You will also find that you no longer moan as much or complain about those things you perceive to be missing in your life.

Make saying thank you, your daily essential prayer. Gratitude, however, is not about jumping up and down with excitement. It comes from the word 'grace' and there is nothing more graceful than being grateful every day to The Absolute in whom you live, and move and have your being.

Chapter 44

THE SECRET IS SECRECY

There is only one real secret when it comes to consciously creating your reality, and that is to keep it a secret. Keeping your mental intentions, desires, goals, and objectives private is one of the most important, yet widely overlooked, factors of intelligently directing your life. The key is say *nothing* to *no one*.

HOW *NOT* TO TEMPT FATE

Have you ever had a strong feeling that something you wanted to happen in your life was on its way, but then you told someone, and it did not happen, despite your having been positive that it would?

Have you ever felt hesitant to say something about a positive expectation because you did not want to 'jinx' it or 'tempt fate' but you went ahead and said it anyway, dismissing your reservations as superstitious nonsense by thinking 'what could possibly go wrong?' And then when your expectation did not come to pass, you blamed the person you told for jinxing you or yourself for tempting fate, or otherwise, you just put it down to bad luck.

Throughout history, humanity has adhered to superstitions to explain the inexplicable. Most superstitions, however, are not based on reason or knowledge. In this case, when something you expected did not happen just because you spoke about it, you would be excused for thinking that fate must have some kind of warped sense of humour but the truth is, it has nothing to do with fate.

Interrupting the Creation Process

There is a very specific reason why verbalising your expectations prevent them from happening, and the answer does not belong in any book of superstition or jinxes. It is not fate you tempt but rather, it is the *creation process* you interrupt when you speak about it too soon. However, when in ignorance of the creation process, one has little choice but to shift the responsibility onto fate and the jinx.

To be able to understand what is happening when you appear to tempt fate, you must understand the creation process. Put simply, the creation process is the transmutation of potential energy into actualised form through *concentrated* thought, and as is the case with all creation in the Physical Plane, this process takes time. You must therefore, allow for the necessary *uninterrupted* passage of time when consciously creating your reality by not saying anything to anyone. To tempt fate is nothing more than *speaking too soon*. And in fact, another way of saying 'I tempted fate' is 'I spoke too soon'. Herein lies the secret of how *not* to tempt fate. Silence is the key.

SPEECH DISPERSES CONCENTRATED ENERGY

Thought belongs to the Mental Plane while speech belongs to the Physical Plane. As long as something you desire or positively expect to happen has not yet appeared in your physical world, then leave it uninterrupted in the Mental Plane for mental creation to take place. It is of utmost importance that you understand that speech *disperses* concentrated mental energy. If you do not understand this, then all your mental efforts to attain your desires may be wasted.

The more you speak about something the more you disperse the mental energy that you previously concentrated in the mental image of your desire. And when there is no energy left to disperse, speaking about the very thing that you not too long ago felt certain about, actually makes it feel untrue. When that happens, you feel deflated and *know* in your heart that you have 'tempted fate', yet cannot quite put your finger on why you feel that way. Speaking about your desires or expectations significantly *weakens* their attractive power because you make use of and disperse the concentrated mental energy that you had endowed them with.

Having said this, speaking about your desires and expectations has nothing to do with *verbally* using auto-suggestions to instruct your subjective mind. You do not speak to your subjective mind *about* your desire but rather you direct it to create it. Auto-suggestions *supplement* the concentrated mental energy in the Mental Plane, whereas just talking about something disperses the energy into the Physical Plane's atmosphere, thereby causing its previous concentrated creative and attractive power to be lost.

Airtight Secrecy

Keep whatever you want to create private and be silent about it. This means not to say anything to anyone. Not to your best friend, your partner or even to your most trusted confidant. This includes not revealing every hope, expectation, and feeling on social media platforms or other internet forums.

Treat your desires and expectations as the most highly guarded secret of your heart, and keep them between you and The Absolute or Universal Mind until they come to pass. It cannot be emphasised enough that the *only secret* to conscious creation is secrecy, and more specifically, *airtight* secrecy. So keep quiet!

The Counterfeit Ego's Reaction

Verbally sharing your expectations, desires and mental practices with others, also inadvertently opens you up to other people's reactions, expectations and beliefs, or lack thereof, in what you are saying and doing. This in turn kick-starts a sense of panic for the counterfeit ego, because now that you have 'said it' you have to 'prove it', which then breeds attachment to the outcome and doubt. This then serves not only to disperse your concentrated mental energy, but also to transmute it into something negative.

'GO AND TELL NO MAN'

The advice to keep your desires private goes against most mainstream books on reality creation that in fact encourage you to do the exact opposite, by suggesting that you speak about your desire to everyone as if it has already happened. I urge you to ignore this advice. If you gain just one thing about reality creation from this book, let it be to keep your heart's desires a secret. Because even if you perform every exercise persistently, and take every necessary mental and physical action towards attaining your ideal, if you speak about your desires and efforts, the energy necessary for their creation is dissipated, and hence you risk wasting *all* your efforts and will have to start over.

What follows are some quotes from prominent authors on the subject of mind power that also insist on secrecy. John McDonald in his book The Message of a Master wrote, "The value of secretiveness lies in the fact that, being impersonal and universal, the [subconscious mind] throws its power in with whatever words it is coupled, and when your plans are expressed verbally, they become released and their force is spent."

In her 1921 book Your Invisible Power, Genevieve Behrend wrote "the moment you speak [your desire] to any living soul, that moment your power is weakened. Your power, your magnet of attraction is not that strong, and consequently cannot reach so far. The more perfectly a secret between your mind and your outer self is guarded, the more vitality you give your power of attraction."

Claude Bristol, in his 1948 book The Magic of Believing, was very clear on the matter. He wrote, "It cannot be too strongly emphasized that you should tell no-one. Don't give anyone an inkling of what you desire. The truth is that when you talk about what you're going to do, you scatter your forces. You lose the close connection you have with the sub-conscious and you frequently find that unless you do as directed, you will have to start all over in your program of achievement. 'Go and Tell No Man' [Luke 5:14] still holds true."

THE BUILD-UP OF ENERGY

Tell a child to keep something a secret and watch them tell someone else within minutes. Most adults, however, do not outgrow this child-like inability to keep a secret, whether it is their own, or someone else's. In fact, the easiest way to spread a rumour is to tell someone something and then tell them to keep it a secret.

The reason why keeping a secret or not talking about something you desire or expect is difficult, is because it creates a build-up of *internal* energy. Most people are uncomfortable with excess internal energy as it creates an inner imbalance. They therefore look for a way to disperse the energy and the quickest outlet is to talk about whatever it is they are not saying.

This explains why secrets are so powerful and alluring, and why most people quickly yield to sharing their secrets, despite their best intentions not to. Rest assured that your need to share your own or another person's secret does not make you a dishonest person. It is simply a matter of not being comfortable with excess energy.

In the case of your desires and positive expectations, the excess energy builds up even further. This is because you increasingly direct your Life Force to the mental image of your intention held within your mind. Not talking about something early on in the process is easier, but the more confident you feel about something, the more difficult it becomes. As your confidence increases, so you become more motivated to persist in your desire's attainment, and the more you believe in your ideal outcome with optimal emotion, then the greater the energy build-up within you, to the point that you feel if you do not tell someone, you will 'burst'.

Make or Break

That *moment* at which you feel that you must tell someone about your expectation is critical, and can either make or break the attainment of your desired outcome. Be very clear that at that very moment your point of attraction is at its *most powerful* and physical attainment is likely to be only a matter of time.

What you should do is use this excess internal energy wisely to power you through obstacles that you may still encounter and to help keep your *focus* on your desired mental image. In contrast, however, this is the exact moment that most people begin to talk and talk, and then talk some more, about their desire and how certain they are about their inevitable success. The instant you do, the excess energy driving your motivation, as well as your creative and attractive power, is immediately dispersed and significantly dissipated.

Other intelligent ways to deal with the build-up of internal energy so as to avoid talking about your expectations, is to do some physical exercise, go for a walk in nature, or simply relax using the relaxation technique for meditation (Ch. 37), all of which help to naturally restore your sense of inner balance. But whatever you do, keep quiet.

TRAINING YOURSELF TO KEEP QUIET

You must train yourself to keep quiet about your desires, positive expectations, or good feelings about something you sense is about to happen for you. This does not mean never having a meaningful conversation with others about your goals or aspirations. Nor does it mean becoming suspicious about other people's intentions for you.

Here is a rule of thumb to stick to. When talking with others about your life, train yourself to keep your conversations to your actual experience of life. In other words, make it a habit to share only those things that you are *currently* physically experiencing in your life or that you have *already* experienced. Do not let what you *say* get ahead of your physical experience. And bear in mind that there is a world of difference between asking for advice and talking about your desires. When you ask for advice about something, you do not have to tell someone your positive expectations or desires. Be intelligent in what you say and what you ask, and know that the *personal* answers you are looking for are within you. There is no better teacher than the inner teacher of your in-tuition.

You can also learn to distinguish between what you should and should not share by listening to your intuition. Listen to and respect the voice within that tells you 'do not say it'. It is not superstitious nonsense. Rather, it is the wisest advice you can come to expect in so far as your desires are concerned. Honour your intuition's advice and you will soon know exactly what you should and should not share so as not to disperse your concentrated energy. The best indication is if the voice within says 'do not say it' then do not say it. And if in doubt, always play it safe by saying nothing.

If what you intend to create involves a group of people, then insist that the people in your group or team keep the intention or goal private and keep any discussions limited to the group. In dealing with groups or teams, imagine the individual minds in the team as a single mind, and the secret of the goal is held within that one mind.

Guilt is a Funny Thing

You may feel a sense of guilt for not sharing something personal that you are expecting or are hoping for with a friend, family member, or partner. Do not, however, give into this misguided feeling of guilt. Just remember that your keeping quiet is based on an understanding of the nature of the creation process, *not* because you do not trust them or want to keep something from them. In fact, not telling them is for *their* benefit as much as it is for yours, because those close to you are likely to benefit from the manifestation of your own desires.

If you find yourself remembering the importance of secrecy mid-sentence of sharing a desire or expectation, then simply change the subject or just pretend you forgot what you wanted to say. But do not tell anyone that you are no longer sharing your desires and have decided to keep them a secret. Keep that a secret too.

Finally, if in retrospect you can think of a few instances of when you spoke about something you expected to happen too soon only for it not to happen, there is no need to be upset. If it is something you still desire and is important enough for you, then simply start the creation process again using the techniques in this book, only this time keep it an air-tight secret.

SHARING NEGATIVITY

A question that often comes up in the context of speech dispersing energy is about sharing negativity. Since speech disperses energy, then it stands to reason that talking about your negative thoughts and fears disperses their creative energy and attractive power. This is true and explains why people generally find it helpful to talk about their negative feelings or problems, because it disperses and relieves them of the negative energy. To put this in context, when you talk about positive expectations or desires you feel deflated because the positive energy within has been dispersed, whereas when you talk about your problems you feel a sense of relief.

Having said this, the problem is that the more you talk about all the negative things in your life, the more you focus on them, and while you may be dispersing the energy of any negative expectation or fear, you are also keeping your overall mental nature negative and creating an image of negativity about you in the minds of others. This serves to keep you stuck in a negative rut and attract those things that resonate with your overall negativity, which in turn, keeps your unwanted circumstances unchanged.

By all means talk to someone that you trust and seek professional help if something in your life is overwhelming you with negativity. The point though is to avoid making negative talk a habit. When you talk about the 'bad stuff', do so with the intention of seeking advice or a solution to your problem, and then *act* on the positive advice you may receive if it resonates with you. In this way, you reduce the negativity of your mental nature rather than increase it.

Make sure, however, that you are not just complaining or moaning, and never think of yourself as a victim of circumstance or otherwise. The last thing you want is other people's pity. By going in search of pity, be well aware that you will find things to be pitied for. Moreover, bear in mind that everyone has their own problems to deal with even if you may not be aware of them, so make sure that you are not simply dumping your own day-to-day negativity on someone else.

It is also helpful to disperse the energy of your negative thoughts through writing. Briefly write down what is bothering you on a piece of paper and then discard the paper. And as you throw the paper away sense how you are also throwing away, or dispersing, all the negative energy inherent in what you have written on it.

Remember also to train your mind to transmute negative thoughts and emotions into their higher equivalents, as and when they arise. Change your perspective by looking for the good in the bad, and be grateful for all that is already going right in your life. And finally, do not dismiss the power of prayer and remember always to consult the silence of your intuition within - be still and know.

LIVE BY EXAMPLE

A final word of advice on secrecy is do not teach this knowledge to others before you have made it part of your life. It is far better for you to walk your talk, than to just talk and talk. Only once you have put the knowledge into action, seen the results, and reaped the benefits, should you *teach it* to others. Better yet, let others ask you how you did it when they see all the wonderful changes taking place in your life. If, however, you try to teach it too soon, you disperse the energy and motivation that it has granted you. Moreover, you are also likely to face resistance to what you are teaching if you do not wholly believe it or have not put it into practice. Not everyone is ready to receive this knowledge and you may find that others attempt to discourage you. In turn, this fuels doubt within you or a need to defend your new beliefs at a time when they have just begun to take root in your mind, and hence are most vulnerable to being uprooted.

Put simply, encourage others for instance to read a book that has benefited you, if you intuitively believe they are ready to benefit from it, and especially if they are faced with an illness. But do not try to force them to read it. Make it your personal motto to live by *example* and let your life be the evidence for this knowledge. Indeed, there is no better way to teach, than to teach by example.

Chapter 45
THE MASTER FORMULA FOR LIFE

There is only one master formula for life and that is to *love* life. A successful life is not measured by how much money you have, how big your house is, what type of car you drive, the clothes you wear, how many goals you have achieved, who you are in a relationship with, if you are single or married, or what others think of you. To measure the success of your life, measure only how much *you love life*. You may have everything in the world, and much more than you may ever need, but if you do not love life, you might as well have nothing. In the same way, you may possess nothing in the physical world, but if you love life, you have everything.

TRUST LIFE

To love life you must learn to *trust* life. Trust that everything in your life is happening in perfect order even if you cannot understand or see the order of things at all times. Do not declare anything that happens in your life as good or bad, or as lucky or unlucky. In this way, you live a life free of judgement and free of self-pity, and so do not give anything in the Physical Plane the power to define your happiness or to take it away when things change.

The Parable of the Farmer

Here is a parable about a farmer from Andrew Matthew's 1997 book Follow Your Heart, which expresses the wisdom of not judging your life or any of your experiences as good or bad, lucky or unlucky.

"There once lived a farmer. He had a son and a horse. One day the farmer's horse ran away, and all his neighbours came to console him, saying: 'What bad luck that your horse has run away!' And the old man replied: 'Who knows if it's good luck or bad luck.' 'Of course it's bad luck!' said the neighbours. Within a week, the farmer's horse returned home, followed by twenty wild horses. The farmer's neighbours came to celebrate, saying: 'What good luck that you have your horse back - plus another twenty!' And the old man replied: 'Who knows if it's good luck or bad luck!' The next day the farmer's son was riding amongst the wild horses, and fell and broke his leg. The neighbours came to console him, saying: 'What bad luck!' And the farmer said: 'Who knows if it's good luck or bad luck!' And some of the neighbours were angry, and said: 'Of course it's bad luck, you silly old fool!' Another week went by, and an army came through town, enlisting all the fit young men to fight in distant lands. The farmer's son, with his broken leg, was left behind. All the neighbours came to celebrate, saying: 'What good luck your son was left behind!' And the farmer said: 'Who knows?'"

Heed the message from the farmer in this parable and do not label anything in your life as good or bad, lucky or unlucky, and be open to *not* knowing yet what it all means. In so doing, you let life flow unhindered and trust life to work out for your highest good. As long as you remain the single director of your will and learn to trust Life, then joy and positivity becomes your natural state of being. In turn, life becomes a process of giving, receiving, and re-giving between you and the abundant Universe without attachment or doubt and without any misguided need to judge your life.

Accept Life

Accept everything that shows up in your life and give nothing too much importance. Learn to say 'it is what it is' in both the 'good' times and the 'bad' times. Not with a sense of resignation but rather, with the sense of being okay with playing both sides of the Game of Life, while acknowledging that nothing is ever permanent.

Saying 'it is what it is' grants you the freedom to focus on your desire, without having to worry about current conditions because you have accepted them for what they are, which really is just a projection of your *past* mental contents. If, however, you refuse to accept life the way it is *first*, then it is more than likely to remain little changed because you are inadvertently *focusing* on exactly how it is.

FLOW WITH LIFE

In a world that is always changing, the only constant is change. Learn to accept and even welcome change and let go of the need to control your life, which itself is a sure sign that the counterfeit ego is running the show. Remember always that your aim is not to control the Physical Plane, nor anything or anyone in it. Rather, your aim is to direct your *own mind*, without concern for your outside conditions.

To embrace change is really nothing more than allowing life to flow. Everything changes, nothing stays the same. Consider these maxims from the Greek philosopher Heraclitus that 'everything is in flux' and 'you can never step into the same river twice', which means that both the water you are stepping into, and the version of the physical you that is stepping into the water, have changed.

You have probably experienced resistance to change in a number of ways. For instance, by trying to hold onto an experience *as it is* because you judge it as good and so do not allow it to change or evolve.

Alternatively, you may also find you refuse to let go of a certain desire that once was very dear to you, even if it no longer resonates with you. By doing so, you become stuck in a moment and go against one of the fundamental principles of nature, which is that *everything* changes.

Let Go of the Past

Endeavour to let go of the past as a place in which you want to be. Even if something from your past does come back into your life, *it* will have changed. Treat it as a *new* experience otherwise you will simply re-live a *version* of the past experience and the outcome will be the same. Instead of trying to revive and re-live the past, live your life in the ever-present *now*, which includes *all* time. Simply focus on whatever you want to experience now as if it *already* exists, because it does, but with no concern for how it was in the past.

There is Nothing to Fear in Change

Adopt a carefree attitude and let life flow. Do not permit yourself to be attached to anything or anyone, and let go of beliefs and desires that no longer serve you. Do not try to hold onto things as they are, or force them back to how they used to be out of fear of losing what you have. Do not permit yourself to become stuck in any moment, no matter how pleasurable or how painful it may be. Keep moving *with* life, and the more you do, the more enjoyable life will become. Albert Einstein put it this way: "Life is like riding a bicycle. To keep your balance, you must keep moving."

Whatever is not allowed to flow and whatever is not allowed to change in a world that is *constantly* changing stagnates, and in time, dies for the lack of renewal. So let your life and your experiences flow and learn to welcome change rather than fear it. Somewhat ironically, nothing seems to change *faster* than what you want to stay the same, whereas nothing seems to change *slower* than what you desperately want to change. Lao Tzu told us that "life is a series of natural and spontaneous changes. Don't resist them; that only creates sorrow. Let reality be reality. Let things flow naturally forward in whatever way they like." Loosen your grip, and allow for all those things you want to *keep in* your life to *flow* and change, and in so doing, you will find to your surprise, that they *stay* in your life and become even better.

Life's Changing Weather

In the same way that the Physical Plane has its seasons, so does life. When life's blessings are shining down on you enjoy and appreciate their warmth in that moment. If life's sunshine turns to rain or its leaves begin to fall, learn to dance in the rain and enjoy life, even if its leaves are falling. And should life's rain turn into a storm, take shelter in the strength of the *undisturbed* I within, and rest assured that by Universal Law, the storm will pass and the sunshine will return.

If you feel 'down and out', remember that the only direction from there is *up*. In fact, albeit somewhat paradoxical, there is great power in hitting rock bottom and knowing that from that point onwards the only direction is up. No matter what challenges you may be facing in your current conditions, and no matter how hopeless things may *seem*, remember that things are seldom what they seem, that no feeling is permanent, and that the darkest hour is just before the dawn.

BE GRATEFUL

When you love life you cannot help but be grateful for everything in your life. Gratitude is about appreciating everything you already have in your life. Know that whatever you appreciate *appreciates* - it grows. Put simply, gratitude is an attitude of grace, and to say grace is to say thank you. Saying thank you, however, need not involve shouting at the top of your voice or expressing over-excitement at the first signs that your desire is being fulfilled. These are extremes that, as all extreme emotions do, cloud your objectivity, waste your Life Force reserves, widen the pendulum's counter-balancing swing, and deny you the grace that comes with gratitude.

Be Graceful

To be graceful is to be filled with gratitude and appreciation, and when you are, you discover an unshakeable sense of inner peace and strength. If, however, you wallow in your problems, wonder why The Universe has 'forgotten you,' or say 'why me?' when faced with a difficult situation, then you trap yourself in a bleak mental prison that blinds you to all the good that already *is* in your life.

Everyone has their share of problems and the grass only *seems* greener on the other side. Recall the words by the Greek philosopher Socrates: "If all our misfortunes were laid in one common heap, whence everyone must take an equal portion, most people would be content to take their own and depart." What matters is how you *perceive* your problems, and when you change your perception, they too will change.

Gratitude for the Mundane

You can learn to be grateful for all those day-to-day mundane tasks that may frustrate you. To do so, think of the *reason* behind why you do what you are not particularly fond of doing, and you will quickly find a reason to be grateful for even the most mundane of tasks. For instance, you can be grateful for having to wash the dishes because it means you have food to eat. You can be grateful for the long commute to work because it means you have a source of income to support yourself. You can be grateful for ironing because it means you have clothes on your back. You can be grateful for the pressure of exams because it means you have education.

In fact, if you did not have all those things you *already* have, you would not be paying the cosmic price for maintaining them. When you can count your blessings in the seemingly mundane, you will know just how truly blessed you are.

Gratitude for the Difficult

You can even learn to maintain a sense of gratitude during difficult times by focusing on all that is already good, by looking for the good in the bad, and by looking for the lessons you can learn from your unwanted circumstances. Wherever possible, treat everything you perceive as going wrong in your life as a blessing in disguise.

Simply recall a past experience which at the time upset you, yet in retrospect you came to appreciate for bringing you to where you are today. In the same way, wherever possible, imagine yourself looking back at an unwanted current experience as a blessing in disguise and be grateful that your life has been shaped by it for the better, even if you cannot yet tell how.

Gratitude for Life

Let go of the idea that 'more is better' and as Wayne Dyer said, ask yourself this: "where is the *peace*, in more is better?" Endeavour to be content with everything you already have, rather than going on a never-ending search for more.

Do not let yourself suffer the many inner imbalances of having many desires. Choose your personal desires one at a time. Ask your heart what you truly want, listen to your intuition, and remember that the Real You desires nothing. As Lao Tzu said, "loss is not as bad as wanting more."

When all is said and done, when you do not let anything define you, there is no need to judge anything as good or bad and you are free to be grateful for the *experience* of life itself. And in so doing, you will no longer have to look for something to be grateful for, because you will already be grateful for everything.

Heed once again the wisdom in the following words by Lao Tzu: "Be content with what you have. Rejoice in the way things are. When you realize there is nothing lacking, the whole world belongs to you."

CHOOSE TO BE HAPPY

As you already know, the only real freedom you have is your freedom of choice. With freedom of choice comes the freedom to *choose* to be happy, irrespective of your circumstances and what your counterfeit ego may be telling you in its futile bid to stay in control.

Happiness in this context, however, does not mean to be a happy go-lucky person, in the same way that positivity does not mean to think good or happy thoughts. Rather, to 'be happy' means to aspire to 'be of good spirit', which is one of the key concepts of Aristotelian ethics based on the Greek word «ευδαιμονία» *(pronounced: evdaemonia)*. Moreover, 'to be of good spirit' means to 'flourish as a human being'. And, since the Real You is Pure *Spirit*, it stands to reason that true happiness is found in aspiring to flourish as the I within.

In turn, by aspiring to the Real You, you become *enthusiastic* about all life. And the word 'enthusiastic' itself has its origin in the Greek word «ἐνθεος» *(pronounced: entheos)*, meaning 'to have God within'. Aspiring therefore, to the Real You increases both your positivity and enthusiasm for life, which in turn affords you with a sense of peace and higher purpose, undisturbed by how much you have or do not have in the physical world.

Let Nothing Define Your Happiness

Choosing happiness is not about comparing a list of all those things that make you happy to a list of those that make you sad, and tallying up the difference. Rather, *choosing* happiness is to *choose* not to allow anything you perceive as good or bad in your *outer* world to define the happiness of your *inner* world. And once again, when nothing *defines* your happiness, then nothing can deny it either. Be wary of what you give your attention to. Think of '*paying* attention' as '*paying* for' whatever you are giving your attention to, and hence receiving it.

Having said this, if an experience in your life is making you sad, and staying positive feels beyond your own personal power, then rest assured that by Universal Law, your sadness will pass. Everybody is sad sometimes, but far fewer people are ever truly happy.

Moreover, let go of any misguided guilt that being happy while others are sad is somehow wrong. You can *only* ever help others find their own happiness, if you yourself are happy. Refusing to be happy until others in your life are also happy serves *only* to maintain the *status quo* of unhappiness in your life and in that of others. Therefore *choose* happiness in the knowledge that your outer world is but a projection of your consciousness, and that everything is possible for you and others, if only you would make use of the greatest gift ever given to you as a spiritual being having a physical experience, which is your freedom of choice to direct your mind.

BE TRULY ALIVE

It is somewhat ironic that one way to ensure you maximise your joy and happiness while having a physical experience, is to realise that one day it will end. When you accept that one day your physical life will end, yet the Real You will go on, you will find that you no longer worry so often, or take every little thing that happens so seriously, or worry about all your possessions and how much you have or do not have, or about what others have in comparison. You will also find that you refuse to waste time *waiting* to be happy, or waiting for what you think *should* happen before you can enjoy your life. Instead, you go out and enjoy life and accept it all as it is, for the experience itself.

Rising Above Life and Death

As human beings in the physical world we tend to view the Cycle of Life as the cycle of birth and death. However, this is a misconception because just as one's death or departure from the physical realm marks one's birth or entrance into the non-physical realm, so one's birth or entry into the physical realm marks one's departure from the non-physical realm. Instead of seeing the Cycle of Life as the cycle of birth and death, which creates an inherent sadness out of fear of the unknown, see it for what it is - The Cycle of Spirit and Form. And the truth is that you never depart from the Spiritual Plane even while in the Physical Plane because you *are* Spirit having a physical experience and not the other way around. There is only ever one real home and that is the Spiritual Plane and since the Real You is eternal, you are never born and never die in any real sense.

Life is the Playground of Your Soul

It is our ignorance of life beyond physical death that makes us fearful of it because non-physical life is not visible to our physical senses. This does not mean, however, that we should focus on death or want to leave the Physical Plane in a misguided attempt to escape life. In fact, metaphysical texts tell us that little changes at first upon physical death, other than no longer having a body and *physical* sensations.

Rising above the opposites of life and death is about accepting that *both* are *part* of the journey, but that *neither* marks its beginning or its end because the journey itself is timeless and eternal. Learn to maximise your experience of the physical journey by being truly *alive* while in the Physical Plane. Few people, however, truly *appreciate* the fact that every day we get to get *older*. Aging is a privilege and one of the greatest gifts of living a full life in the Physical Plane. As is the case with all things, if you resist and fear getting older, it seems to be the only thing that happens to you, whereas when you learn to age *gracefully* while aspiring to the *ageless* I within, you remain forever young and it shows.

You Cannot Imagine Not Being
The only thing you cannot imagine is yourself 'being dead'. You can imagine a 'lifeless' body but it would still be the Real You observing it. In other words, you can never imagine yourself as *not being* because the part of you that *is*, can never *not be*. When you identify life with the cycle of birth and death you make yourself *mortal*, whereas when you identify life with the cycle of Form and Spirit, you come to know the truth that you are in fact immortal and eternal. This mental attitude empowers you to rise above the greatest fear of all that is death, and grants you the freedom to be truly alive while here in the Physical Plane, something that existing alone cannot do.

While the I within is eternal, the *personal* you having the physical experience in the Physical Plane will never be repeated. So make the most of your life by truly *being alive*. Seize the opportunity to enjoy your physical *experience* as a human being. See your physical life as the playground of your Soul and endeavour to play the Game of Life well, before you get to return home thoroughly exhausted, with joy in your heart and gratitude on your lips for a life well lived.

THE ART OF TOP-DOWN-LIVING
The essence of Top-Down-Living is to live life from the top, which means to experience life from the vantage point of who you are *at* the top - the unchanging I within. To live from the I within is to awaken your will and become the objective director of your subjective mind, and all your ever-changing mental contents. As the I within, you do not permit *anything* in the ever-changing Physical and Mental Planes to define who you *know* you are in the unchanging Spiritual Plane.

You know that your will and your intuition are the masculine and feminine *father and mother* principles of the I within. They are intended to guide you and ultimately protect and nurture your physical being in the physical world. When you direct and guide your thoughts and emotions with the power of your will, and choose your desires one by one based on the wisdom of your inner *knowing*, then you become the master of your mind and in turn, of your life.

Instead of wondering if the Universe will grant you your desire, realise that your will is a focalised centre of Cosmic Will and that your mind is a creative centre of the One Universal Mind. In this way, you co-create your experience of reality *through* Universal Mind, knowing in your heart that all things are possible for you, for you will have attained mutual recognition with the single creative source of the entire Universe, in which your will is a centre.

The Master Formula for Reality Creation

As the master of your mind and your life, you are *not* concerned with controlling or changing your outside conditions. Instead you accept them as they are because you know there is no point in trying to change or manipulate a *projection* of consciousness. Doing so can be likened once again, to trying to change an already printed photograph and expecting the changes to be reflected the next time you develop it from the original. To change something in the Physical Plane, while operating at the degree of positivity of the Physical Plane, requires *physical force*. In contrast, to change the Physical Plane in a lasting way and without physical *force* requires that you change the 'original' from which your experience is being projected, which is the mental image in your mind. Since the Physical Plane is *below* the Mental Plane in degree of positivity, it must, by Universal Law, submit to and follow the lead of your mental changes.

It cannot be stressed enough that there is no need to try to *change* the Physical Plane itself by working with outside conditions or trying to manipulate people, and in fact there is no point in doing so. The Physical Plane 'is what it is' and there is nothing you can do about it at *its* level. You must rise *above* its level and change the mental image held in *your* mind, not in the mind of others. Focus on an altogether *new* possible future as if in the *present* moment, without any concern for your current outer conditions, which themselves are simply the projection of a possible future you once focused on. In other words, your current conditions are *not* any more real than the projected movie you watch on the screen in a movie theatre. Have no concern, therefore, for what you are observing in your outer world. Accept it as it is, and do not let the *unreal* define the *real*. Focus instead only on what you *desire* to observe by imagining conditions as you desire them to be, and be *patient*. In so doing, what you observe in the physical plane will in time follow suit.

Multiple Streams of Joy

Broaden your horizons by having several *personal* interests, even while pursuing your one desire. When you have multiple interests you have multiple streams of joy, and if one stream should dry up, joy will still flow into your life from the other streams. In so doing, your joy does not depend on attaining your desire. Better yet, be joyful as a way of *being*, independent of what is going on in your life. In this way, you will find your desires flowing to you with far less effort and free of obsession and doubt.

Take Nothing Personally

Do not take others' actions or words towards you personally. No matter how personal they may seem, remember always that the Real You is *undisturbed*. Only the counterfeit ego has a vested interest in taking things personally. This does not mean, however, to put up with others' hurtful words or actions. Instead, it means to deal with them *impersonally* rather than internalise them. This in turn empowers you to respond intelligently to whatever is going on in your outer world, rather than to react emotionally. A rule of thumb is, if you are taking it personally, it is the *personal* counterfeit ego that is doing so.

The less you take things personally, then the less personal they become, and in time, you will find that others no longer say or do things that *personally* upset you anymore. Moreover, remember that since Universal Mind is *impersonal*, nothing that shows up in your life is a *personal* intention on Its part towards you. In fact, it is only ever *your* intention, whether conscious or not, because it is your thinking that directs Universal Mind.

Expect Nothing

Endeavour wherever possible to expect nothing from others. In so doing, you will find that you are seldom disappointed. Relationships free of expectations usually prove more rewarding because no one feels under pressure to perform. You will also find that most people are willing to *gladly* do things for you when it is not expected of them because they are *free* to *choose* to do so. This does not, however, mean not asking others for help or not being willing to receive, but rather it means not *insisting* on it. Not expecting anything from anyone is of course not always practical in your day to day life. So strike a balance between expecting nothing and expecting others to do what is expected of them, but endeavour to lean towards the former and to give others the freedom of choice.

Moreover, while you can confidently *expect* the creation of your *personal* desires, do not *depend* on their fulfilment to complete you. In the words of the Greek author Nikos Kazantzakis, "I hope for nothing, I fear nothing, I am free." In other words, when you *desire* nothing, you have nothing to *fear*, and so you are free, and this indeed underpins the power of the I within.

Assume Nothing

Let go of your assumptions because while you may or may not believe what you are told, you never doubt what you assume, and so most of your misunderstandings and disappointments are as a direct result of your assumptions. Instead of assuming you have understood someone's words, ask them for clarification. And instead of assuming others know what you want, be willing to tell them. Essentially, to assume is to live at the level of your sub-conscious *assumed* beliefs, whereas conscious living is about endeavouring to *know* what is *really* going on in your life, rather than assuming you already know.

Do Not Compare Yourself to Others

Comparing yourself to others traps you in a roller-coaster ride, on which your self-worth is flung around by others' opinions, words, and actions. Even if you do feel better than others by comparison, the strength you gain is a temporary counterfeit ego-boost disguising itself as authentic inner power. Once the 'ego'-boost begins to fade, as it will, so your insecurities re-surface, thereby re-triggering your need for reassurance that sends you on a futile search for inner strength in the one place you will never find it - outside yourself.

If you compare yourself to others, you are likely to find that you also look to others for their approval. Needing others' approval makes you doubt yourself and your decisions. It drains you of a sense of individuality and leaves you never quite sure of who you are and what you really want. The good opinion of others may feel 'good' in the short run but can only leave you feeling 'bad' in the long run. Someone else's stamp of approval can be likened to an ink stamp on your skin that is quickly washed off with the first sign of rain. Put simply, whoever you need to 'stamp' you, owns you. When all is said and done, compare your *personal* self only to your Real Self, and let the I within be your only aspiration.

A New Vocabulary

Remove the opposites of 'good and bad' and 'success and failure' from your vocabulary. Give nothing in your life so much importance that it defines your *happiness*, because one day, it may become what determines your *sadness*. In the words of Kahlil Gibran, "When you are joyous, look deep into your heart and you shall find it is only that which has given you sorrow that is giving you joy. When you are sorrowful look again in your heart, and you shall see that in truth you are weeping for that which has been your delight."

When you judge something going on in your outer world as being good, it makes you feel happy; and when you rejoice in your outer world success, it makes you feel successful. But in so doing, you give those very things the power to make you feel sad or a failure, if and when they change, as all things do. Likewise, when you judge something as being bad or wallow in your perceived failure to achieve something, then you are *depending* on those very things to change in order to allow you to feel happy and successful again. Do you see the futility of it all? Label nothing therefore, as being good in your outer world, and in so doing nothing can make you feel bad. And likewise, give no worldly achievement the power to make you feel successful, and in so doing nothing can make you feel a failure.

When all is said and done, let the *only thing* that makes you feel good and successful be the *knowledge* that you are the unchanging and undisturbed I within. And since *it never* changes, then neither can your 'feeling good' about life change. In turn, your life will become more successful than any physical world success could ever make it, and even more so since your success will no longer depend on outer world things that, by Universal Law, will change.

EINSTEIN'S FORMULA FOR SUCCESS

To be successful in your personal life is not to work yourself to the bone in pursuit of your goals. A life of all work and no play is just as unsuccessful if not more so, than a life of all play and no work. Endeavour therefore to strike a balance between work and play by adhering to Albert Einstein's following formula for success.

"If A equals success then the formula is A = X + Y + Z, where X equals work, Y equals play, and Z equals keep your mouth shut." The beauty of Einstein's formula for *personal* success is in its simplicity. Work first and then play, and in everything you do, speak less and keep quiet about your desires, dreams, and aspirations.

Work Hard and Play with Abandon

In whatever work you do, endeavour to cultivate a strong work ethic of persistence, strength of character, honesty, and integrity. Know that if you cheat others or deliberately keep them 'down' in order for you to get ahead, then that is your mental frequency and is what will be attracted to you in time. In contrast, when you keep your own goals in mind and pursue them with integrity, while also taking the time to help others along their way where possible, you will find that Life will gladly take you where you want to go, because you too will have gladly helped Life to take others where they want to go. Always do your best but remember that your best will not always be the same at every given moment, so be gentle with yourself.

Finally, in all your pursuits and hard work, make time to play. But to play does not mean to relax. It actually means just that - to *play* – and do so with the same sense of abandon with which you played when you were a child. Walk barefoot on the grass, feel the wind blow on your face, let the sun warm your skin, taste the rain, sing out loud, have fun, and laugh often.

Put simply, when you work, *focus* on your work with the power of your will as a self-directed adult, but when you play use the power of your child-like *abandon* and let everything go. Remember always to play the Game of Life gracefully. Do not be so concerned about *you* winning, as much as you are about enjoying it, playing it well, and wanting everyone else to win *with* you.

THE MENTAL GARDENER

There are many lessons to be learnt for the conscious reality creator by studying how a skilled gardener creates and maintains his garden. The darkness beneath the soil can be compared to your subjective mind where creation takes place, and the seeds planted within the soil are the mental images you impress on it to be created. The water, which is necessary for the seeds' growth, is akin to your emotions with which you nourish your mental image. And the flowers and plants which in time emerge above the soil can be likened to those outer world experiences that appear in your life, which too are the outcome of your mental images. In other words, the invisible mental realm is *within* the soil, and the garden that emerges *above* the soil is the visible physical realm of your experience of reality.

Planting Your Mental Seeds

To prepare your mind as would a gardener his soil, loosen your mental soil by not holding onto anything too tightly and not giving anything too much importance. Remove mental weeds by uprooting limiting beliefs, doubt, and attachment, and add 'organic matter', by maintaining a sense of positivity, faith, and balance. In the same way that most seeds prefer soil of neutral pH levels, so it is that mental seeds prefer a mental soil of balance or equilibrium. Consciously *choose* the mental images you plant in your subjective mind one at a time and *know* why you are choosing them, just like the gardener carefully selects the seeds he will plant and their purpose for him.

Creating Your Garden

When a skilled gardener plants a seed in the soil, he leaves it in the soil's darkness with *confidence* that it *will* grow. He does not wonder if it is or is not growing, even if he does not see any activity above ground for some time. He does not over-water it in the hope it will grow faster, because he knows over-watering will drown it and give it little chance of growth. Nor does he dig the seed up every ten minutes to see if it is growing, or pull on its first shoots that emerge to hurry it along. In the same way, endeavour to become a skilled mental gardener. Tend to your garden lovingly every day. Water its seeds with enough emotion but do not allow your mental soil to become 'emotion-logged', lest your mental seeds 'drown'. If you find you have over-watered your seeds, let the excess emotion be drained away by emotionally calming yourself before watering again.

Remove mental weeds of negative thoughts and doubt lest they mingle with the roots of the mental seeds you have planted. If left to grow uninhibited, they will hinder and even stop the growth of your seeds. When the first signs of growth appear in your outer world be joyful, but do not become overly-excited and do not try to *force* things to go faster. Instead, have patience and enjoy every step. Remember that patience is a willingness to *endure* the internal imbalance of desire and to *wait* for its fulfilment, while doing whatever it takes to attain it. In other words, patience is a willingness to *persist* even when things are slow because you *know* that every creation in the physical world takes *time* to be created, and so you gladly allow for it.

Maintaining Your Garden

When your desire is physically created, enjoy it and be grateful. Share it with others but do not talk about your mental seeds because that is akin to a gardener uprooting the seeds he planted instead of letting them grow. Also bear in mind that some flowers in life's garden will bloom in the spring and may wither away as autumn approaches, but they will *grow* again as long as you allow them this *change*. Others, however, may bloom but once but again be grateful for their beauty, albeit transitory. Witness the changes in your life's garden and notice how every change adds to its overall beauty. Intelligently care for your garden while also allowing for change. In so doing, you will find there will be few *unwanted* changes, while *most* changes will be in the direction of the greater expression of all life in your experience of reality. In time, when the roots of your garden are deeply grounded, it will be able to sustain itself with less effort on your part, and you will reap the rewards of its bounty and gladly share them with others.

LIVE AND LET LIVE

Living from the I within and knowing your true nature is not about believing that you are now above or better than others because you have 'figured it all out' and they haven't. Nor is it about arrogantly believing or proclaiming that you are God, or thinking that you are invincible and that nothing can touch you or get in your way. This attitude is an extreme that is best avoided, and is in fact more self-destructive than not knowing your true nature at all.

In contrast, knowing yourself is accompanied by an inner calm and peace of mind and by reverence for The Absolute. When you are truly grateful to The Absolute for everything in your life and are in awe of the sheer infinite wonder of the Universe, then there is no room for self-righteousness, conceit, or arrogance.

Moreover, being the I within is not about having power over everyone else. Only the counterfeit ego needs power, and to need power is to believe that it is outside of you, whereas in truth, All Power is within you. Indeed, true power resides in the mind that has no need for power.

Everyone Has Their Own Dream

Do not allow for an inflated sense of self-importance to cloud your mind. Avoid the narcissistic trap of believing you are the only one who matters since your experience is a dream of your Real Self. This is buying into separateness to an extreme and has nothing to do with the unity of I consciousness. Bear in mind that everyone has their own dream. Even if we have yet to fully understand the 'mechanics' of how shared reality works, a good place to start is to see everyone and everything as *reflecting* a part of your consciousness back to you. Focus your desire for change *inwards* not outwards, and give everyone the same importance you give to your personal self.

Seeing your experience as a projection of your consciousness is not narcissistic. It is not about feeling guilty, allocating blame, becoming a control freak, putting up with the others' hurtful actions, or going on a power-trip. Rather, it is about taking responsibility for your *own* life and for changing your *own* reality by directing *your* mind. It is about being kind towards everyone you meet, not out of pity or a sense of superiority but out of recognition that they too are spiritual beings having a physical experience. It is about recognising the true non-dualistic nature of reality that All is One, meaning we are all connected, not only to each other but to all of Nature and to everything in the entire Universe. You know that what you do to others, you do to yourself. And the way you treat Nature, you in fact treat yourself.

Finally, it is to know that great power comes with great responsibility and, while you are free to choose your thoughts and actions, you are not free to choose their consequences. When all is said and done, live and let live.

ROW, ROW, ROW YOUR BOAT

Oftentimes you find profound truth in the simplest of places. The following nursery rhyme is no exception. "Row, row, row your boat, gently down the stream; merrily, merrily, merrily, merrily, life is but a dream." These few words, intended for children, hold a profound message for anyone who understands them, irrespective of their age.

'Row, row, row...'
To 'row, row, row' is to take action in three ways. *Spiritually,* by aspiring to the I within, *mentally* under your will's direction and intuition's guidance, and *physically* by way of inspired action that takes you towards your goal. Aspire to the I *first*, then direct your mind, and then all your actions will naturally follow your will's command.

'...your boat'
'Your boat' can be likened to your physical body. It is your *body* but remember it is *not* the Real You. Your body allows the Real You, who is the spiritual being, to have a physical experience as your *personal* self in your physical life. Knowing that your body is the necessary vehicle for your physical experience, you honour it as the temple that houses your Spirit.

'...gently down the stream'
To row your boat 'gently' reminds you not to force anything in the Physical Plane and not to manipulate anyone. It is also a reminder to be gentle with yourself and to be kind to everything and everyone you may meet along the way. To go 'down the stream' is to *flow* with life and allow for change on your journey. At the same time, it is to row *around* the obstacles you may encounter in your life, rather than allow them to keep you stuck in the moment.

'...merrily, merrily, merrily, merrily'
'Merrily, merrily, merrily, merrily' is a reminder to maintain a *positive,* care-free attitude of love, courage, and joy, with confidence and trust in Life to take you towards your *chosen* destination. To be merry is to be in good spirit as you aspire to flourish as a human being,

while knowing that nothing is permanent in a world that is always changing. Ultimately, to be merry is to *enjoy* the journey.

'...life is but a dream.'

Finally, 'life is but a dream' tells you in no uncertain terms that your experience of reality is a *dream*. Not that it is *like* a dream but rather, it *is* a dream. In other words, life is a projection of the consciousness of the Real You, in the same way that your dreams are a projection of the consciousness of your personal self. It is you who must wake up *within* your dream and begin to dream lucidly. This means to *live consciously* and to be *awakened*. And when you are awakened, you hand the oars of your boat over to the I within, whose dream it is, and you begin to truly *live* your dream, which is the Adventure of I.

THE OPTIMIST'S CREED

It is well worth repeating the so-called Optimist's Creed from the 1912 book Your Forces and How to Use Them by Christian D. Larson. Once again, read it carefully with your full attention and make it a promise to yourself, every day and in every way.

Promise Yourself

"Promise Yourself to be so strong that nothing can disturb your peace of mind. To talk health, happiness, and prosperity to every person you meet. To make all your friends feel that there is something worthwhile in them. To look at the sunny side of everything, and make your optimism come true. To think only of the best, to work only for the best, and to expect only the best. To be just as enthusiastic about the success of others as you are about your own. To forget the mistakes of the past and press on to the greater achievements of the future. To wear a cheerful expression at all times and give a smile to every living creature you meet. To give so much time to improving yourself that you have no time to criticize others. To be too large for worry, too noble for anger, too strong for fear, and too happy to permit the presence of trouble. To think well of yourself and to proclaim this fact to the world, not in loud word, but in great deeds. To live in the faith that the whole world is on your side, so long as you are true to the best that is in you."

LOVE FOR LIFE OR FEAR OF LIFE

There are essentially two ways in which you can live your life. The mental scale of your inner world bears down either in favour of a '*love for* life' or a '*fear of* life'. Love is the most attractive force in the

Universe, and fear is the most repelling. While love attracts her kind to you, fear keeps love's kind away.

Love's Children and Fear's Brood

Love and fear are the two mental parents of all mental states. Love is the mental parent of *positivity* and among love's many children are faith, joy, desire, confidence enthusiasm, inspiration, hope, courage, trust, strength, kindness, calmness, success, and gratitude. Fear on the other hand, is the mental parent of *negativity*, and among fear's brood are worry, discontentment, cowardice, hate, jealousy, malice, anger, failure, attachment, obsession, self-pity, shame, and despondence.

When you rise above fear, it will take its off-spring away with it. But as long as fear masters you, there is little progress you can ever hope to achieve. In contrast, when love is your guide, there is nothing that you cannot achieve. Indeed, there is no man more free than the man free of fear. You may have heard of the saying 'there is nothing to fear but fear itself', and there is great truth in this. But let me tell you a little secret, fear in fact need not be feared. By its own *inherent nature*, it is the weakest of cowards and will flee at the first signs of your standing up to it and commanding it 'to be gone'.

Fear and its brood are so far beneath the degree of positivity of Love and her children, that they cannot but *submit* to your command and leave your mental world. When you raise your mental frequency to the degree of *Love for Life*, then fear will become a distant memory of an unwelcome stranger who once used to visit you.

FALL IN LOVE WITH LIFE

Fall in love with Life. Let her be your *first* real Love in the Physical Plane. Love her with all your heart, pursue her, dream about her, nurture and protect her, always be kind to her, only speak well of her, aim to please and impress her, shower her with every gift you have to give, and let all your desires be born of a desire to make *her* happy.

Above all, love her without condition. Love her so much that you allow her to be herself. Set her free. Do not smother her with your needs. Have no demands of her. Do not be attached to her and never fear losing her. Know in your heart that she is already yours and loves you just as much as you love her. Fall in love with her over and over again, and love her more deeply every day. When you truly fall in love with Life with all your heart and mind, you cannot help but fall to your knees in gratitude to The Absolute for having given Life to you. And ultimately, when you love *All* Life without condition, you begin to rise upwards to the Love of The Absolute Itself, which is Absolute Love.

Chapter 46
ABSOLUTE LOVE

All is Love. You have probably heard this expression that *All is Love*, some time in your life, also phrased as 'God is Love' or 'Love is the force that sustains the Universe'. You may have also dismissed all these statements as feel-good declarations which have little or no evidence to support them. Nothing, however, could be further from the truth. These are by no means idealistic feel-good statements but in fact, have their foundation in a deeper understanding of the true nature of The Absolute.

ALL IS LOVE

What follows is a logical explanation of why All *is* Love and God *is* Love, and why Love is indeed the force that sustains the Universe. What is written here is inspired by the early 20th century writings of Judge Thomas Troward, and also offers you a deeper understanding of your own true nature.

Since the Universe is a *creation* of the Mind of The Absolute, then creation must be the *purpose* of Universal Mind. And since what is created is *Life*, and All is *Mind*, then Universal Mind *is* Life Itself, both visible and invisible. And since Universal Mind is the Mind of the Absolute, then All Life is *in* the Mind of God.

Now, since The Absolute is all there is, and there is nothing *outside* of It, then it stands to reason that The Absolute must be equally in *favour* of *All Life*, because anything less would be to oppose Itself. Something that is Absolute *and* is in favour of All Life, must *love* All Life equally and without condition, because not to do so, would again be to oppose Itself.

Unconditional Love for All Life equally is Absolute Love. Therefore, the *nature* of The Absolute must, by definition, be Love, and so 'God *is* Love'. And since All *is* God, then 'All *is* Love'. Love must also be the *nature* of the *Mind* of The Absolute. And since Universal Mind's *Life Force* is what sustains the entire Universe, then it stands to reason that '*Love* is the *force* that sustains the Universe'.

ABSOLUTE LOVE *IS*

Absolute Love *is*. It stands *alone* and has no opposite. In fact, the origin of the word 'alone' is '*All One*'. Absolute Love is not the same as the personal love of loving something but not loving something else. Although we refer to love as an emotion, the love we talk about in the

274 | The Adventure of I

sense of adoration for something or someone, is not Absolute Love but instead, it is *relative* love subject to its opposite of hate. In contrast, Absolute Love is Divine in nature. It is a state of *being* devoid of personal preference. It does not rise or fall in accordance with the subject, circumstances, or specifics.

Remember always that Absolute Love has no opposite. It cannot be compared to a state of non-love and it does not discriminate between what is loved and what is not loved. Absolute Love is not an emotion but rather it is the absence of all the ever-changing emotions of the relative world. This is because love in the relative world is *exclusive*, whereas Absolute Love is All-Inclusive.

Since The Absolute's Love is *Absolute*, It does not love one aspect of Life any more than any other, and nor does It love one aspect of Life less today than It did yesterday, or more than It will love it tomorrow. Remember that the Absolute is wholly unconstrained by time and space, and so It must Love every aspect of Itself equally, infinitely and eternally.

ABSOLUTE LOVE FOR YOU

Since your mind is a centre of Universal Mind, and Universal Mind *is Life*, then your Life is a focalised centre of the One Life. Moreover, since The Absolute is infinite and is present in *your every cell* in Its *entirety*, then it stands to reason that It *always* Loves you Absolutely and is always in favour of your life.

The truth is that The Absolute loves you *Absolutely*, no matter how many mistakes you have made, no matter what thoughts you think, no matter what you desire, no matter how much you love yourself or not, and *irrespective* of whether or not you realise Its Absolute Love for you. Moreover, The Absolute is always in favour of *your* life, as much as It is in favour of All Life.

It also stands to reason that since the Real You is created in the image of The Absolute, you too should aspire to be in favour of your life and All Life, and with a Love that is Absolute for yourself and for everyone and everything.

The Circle of Absolute Love

The Circle of Absolute Love begins and ends with Self-Love. Indeed, the Golden Rule, which is the common thread found in most of the world's sacred and religious teachings is 'to love your neighbour, as you love *yourself*'. You are likely to have heard the Golden Rule many times, expressed in different ways, thinking it is about loving *others*. But look a little closer, and you will find at its centre the command to love *yourself*. In fact, it suggests that loving yourself is a *prerequisite* to loving others because you can only *truly* love others in the same measure that you love yourself.

As you already know, real Self-Love is founded in identifying with the *Real* You who *knows* All is One. Self-Love has nothing to do with accepting your imperfections and loving yourself in spite of them. But rather, Self-Love has everything to do with identifying with your inherent complete *perfection* to which nothing can ever be added, and from which nothing can ever be subtracted.

When you love yourself as the I within, you love All Life because from *your* perspective, All Life is a projection of your consciousness. To love All Life is to love Universal Mind because It *is* All Life. And to love Universal Mind is to love The Absolute because *It* is the *Mind* of The Absolute. In so doing you complete the Circle of Absolute Love, because to love The Absolute is to love yourself, because *you* are created in Its image, and It is within you in Its *entirety*. Self-Love therefore, is the Alpha and the Omega of Absolute Love. Ultimately to love yourself is to find that the Kingdom of Heaven is *within*, as all the greatest masters who ever walked the Earth told us.

LET YOUR LOVE BE ABSOLUTE

To begin to know The Absolute within, let your Love begin to be Absolute. When you rise above the illusion of duality of the relative world of opposites, you will find a love for everyone and everything that is free of all judgment, and your life will become the highest expression of joy. When you commit your Love to The Absolute, knowing that you are loved *absolutely* always and without condition, you will find an inner strength and peace of mind that can never again be disturbed by outside things and circumstances.

Service to Others

As conscious creation becomes part of your mindset, you will know that you can indeed have all those material and non-material things you once deemed so precious and out of reach. In so doing, you will find that creating your own desires only will no longer appeal to you as much, for they will have lost some of their allure.

Instead, your focus and the direction of your Life Force will shift towards the greatest of all ideals, which is *service to others*. To serve others, however, you must first come to know how to serve and love yourself, because it can only ever be a joyful experience when it has its foundation in self-love and self-care. In the same way that you cannot truly love others if you do not love yourself first, you cannot truly serve anyone either, if you are not willing to serve yourself. And to serve yourself is to serve your *Real* Self.

When the day comes that you *know* in your heart that you *have* Absolute Love, then you will know that you already have everything. In knowing so, instead of asking The Absolute for what *you* want, you will ask The Absolute what *It* wants from you. And you will find that the answer is always unchanging: Love. Indeed, Absolute Love is mankind's destiny and it is the only destination that is infinitely greater than the journey.

BUT THE GREATEST OF THESE IS LOVE

There is no more complete description of Absolute Love than that found in 1 Corinthians 13 of the New Testament Bible, as written below. Knowing what you now know about the Spiritual Plane of *unity*, as well as the relative realm of the *parts* of the whole being reflected in a *mirror*, carefully read the following passage.

"If I speak in the tongues of men or of angels, but do not have Love, I am only a resounding gong or a clanging cymbal. If I have the gift of prophecy and can fathom all mysteries and all knowledge, and if I have a faith that can move mountains, but do not have Love, I am nothing. If I give all I possess to the poor and give over my body to hardship that I may boast, but do not have Love, I gain nothing.

Love is patient, love is kind. It does not envy, it does not boast, it is not proud. It does not dishonour others, it is not self-seeking, it is not easily angered, it keeps no record of wrongs. Love does not delight in evil but rejoices with the truth. It always protects, always trusts, always hopes, always perseveres. Love never fails.

But where there are prophecies, they will cease. Where there are tongues, they will be stilled. Where there is knowledge, it will pass away. For we know in *part* and we prophesy in *part*, but when *completeness* comes, what is in part disappears.

When I was a child, I talked like a child, I thought like a child, I reasoned like a child. When I became a man, I put the ways of childhood behind me. For now we see only a *reflection* as in a *mirror*, then we shall see *face to face*. Now I know *in part,* then I shall know *fully*, even as I am fully known.

And now these three remain: Faith, Hope, and Love. But the greatest of these is Love."

Chapter 47

FREEDOM

The knowledge contained in this book when truly understood and correctly applied, can create miracles in your life. If, however, you do not apply it, there is little it can offer you because it is only ever the application of knowledge that can unlock its power. What determines *how* you apply this knowledge is your *mind* and how you use it.

James Allen said it best in his 1902 book As a Man Thinketh, in which he referred to our conditions or outer world environment as our 'looking-glass', which is Old English for 'mirror'. Give the following words your *full* attention. Read them carefully and let them take root within your mind and stay with you always.

"Mind is the Master *Power* that moulds and makes. And Man *is* Mind. And evermore he takes the Tool of *Thought*, and shaping what he *wills*, brings forth a thousand joys, a thousand ills. He thinks in *secret*, and it comes to pass: environment is but his *looking-glass*."

In applying the knowledge contained within this book, you must endeavour therefore to apply your mind *correctly*, and to do so, you must be in the *correct* state of mind. In fact it is arguably better to be ignorant of this knowledge than to apply it in the *incorrect* state of mind. While the incorrect state of mind 'brings forth a thousand ills', the correct state of mind 'brings forth a thousand joys'. The correct state of mind is that of the I within, and it is *within* your reach at every moment. All you have to do is mentally merge with the Real You.

IN TWO MINDS

The incorrect state of mind is a mind that is frantic and attached. It is accompanied by a refusal to accept life *as it is* and also by a need to control everything, and at times, everyone. This mind belongs to a person who lives in an overwhelming, emotional world of passions and desires. He mentally dangles off Rhythm's pendulum that swings him between varying degrees of doubt and attachment, hate and obsession, self-pity and over-exuberance, suspicion and naivety, and shame and arrogance.

In this state of mind, you know nothing about the undisturbed I within, but instead you are mentally pulled about in all directions by the incessant and taunting chatter of your controlling counterfeit ego. In leaving the power of your will idle, you have no mastery over your mind. Instead, you are a slave to your ever-changing desires, fears, and emotions, as well as to the will, desires, and opinions of others. And in so doing, you serve them all obediently, while mistakenly thinking you are free. This is the mind of *lower* positivity, which is forever looking outwards for its power, but for which no amount of power is ever enough.

In contrast, the correct state of mind is a mind that is calm and detached. It is accompanied by a love for life *as it is*, and a willingness to let life flow. This mind belongs to a person of will power, self-discipline, and strong character. In this state of mind, you are at the helm of your will power, you listen to your intuition, you engage your reasoning mind, and aspire to be in a state of optimal emotion of joy, love, trust, faith, courage, and confidence. You know that whatever you *need* to control, in fact controls *you*. You *know* that you desire *nothing*, yet are always ready to *direct* your mind to attain anything for the *personal* experience. This is the mind of *higher* positivity, which only ever looks *inwards* and finds All-Power within, and in so doing, you begin to approach the *Entelecheia* of 'perfection within'.

All human beings have both minds within them. The first is your Lower Mind and belongs to your *counterfeit ego*, created in the image of the *limited* personal self. The second is your Higher Mind and belongs to your *Real Ego* of your Real Self - the Observer - created in the image of The *Limitless* Absolute.

IN ONE MIND

Your Higher Mind *observes*. It *never* fights your Lower Mind and *never* forces it into compliance. It loves your Lower Mind absolutely. Your Lower Mind, however, is burdened with outer world fears, which feed its desperate need to be in control. Misguided in its belief that power is finite, it uses tactics of force and manipulation to take it away from others, and also depletes its own limited resources. In its bid to stay in control, your Lower Mind ignores the whispers of the quiet voice of your intuition, and instead drowns it out with its incessant taunting and controlling chatter. It resists the direction of your will, and with its childish tantrums to get its way, it fights your Higher Mind. But again, your Higher Mind does not fight back. Instead, the I within remains still, unchanged, and undisturbed in the vast silence of nothingness. It lovingly watches, waiting for the day you will let go, accept its guidance, and become One with It...

...and when you do, you will be free, for you will have found God within, and with gratitude on your lips, peace in your mind, and Absolute Love in your heart, you will say
I AM I.

*The end of the Adventure of I
and the beginning...*

BIBLIOGRAPHY

ALLEN, James, *As a Man Thinketh*, 1902

ANONYMOUS, *The Arcane Teaching*, 1909 *

ANONYMOUS, *The Arcane Formulas*, 1909 *

ATKINSON, William Walker, *Practical Mental Influence*, 1908

ATKINSON, William Walker, *Suggestion and Auto-Suggestion*, 1915

ATKINSON, William Walker, *The Secret of Mental Magic*, 1907

ATKINSON, William Walker, *Thought Vibration*, 1906

BEHREND, Genevieve, *Your Invisible Power*, 1921

BRISTON, Claude, *The Magic of Believing*, 1948

COUE, Émile, *Self-Mastery Through Conscious Autosuggestion*, 1922

FERSEN, Eugene, *The Science of Being - Seven Lessons*, 1923

FERSEN, Eugene, *The Science of Being - Twenty Seven Lessons*, 1927

GIBRAN, Kahlil, *The Prophet*, 1923

GIORBRAN, Gevin, *Everything Forever*, 2007

HAANEL, Charles F., *The Master Key System*, 1912

LARSON, Christian D., *Your Forces and How to Use Them*, 1912

MAGUS INCOGNITO, *The Secret Doctrine of the Rosicrucians*, 1918 *

MATTHEWS, Andrew, *Follow Your Heart*, 1997

MCDONALD, John, *The Message of a Master,* 1920s

RUSSELL, Walter, *The Universal One*, 1926

RUSSELL, Walter, *Home Study Course*, 1950

SILVA, Jose and STONE, Robert B., *You the Healer*, 1989

SMOTHERMON, Ron, *Winning Through Enlightenment*, 1980

THE THREE INITIATES, *The Kybalion*, 1908 *

TROWARD, Thomas, *The Edinburgh Lectures on Mental Science*, 1909

TROWARD, Thomas, *The Dore Lectures on Mental Science*, 1909

TZU, Lao, *The Tao Te Ching*, ~6BC

WEED, Joseph J., *Psychic Energy*, 1970

* *Written anonymously at the time by William Walker Atkinson*

For more writings and products
from Tania Kotsos or to contact her,
please visit her website:

Mind Your Reality

www.mind-your-reality.com

Here's to Your Adventure!

Thank You and
Be Well Always
Tania Kotsos

Printed in Great Britain
by Amazon